The
Good,
the Bad,
and Me

ELI WALLACH

The Good, the Bad, and Me

In My Anecdotage

Harcourt, Inc.

Orlando   Austin   New York   San Diego   Toronto   London

Requests for permission to make copies of any part of the work should be
mailed to the following address: Permissions Department, Harcourt, Inc.,
6277 Sea Harbor Drive, Orlando, Florida 32887-6777.

www.HarcourtBooks.com

Library of Congress Cataloging-in-Publication Data

Wallach, Eli, 1915–
    The good, the bad, and me: in my anecdotage / Eli Wallach.—1st ed.
      p. cm.
    1. Wallach, Eli, 1915– 2. Actors—United States—Biography. I. Title.
    PN2287.W247A3 2005
    792.02'8'092—dc22   2004023121
    ISBN-13: 978-0151-0489-6 ISBN-10: 0-15-101189-3

Text set in Janson MT
Designed by Lydia D'moch

Printed in the United States of America

First edition
K J I H G F E D C B A

To the love of my life, Anne Jackson

To Peter, Lucinda, Roberta, Katherine,
and my three grand grandsons, Jason, Tyler, and Sean

Contents

Prologue

ONE DAY IN 1958, I had just returned to New York from two months on the road touring with Tennessee Williams's play *The Rose Tattoo*. When I got in the door to my apartment, the phone was already ringing; it was my agent Peter Witt on the other end of the line.

"Don't unpack," he said. "I have an offer for you."

Witt told me that the producers of the dramatic television series *Climax!* wanted me to play opposite Don Ameche in the episode "Albert Anastasia: His Life and Death." I was to play the title character, the legendary head of Murder Incorporated. Anastasia, nicknamed the Mafia's "Lord High Executioner," had been gunned down in the Park Sheraton Hotel barbershop on

Seventh Avenue in Midtown Manhattan one year earlier in 1957. I remembered hearing stories about Anastasia and seeing the pictures—Anastasia's bullet-riddled body lying in a pool of blood on the floor of the barbershop—and I remembered the banner headlines of the tabloids, the *Daily News*, the *Daily Mirror*, the *Journal-American:* MURDER INC. BOSS RUBBED OUT! I looked forward to taking on such a challenging role. And yet, for one of the first times in my career, I was at a loss as to how to bring the man to life.

That night I went to Sardi's on West Forty-fourth Street. Sardi's was the in spot where actors could meet, talk, and have a late dinner. The walls of the main dining room were covered with caricatures of those who had had a success on the Broadway stage. Martin, the maître d', would often try to get me to sit on the banquette below my caricature, which was sandwiched between drawings of Gwen Verdon and Carol Channing. "Thank you," I would always say, "but I'll sit at the table by Miss Jackson," and I would sit beneath the caricature of my wife, Anne Jackson, whose image appeared between those of Henry Fonda and David Wayne.

Every night at Sardi's, Leonard Lyons, the *New York Post* show business reporter, would drop by after the evening's shows had let out. He'd wander from table to table, gathering tidbits for his column, which was called "The Lyons Den." Well-dressed, balding, and mild-mannered, Lyons would never sit down at anyone's table. Pad in hand, he'd ask questions of the actors. Actors liked being mentioned in Lyons's column because, unlike the hatchet gossip collectors who distorted every remark they made, Lyons was fair and clear. On this particular night, he spotted me sitting alone at the table underneath my wife's caricature.

"What are you up to?" he asked.

I told him I was going to California the following week to play Albert Anastasia on *Climax!* When I said I was having trouble figuring out how to play the role, his eyes twinkled.

"How would you like to meet my friend Sam Liebowitz?" he asked.

As a young attorney, Judge Liebowitz had helped to defend Anastasia on two murder charges and won an acquittal. I could hardly catch my breath. I thought I would get a chance to learn inside information about the man I was going to play. Lyons told me that he'd call the judge and arrange everything. Then he pocketed his pad and moved on to another table.

A few days later, I was standing in the Brooklyn Supreme Court in the chambers of Judge Liebowitz.

"Lyons tells me you're going out to Hollywood to do a TV show about one of my former clients," he said as he shook my hand—he had a firm grip. "I'll have some good stories for you about Al."

In the courtroom, Liebowitz wore a long black robe. He looked a foot taller than he did in his chambers. He nodded to me, patted the bench, and beckoned me to sit beside him.

"Come sit," he said. "I have a few cases to dispose of first."

Judge Liebowitz seemed excited about being in the presence of an actor. He made quite a show of banging his gavel as he berated a young girl charged with soliciting a police officer and a matronly woman charged with shoplifting. At the end of the day, the judge shook my hand, his grasp stronger than ever.

"Come visit me again," he said, and departed.

Outside, it was raining. I stood on the steps of the courthouse, looking up at the statue of the lady of justice. I didn't mind getting wet; the droplets seemed to wash away all that I had seen in the courtroom. But then I thought, "Wait a minute. The judge put on quite a show for me, but I didn't learn a damn thing about Al."

Sitting by the window in a California-bound jet, I began to thumb through a paperback volume about the Mafia to learn more about Anastasia. He had been born in Italy and had worked his way up through the ranks of the Mob to become the feared head of Murder Incorporated. His job was to maintain order and loyalty for the bosses. If someone deviated from that path, Anastasia would take him for a ride. No one ever returned from that trip—the body would simply be dumped into the East River. Once I was done reading the book, I was still in a quagmire. "How do I play this part? How does one play a murderer?" I asked myself. "Does the act of murder give him a thrill? Do his hands sweat? Does he have any pity for the victim?" The more I racked my brain, the more I came up dry.

When I arrived in California, I was driven directly to the wardrobe department of the studio. The costume designer greeted me warmly.

"Albert Anastasia," he said, "I've got plenty of good-looking suits for you."

The costume designer also told me that he had a film of Anastasia's brother Tony being questioned by the Kefauver Crime Committee. "Why don't we go in and take a look," he said. "It might help you find something out about the Anastasias."

As we sat in the airless screening room, the grainy film started to roll. I watched as the prosecutor began to interview Anastasia's brother.

"Please give me your name and occupation," he said.

"My name is Tony Anastasia," the man replied. He had a thick Italian accent and he spoke in a high tenor voice. "I'm the head of the Brooklyn Longshoremen's Union, and I ain't gonna answer no questions I don't like."

"Well, just tell me where you live at present," the prosecutor said.

"I live at 167 Union Street," Anastasia snarled at the prosecutor.

"You can shut the film off now," I told the costume designer. "I was born at 166."

1

An Actor Grows in Brooklyn

UNION STREET was a wide main artery running from Prospect Park past Park Slope down to the docks of the East River. Number 166 housed Bertha's, a small toy, candy, and stationery store named for my mother. A long glass counter ran the length of the store. There was an icebox for soda pop and a pay telephone. On the back wall of the store were shelves, which held toys, big jars of Indian nuts, and cigarettes. The store was always busy in the late afternoons, when longshoremen would drop in after a day of unloading ships' cargo. Over their shoulders, many of them would carry big crooked iron hooks, which seemed to be part of their uniform. They'd drink sodas, make phone calls, buy cigarettes, eat the tiny Indian nuts, then spit the shells all over the floor.

I lived in the rear of the store with my parents, Abe and Bertha, my older brother and sister, Sam and Sylvia, and my younger sister, Shirley. Mom and Pop had a bedroom with a big window that looked out onto the alley. Sam had his own bed, and there was a cot for me next to it. Sylvia and Shirley shared the last bedroom. There was one toilet for the six of us. Sam called it the throne room. We all soon learned how to take care of our needs there— no reading, no wasting time, just do your duty, flush, and get out.

My baby sister, Shirley, and I used to argue a lot. Sometimes I'd steal her milk bottle. And at dinner we would fight over the wishbone. We'd each hold one end and pull it apart, and the winner would get to make a wish. Even in my earliest memories, my wish was always the same: I wanted to be an actor.

◎ ◎ ◎

I was born in Brooklyn on December 7, 1915, back when the streets were still lit by gas lamps. As soon as it began to get dark, the lamplighter would appear. A little man with a thick black mustache, he carried a long stick with a flint on the end of it. He'd push the stick into an opening of a glass bowl at the top of a lamppost, and a blue-green flame would light up the gas and throw big circles of light down on the street. Right in front of our store, a streetcar ran down the center of Union Street powered by an electric wire overhead.

My father, Abe, had been a tailor in southeast Poland and had met my mother, Bertha, in their small town of Przemyśl. He had come to America in 1909 and opened the store with the financial backing of his brother Michael, a wealthy furrier who lived in Bensonhurst. Then Abe sent for my mother and my brother Sam. Sometimes Abe would tell us stories about growing up in Poland—Cossacks riding into his village, robbing stores, and killing Jews. He was a wonderful storyteller, but he also had a volatile temper and suffered from severe headaches. Often I remember him holding a hot glass of tea next to his throbbing temple. One night Sam and Sylvia were arguing as I lay between them on the sofa bed. "Quiet," Pop yelled. "Quiet or I'll throw the glass!" That yell from my pop just seemed to add fuel to their arguments. They argued even more fiercely, and Pop threw the glass like a fastball pitcher. Sam yelled, "Look out." I did—and I got hit. My pop was very upset. "Get him to the doctor," he ordered. Sylvia walked me to the hospital, crying. "I will not walk on the same street with you if you cry," I told her.

"I'll stop," she said, taking me by the hand, as we went to the hospital. I received three stitches over my left eye. When we returned to the store, my pop handed me a three-scoop ice-cream cone—one scoop for each stitch, I guess.

◎ ◎ ◎

We were the only Jewish family in our working-class neighborhood, which was predominantly Italian, and my earliest childhood memories are filled with vivid images of Union Street. Sometimes an organ grinder would appear on the street with a live parrot perched on his shoulder. "Fortune! Fortune! I'll tell you a fortune," the fortune-teller would call out, and customers would gather around him.

"Come on, let my parrot pick a card for you," the fortune-teller would say, and if you paid a nickel, the parrot, after a nod from his owner, would bend down and come up with a card sticking out of his beak: "There's your fortune! Read, read! All of it is true!"

Sometimes a photographer would set up his tripod just outside of our store. Under his camera, there would be a tin can filled with developing fluid.

"Ten cents," he would say. "You sit on my pony, I take-a your picture and develop it right here." I always watched him, and one day I got up the courage to have my picture taken. I gave him a dime, mounted the pony, and pretended to be a cowboy riding out to round up cattle or joining a posse chasing bandits.

At one time or another, everyone in our family worked in the store. Sometimes Pop would go across the river to New York's Lower East Side to buy supplies, and Mom would take care of customers. My tasks included emptying the water out of the basin underneath the iceboxes, taking out the garbage, sweeping up the shells from the Indian nuts, and walking my little four-wheeled wagon to the newspaper dealer on Harrison Street and piling it up with Sunday papers for the store.

Early in the mornings, I'd stand in front of our store and watch the white-jacketed milkman. He'd hop off his wagon, leaving the reins draped off the horse's back, and stop at each doorway. He'd drop off the milk, and his horse would walk slowly down the street, timing its stops exactly with the milkman returning to reload his tray. The milk came in bottles, and at the top of the bottle, there was always heavy cream. Another one of my jobs was to shake those bottles and put them in the iceboxes in our kitchen and in the store.

Twice a day, the fruit wagon would stop near our store. The

wagon had elegantly painted side panels depicting churches, mountains, and trees. A big scale with large white numbers dangled from the rear of the wagon. The horse's ears would stick out through the holes in his straw hat. The fruit man would stand up and ring a big bell, crying out, "Fruit! Fresh fruit! Melons, bananas, oranges, apples!" Mom would always send Sylvia out to buy a bag of fresh fruit that she would then put out on the sideboard in our kitchen.

Horses were everywhere in those days, hauling fruit, milk, and ice. And they often left their calling card on the street—big clumps of horse shit. On cold days, steam would rise from the pile. Three times a day, the street cleaner would arrive in a white hat and jacket, pushing a big two-wheeled ash can. He'd deposit the manure and move on. The manure would be sold later as fertilizer.

Mr. Dante the wine-maker had a shop near our store. One day he hired me to help him slide crates of grapes down a board into the cellar, where he would catch them.

"Come down and watch," Mr. Dante said to me.

We emptied the grapes into a large round vat that stood on a wooden frame about three feet from the ground. Two overweight ladies who looked like they had mustaches stood waiting, with their skirts rolled up above their knees. Dante turned on his phonograph, and the women began stomping the grapes to the rhythm of a tarantella. The juice flowed from the holes in the bottom of the vat into big bottles.

"Here's a bottle from last year's pressing," he said. "My regards to your pop." He also gave me a whole new shiny quarter. On the way home, I wondered if I should tell Pop about those ladies; I wasn't sure if they had washed their feet.

A few blocks away from our store, there was a theater called La Luna, where I saw my first stage production when Pop took Sam, Sylvia, Shirley, and me to see an Italian puppet show. The walls of La Luna were covered with giant canvas paintings of fearless warriors on horseback, driving spears into the necks of animals. The canvases seemed to drip blood. The puppets in the show were life-size; their big glass eyes moved as they looked out on us and yelled in Italian. I was frightened by the show, and that night I couldn't fall asleep because I was afraid the puppets would get me—their eyes kept staring at me.

Even more exciting than the puppet shows were the Italian fiestas held on Union Street honoring the lives and accomplishments of saints. Pushcarts would suddenly line both sides of the street. Each cart contained delicacies—candy, plates of food. One time there was a man in a black apron with a big knife opening clams and oysters. Then we'd hear the band playing the Italian national anthem, and up the street would come floats and big, brawny longshoremen bearing huge statues of Jesus and Mary and other saints. Jesus would have his arms stretched out on a cross, a crown with thorns around his head, bloody tears trickling down his face. Mary would be wearing a colorful blue, green, and red dress—she looked a little like my mother.

At one of those fiestas, I tugged at Pop's shirt. "Pa," I asked, "why don't we have parades like they do?"

"Well," he said, "they have a different God and their God likes parades." I knew that wasn't the real answer, but I accepted it.

But the best part of Union Street was the funerals. At the first solemn drumbeats, people would line the sidewalks. Our family would go out in front of the store to pay our respects. A large band with drums, trumpets, and saxophones would march by us, all of the musicians walking very slowly. Then a beautiful hearse would follow, drawn by two horses wearing large plumes as black as their shiny flanks. The sides of the hearse were made of glass so you could catch a glimpse of the ebony casket covered with a blanket of red roses. Silently parading behind them were the mourners, all the women wearing black scarves.

Once when I was watching a funeral, I asked Sam if he thought our mom and pop would get such an exciting one. Sam was a mentor to me and my sisters, and later he would be the first member of the family to go to college. He would always come home expressing very radical views. Fuming at Sam's political remarks, my father would hold up his newspaper. "This paper tells the truth," he would say. "It's the *Jewish Daily Forward*." And Sam would always goad him with this smart comeback: "No, it's not. It's the *Jewish Daily Backward*."

Sam always played classical music on our record player, and before the record would finish, he'd say, "Now that was B Major or B Minor Schubert or D-flat." I would never know what he was talking about. I always thought he was grading papers as a schoolteacher. Nevertheless, Sam seemed to have the answers to most of my questions, so I asked him why Jews didn't get such fancy funerals.

"Jews are not embalmed," he said.

"They're not?" I asked, even though I had no idea what the hell *embalmed* meant.

"Well," he said, "it's got a lot to do with blood. It's too complicated to explain." But as soon as Jews died, he said, they were put in a plain wooden box and lowered into the ground at the cemetery.

"Why do we have such crazy rules?" I asked. "No parades? No funerals? Do you have to be Italian to get a band or a big black hearse?"

Sam was also the one I went to when I wanted to know about babies and how they were made.

"Well," he said, "you take your penis and put it in the girl's hole."

"What?" I asked him. "I thought the penis was only for peeing."

Sam shook his head. "All right," he said, "I'll explain it technically. You have two balls below your penis. The balls manufacture sperm; it's like seeds. And when the penis is in the girl, the balls send a message to the brain to switch from the peeing penis to the sperm penis. Nine months after that deposit in the girl, she gets a baby."

I couldn't believe it. Why couldn't God devise a simpler method? Why not a penis for peeing and one for planting the seed? That would solve the problem, I thought—no switching.

◎ ◎ ◎

In the fall of 1920, on the day I was supposed to begin kindergarten, I remember watching my mom lighting the stove, heating the water, and putting it into a tub, the same tub she used to do the laundry. She was a beautiful woman—small, kind of chubby with short black hair, big brown eyes, and a wonderful smile. I loved to hug her.

"You're going to school today," she said.

She said that Shirley, who was three, would stay with Abe in the store, and then she helped me get dressed in my short pants, white shirt, and my good shoes. Public School 46 was just across the street. It was a big gray building with bars on the windows and an American flag hanging over the front door. As we crossed the street, I started to cry.

"Stop it," she said. "People are watching."

"I don't care. I don't care," I said. "Once you go in there, you never get out."

"Sam and Sylvia went in there and they got out," she said.

As we neared the front door of the school, I grabbed my mother around her waist.

"Please don't let me go in there," I said. "I don't need to learn anything."

"Darling, I'll be waiting for you," she said. "I'll be here when you get out. You can look out the window and see me standing there." She smiled and waved to me as the teacher came out and took me into the classroom.

After a month or two, I began to enjoy kindergarten. I made crayon drawings of streetcars, horses, and steam rising out of manure piles. I was so pleased when my teacher would hang my drawings on the wall. I even got permission to cross the street by myself.

֎ ֎ ֎

At the age of ten, I helped to form a gang called the Union Street Toughs. There were seven of us. Joey Feliciano was the ringleader. Then there was Frankie Galante, Mickey Riley, Lilly Mangano, Fatso Tommy O'Neill, Georgie Albano, and me. I was the only Jew in the gang, but I was known as Chink because my eyes became slits when I smiled. Sometimes when the streetcars would rattle past our store, a tiny wheel would disengage from the overhead electrical wire that supplied the power and send blue and white sparks cascading onto the street. The conductor would rush to the rear of the car to guide the wheel back onto the wire, and Joey would appear from out of nowhere, whistling a secret code.

"Hey, Chink," he'd say to me, "you got some pennies?"

"Yeah."

"So let's do it," he'd say.

While the conductor was busy at the rear of the car, we would lay our pennies on the track. As the trolley passed, the conductor would shout, "I know what you guys are doing—you're gonna end up in jail."

As soon as the streetcar would pass, we would pick up the flattened pennies and file them until they looked like nickels—perfect for making telephone calls.

"These fake nickels better not be used in our store's phone," I would warn Joey. "My father and the telephone company would kill us."

"I'm taking them home," he would tell me. "I'm giving them to my pop; he can use them."

When we were all about eleven, the whole gang would meet and play games like ringalevio—where one person would hide while the others tried to capture him—or ride the pony, where we would pile up on each other until somebody fell. When it snowed in Brooklyn—which seemed to happen a lot when I was growing up—our gang would split up, and we'd choose sides and build snow forts on either side of the street. I loved when the garbage truck would come with a big snowplow in front of it and scoop up all the snow and get it out of the way. After that, we could create great little tunnels running alongside the street where we could hide. After the trolley would pass, we would unleash our snowballs at each other. We never gave a damn who won our battles, but after they were over, we'd cook Mickeys (sweet potatoes). Many nights after school, we'd choose up sides and play stickball. A sewer cover was home plate. The other three bases were marked out in chalk. The bat was a cut-down broomstick handle, and the tiny red ball was one we had used for handball games. On Friday nights, I was supposed to come home early for *shabbos* dinner, which sometimes conflicted with my stickball schedule.

On *shabbos* at home, meals were almost always the same: chicken, chicken soup, and challah. Once in a while, my mom would bring a live fish home from the fish store, and our tub would be its new home. After school I would play with it as it swam over and under my hands. One night while I was listening to the *Eddie Cantor Show* on the radio, I saw my mom tiptoe to the bathroom with a wooden mallet. She soon emerged with something wrapped in a newspaper. "Tomorrow we'll have fish for dinner," she announced proudly. I ran into the bathroom and saw the water swirling down the drain—the fish was gone. I had been on good terms with that fish—I wouldn't eat seafood after that. In fact, I became a very fussy eater, never even tasting shrimp until I was an adult.

On one particular Friday night, I'd been playing stickball with my gang when I noticed the sun was getting ready to set. After my turn at bat, I said, "Listen, guys, I've got to go home now."

Joey Feliciano walked up to me and put his nose against mine. "Sure, sure," he said. "Leave the game, you rat."

The rest of my team gathered around. "Why can't we finish the game?" they asked.

"Well," I said, "it's important to my family that we all eat together on Friday nights. It's a holy day for us."

"Yeah sure," said Mickey Riley. Then they yelled at me: "You eat meat on Fridays. That's God's flesh—you killed Jesus." And Joey, for good measure, added, "And you're missing a piece of your prick."

I hadn't realized that.

I ran home. My mother was just lighting the three candles for *shabbos*. I remember how beautiful she looked when she did that, how she would move her hands slowly over her eyes, then cover them and sing some mysterious words.

"What did you wish for this time?" I asked her when she was through.

"I asked God to help us to be a healthy and happy family," she said. "Now we'll eat."

"Can I ask you a question, Mom?" I asked.

"Yes, darling," she said. "What?"

"Did we kill Jesus?"

"Who told you that?" she asked.

"The guys on the team said we did it."

"No, no," my mom assured me. "That's just a silly story."

"I gotta ask her," I thought. "I just got to."

Finally, I came out with it: "Well, how come I got a part of my pee-pee missing?" Pop, Sam, and the girls tried to stifle their laughter; they wanted to see how my mom would answer that one.

"All good Jewish boys have that done when they're born," she assured me.

"Does it hurt?" I asked.

"No, no," she said.

"Well, then, how come Frankie, Mickey, and the other guys didn't have it done?" I asked. "Is it because we really killed Jesus?"

"Eat, eat," my mother said as the candles burned lower.

@ @ @

At PS 46, I learned how to recite the Pledge of Allegiance and how to do multiplication tables. I also learned how to read, which was partly responsible for my initial dreams of being an actor. I loved reading about Sinbad the Sailor and Ali Baba and the Forty Thieves. Fairy tales were my favorite.

I enjoyed reading the comics in the newspapers too. My brother, Sam, had learned that during the newspaper strike in New York, Mayor Fiorello La Guardia was going on the radio to read comic strips to children. Sam contacted the head of the Union Street Boys' Club, which was just down the street from our store, and told them that his brother (me) loved to read the comic strips aloud. I was invited to come and read to the boys at the club twice a week after school—*Mutt and Jeff, Popeye the Sailor, Tarzan*. I would get great pleasure from watching the kids' faces as I dramatized each panel of the comic strip using different voices.

After a while I graduated from comic books to *Tom Sawyer* and

Horatio Alger and then my all-time favorites: detective and crime story magazines, such as *True Detective* and *Crime Busters*. These magazines described lurid killings and always contained photos and maps detailing where and how crimes took place. I always imagined I was the one who was called in to help solve the crimes.

Sam once saw me thumbing through those magazines. "Listen," he said. "Why do you read that junk? Why don't you get some good books to read?"

I didn't dare tell him about the magazine that Joey Feliciano had loaned me. The cover said *Burlesque* and there was a picture on the front of a smiling girl, naked to the waist. I used to hide in the closet and read the stories about those showgirls. But Sam's warnings did take root, and I began to really study in school. I did fairly well and was allowed to skip sixth grade, after which I was sent to Public School 6, Nathan Hale Junior High, which was a fifteen-minute bus ride from home. I liked the school very much, especially a teacher named Miss Leary. I remember her smiling when I first entered her classroom.

◎ ◎ ◎

Movies always made a deep impression on me. On Saturdays the Union Street Toughs would go to the Rialto, a movie palace about three blocks from my house. The Rialto had a big marquee with red and green lights flickering on it, and I would pay for my admission with the dime I had earned during the week from completing my tasks at the store. We would all sit on wooden benches in the smoke-filled theater and watch Westerns starring

Tom Mix, Hoot Gibson, and William S. Hart, who became my heroes, and serials, such as *The Perils of Pauline,* starring Pearl White. I remember one episode where a mustachioed villain had tied Pauline to the train tracks. As the train bore down on her, my fists clenched nervously. Suddenly, the screen went white. Then the big announcement appeared: "What will Pauline do? Will she be killed? Come see the next episode!"

While the next reel was being loaded on to the projector, a man would walk up and down the aisle with a spray can, showering the air with a sweet-smelling spray that was supposed to eliminate the odors that came from the cigarette smoke and all the longshoremen sitting in the audience. I hated that smell, but I was always determined to find out what happened to Pauline.

One time I came home after a particularly bloody foreign legion film, *Beau Geste* (the 1926 silent version starring Ronald Colman). I lay on my bed and began to fantasize. Reenacting episodes that I had seen in movies always gave me a sense of power. I always seemed to be crawling around on the bed wounded, shot, or about to be sentenced to death. My light tan blanket was the Sahara desert, and I began crawling over the sand dunes as a proud member of the foreign legion surrounded by enemy Arabs. Suddenly, a shot rang out and I was wounded.

Bleeding profusely, I began moaning. I remember my mom knocking on the door; she was used to these reenactments.

"Come," she whispered. "Come, it's time to eat."

"I'm bleeding, Ma," I said. "I can't move."

"Please," she said, "the food is getting cold."

I lifted my bleeding arm. "Go, go, it's too late for me," I said.

Shaking her head, Mom closed the door. I knew that she'd set a plate of cold food aside for me—my wounds healed miraculously, and I went to the dinner table and sat at my usual place. By then, Pop was the only one there. He looked at me for a long time. His eyes narrowing, he said, "What were you doing in there? You got shot again? What kind of games are you playing? When you grow up, I want you to go to college and I want you to study to be a doctor or a lawyer."

@ @ @

Back when I was a little boy, I used to love to climb into our store window and curl up, pretending I was a cat. One night there was a terrible rainstorm while I was lying up there in the store window. I saw a man kneeling in the middle of the street, his hands above his head. Standing over him was a dark figure holding something in his hand. There was a flash of lightning, and in that flash, I saw a gun. I jumped out of my window perch and hid under the counter. I heard a clap of thunder and then a shot. My heart stopped. Pop rushed in and dragged me to the back of the store.

"You didn't see anything, you understand?" he said to me. "You saw nothing."

"I was under the counter, Pop," I said. "How could I see?"

One day several years later, Pop sat us all down and stood at the head of the table. He said we were going to have to sell the store and move. He explained that Union Street was getting too dangerous and that his close Italian friends had warned him to leave because the internal fights of the Mafia were spilling over into our neighborhood. Pop knew that this was a serious threat, so he searched for several weeks and found a house for us on Bedford Avenue in Flatbush, two miles away from our store. I met with my gang after the news my father gave us and explained that we had to move. I didn't tell them why; I knew that you never squealed, and I wasn't about to.

I had a sad parting with my friends, but I was happy that we were going to a real house now. It seemed like a mansion to me— it had a stoop with four steps leading up to the front door. Mom and Pop had their bedroom, my two sisters had theirs, and Sam and I were to share a small room. Now we had a toilet and a bathroom on each floor and even a dumbwaiter that, with a pull of the rope, would send plates of food from the kitchen to the dining room. Pop evidently was not going to work anymore—he received an adequate income from renting out the top floors of the house. Just across the street was a big building with a huge sign— EBINGER'S: BROOKLYN'S BEST BAKERY. Ebinger trucks would return from all the branch stores after picking up unbought breads and cakes that were sold the next day by the main store. We had plenty of Ebinger's leftovers. The smell of the bakery permeated the whole block. After that, I never enjoyed bread, cakes, or pies unless they were one day old.

When I was thirteen, Pop told me that I would be bar mitzvahed—he said it was the rite of passage for all Jewish boys, even though I don't recall my brother ever being bar mitzvahed.

"You'll be a man," my father said.

This puzzled me, for other than watching Mom do the *shabbos* ceremony every Friday night or being told that I had to fast on Yom Kippur to atone for my sins, we weren't a particularly religious family. Besides, I never could remember any sins I'd committed—maybe once or twice when I had stolen my baby sister's milk bottle or made up lies about how I was doing in school. Nevertheless, I now had to go sit with the rabbi at a shul called Shara Torah. The rabbi was a short man with a heavy beard who wore thick glasses.

"Now, my boy," he said to me during my first lesson. "We're going to learn a passage from the Torah. You'll learn to read it and say some prayers."

He breathed into my face, and I could smell his whole dinner. He towered over me, then leaned in close. "Repeat what I say," he said. Even his clothes smelled of onions, and the letters on the page looked like Chinese writing. Everything he said sounded weird.

"You will lay this tefillin," he said, as he handed me the little black box with its long leather straps. "This goes around your forehead, and these straps you wind around your right arm from your wrist to your elbow. You get it?"

After a while I was able to escape the rabbi's breath, but still all this winding and unwinding with the leather straps didn't appeal to me.

"Each morning, you hear?" he said. "Each morning you will do this after you're bar mitzvahed."

The whole family turned out for the bar mitzvah ceremony, which took place in the shul. I wore a black suit and long pants. That was unusual for me, because I almost always wore knickers. There weren't many people who attended my bar mitzvah, but I decided, "Okay, here goes." I tried to read from the Torah; it wasn't easy. The rabbi's eyes went heavenward as if to say, "What am I doing with this boy?" As I stumbled over the passages, he dug his finger into my back. "Good, good," he said. Afterward, Pop gave me $12 and my mother gave me an elegant fountain pen. My sisters smiled and congratulated me.

For ten days, I tied the straps around my wrists and forehead. And then I gave up. "I can't go on with this," I thought. "I'll fake it." So one morning, I closed the door to my bedroom, left the leather equipment on my bed, and began to pray loudly. My mom heard me. She opened the door and her eyes teared up.

"What are you doing?" she asked. "Why don't you do the ritual?"

"I can't," I said. "I just can't. First, I don't understand what I'm saying, and, second, I already know I'm condemned so all the prayers won't help."

Mom shook her head sadly. "I don't know what will become of you," she said.

"I'll be all right, Mom," I said. "I'm over thirteen and I'm a man now."

@ @ @

After junior high, I entered Erasmus Hall High School, which was located two blocks from our house on Bedford Avenue. It consisted of a huge square block that enclosed a large green campus. The buildings were covered with ivy. Despite all the trappings, I never enjoyed high school. I hated doing homework and I didn't join any clubs. I missed my gang from Union Street. The only thing I liked doing was going to the library to read.

But after my second term, I made a crucial discovery: The Flatbush Boys' Club—just a block from my house—was a great escape from high school. Here, I could swim in the indoor pool and play Ping-Pong. I also joined the Dramatics Club, where, for the first time, I could really make believe onstage.

Mr. Bradley, who not only taught swimming but ran the theater, cast me in my first play, *Fiat Lux* (Let There Be Light). I was to play the starring role—an old man angry with God for allowing his child to die. The first day of rehearsal, I sat on the stage with the whole cast—two guys and one girl. Mr. Bradley showed us a drawing of what the set would be—a small room with a fireplace and some very old furniture.

"Let's read the play," he said. "And don't act; just read it."

Two days later he began to show us where to move and where to sit. As rehearsals progressed, I began to develop my character by thinking of old men I could play, how they walked and talked. I began to fashion the old man I was playing after my pop, especially his temper. I also based the character partly on Leon Stock, a relative of ours who was an insurance man. Stock carried six pens in his vest pocket and wore spats; he would come by every week to collect the $5 premium on my parents' life insurance policies. (Decades later I would use Leon Stock in part as the inspiration for the role of Gregory Solomon, the furniture salesman in Arthur Miller's play *The Price*.)

Memorizing was easy for me. The part of the show I liked best was when I got angry with God for taking my daughter. Posters were put up all over the neighborhood announcing the play. My name stood out in big black letters. I got tickets for my mom and pop and my two sisters. Sam sent his regrets; he had a date or an exam. On opening night, I sat in the dressing room. Mr. Bradley had ordered a special gray wig, a beard, and eyebrows, and he pasted them all on for me. I kept staring at the red curtain, waiting for it to go up. My hands were shaking. I could hear people whispering in the audience. The stage manager looked at me sitting by the fireplace, nodded his head, and the curtain went up. I took a deep breath, and there in the front row were my buddies from high school and the club.

The play was going along fine, but then I heard one of my friends whisper loud enough for me to hear, "That's not an old man; that's Eli." The second guy giggled—"He hasn't got a real beard; it's just pasted on." For a moment, I wanted to jump off the stage and let them have it. But a voice inside me warned, "Be that old man."

I turned my eyes heavenward and let God have it instead. "You took my only child," I sobbed. "I don't believe in you anymore. All is darkness."

That seemed to silence my front-row critics. I enjoyed the applause we received at the end of the play. During the curtain call, I kept looking out front trying to find where my parents were sitting. After the show my pop said, "You were very good." Mom said, "I cried when you got angry." My sisters brought me flowers, and Sylvia asked for my autograph.

Now I knew I could be an actor.

◎ ◎ ◎

After I graduated from Erasmus Hall High School in 1932, Sam—who was now a college graduate after completing his degree in economics at City College and was working as a teacher and a playground director—asked my pop to call the family together to plan for my sisters' and my education. Sam said that Sylvia and I would be going to college in the fall.

Pop shook his head. "We can't afford it," he said. "The store is gone, and it will be difficult to raise money."

Mom, who always worried about our financial state, started to cry. People were selling apples on the street now, and a lot of men who had lost money in the stock market were jumping out of windows. "It's the Depression," my mother said. "We have no one to help us."

Sam said that he had investigated about ten colleges and that the University of Texas at Austin was an oil-rich school that charged only $30 a year for out-of-state applicants.

"Texas?" I said. "That's where cowboys come from. Why would cowboys go to college?"

Sam ignored my remark and reminded us of his degree in economics; he said he would be able to work out all questions of money. "Texas is offering an education to all who seek one," he said. "So no ifs, ands, or buts, you're going to college!"

Pop tried to wrest control over the proceedings, but he knew that Sam had worked out an unbeatable scheme. I kept silent, never mentioning my dream to become an actor.

2

The College Years

To get to the University of Texas, Sylvia and I had to travel by boat, taking a freighter that also carried passengers. We were put down in steerage. I never dreamed that this was the way one traveled; it reminded me of the stories Pop told me about how he traveled to America, also in steerage. Our first stop was Miami. I remember that the whole city seemed deserted; every building looked as if it were under construction, and it seemed to me as if all of America had gone broke. Our final stop was Galveston, a large port city on the east coast. From there, we took a train to Austin.

Miraculously, Sam had found boardinghouses for us. Mine was a three-story wooden structure painted green with white shutters.

I was to occupy a screened-in porch on a tree-shaded street. As soon as I arrived, I met my roommate, a tall tobacco-chewing fellow named Charley Young.

"Where y'all from?" asked Charley.

"Brooklyn," I said.

"Say something in 'Brooklyn,'" he ordered.

For some reason, the words of a song popped into my head: "Tea for two and two for tea," I said.

Charley looked at me suspiciously. "You chew tobacco?" he asked.

"I never tried it," I said. "But if you want, I'll give it a go."

He handed me some curled-up tobacco and told me to put it under my lower lip. "I'll join you," he said. "First one who spits is a loser."

Within ten seconds my mouth was filled with a vile-tasting concoction. But rather than spit, I swallowed, then promptly ran to the bathroom and threw up.

"You lose," he said, "but you're a good sport for trying. You can have the bed closest to the screen; it's cooler there."

The meals that were served at the boardinghouse were much like I imagined the ones cowboys ate: black-eyed peas, greens (which I hated), and a lot of meat loaf, chicken, and hamburgers. Eight of us, all men, would sit around a long table. There was one rule at the table—if you asked someone to "please pass the peas" and did not take the plate as it was passed to you, the passer could drop the plate, and it was your job to clean up the table. The room and meals cost $40 a month. Because I didn't have much money, I lowered my room-and-board costs to $30 a month by skipping breakfast and fasting on Sunday. I'd never fasted before—even on Yom Kippur at home, I always cheated by hiding Italian anisette cookies under my pillow—but doing it seemed to sharpen my reflexes. Still, I sure was hungry most of the time.

For the first few months in Texas, I felt as if I'd landed on another planet. In Brooklyn I had lived in a mixed neighborhood: Italians worked on garbage trucks; the cops were Irish; Jews ran the candy stores; Greeks ran the little restaurants. Here, everyone looked tall and strong, spoke slowly, and wore boots. During my first semester, professors were always calling on me—not because they wanted an answer to their questions necessarily, but because they wanted to hear my Brooklyn accent.

Austin was deserted at Christmastime; most of the students went to their hometowns for the holidays, so Sylvia and I went to the movies and museums. One time we even took a side trip to San Antonio to visit the Alamo, a shrine for the heroes who had fought the Mexican army. After New Year's we went back to school—I didn't do much socializing. After dinner my roommate and I would dig into our schoolwork.

While I was in school, Sam continued to be one of my best teachers. He laid down one rule for me: Once a week I had to read a book and send him a book report. I'd airmail the report to him; he'd read it and return it with a grade in the upper right-hand corner. I usually didn't get A's from Sam; still, these reports whetted my appetite for reading. Sam opened my eyes to Sinclair Lewis, Jack London, and Ernest Hemingway. Maybe he was trying to turn me into a writer, but I still wanted to be an actor.

After my first year at the University of Texas, Sylvia returned to New York, where she would attend Brooklyn College. I landed a job as a counselor at a boys' camp in the Berkshires. Camps in those days always had Indian names; ours was Orinsekwa. I always wore my University of Texas belt buckle; it was silver and had the school's mascot, a longhorn steer, carved onto it. I was the assistant to the dramatics coach, teaching acting lessons and supervising the building of the sets for weekly shows. I also wrote wild scenes about cowboys and Indians for the campers to perform. I was responsible for eight boys, most of them from privileged homes; they seemed to enjoy the work I assigned them: sweeping the floors of the tents, making their beds.

By the end of summer, with my salary from the camp and tips from the parents of the campers, I was ready to return to Austin. Hitchhiking was the cheapest mode of travel in those days, and the only way to get back to Texas without depleting my nest egg (tuition, room and board). Hitchhikers usually went solo; I stayed away from crowded areas where the hitchhikers gathered. I developed a technique for catching a ride. I'd sit on my little suitcase on the side of the road, looking forlorn and holding up a sign that read: TEXAS. I'd shyly raise my right thumb and point it at the oncoming car. Trucks were the best rides to catch; their drivers went long distances and they were happy to have someone to talk to. Usually, it took me five days to make the trip with stopovers in little motels.

Once I had returned to my old boardinghouse, I walked over to the registrar's office with my $30 tuition. He stamped some papers, asked if I was ready to start my second year of classes, then informed me that the fee for out-of-state students had gone up; it was now $100.

I stared at the registrar.

"I'm sorry," I said. "I have the $30 tuition and money for room and board, but not for the fortune you're asking. So I guess I'll have to hit the road and go back home."

"No, stay on," said the registrar. "We'll work out a plan to keep you here."

The dean of students was a lovely little man named Shorty Nowotny. He arranged for me to find work with the National Youth Administration, a federal program designed to help needy students work their way through school. It was headed by Lyndon B. Johnson, in Washington, D.C. Years later I loved to tell my New York friends that I worked for LBJ before he became a senator, vice president, or president.

I worked several jobs while I was a student: mopping up as a janitor in the student union building; sitting in the library typing up memoirs of old cowboys and their battles with the Indians in the Southwest; selling soft drinks at football games on Saturdays. For that job, I remember walking around the stadium my first day with a big pail of glass soda bottles. I was afraid that someone in the stands would recognize me, and I could hardly get the words out of my mouth. "Coca-Cola! Pepsi-Cola!" I whispered. Then I thought, "Who the hell cares who you are? Just sell the damn stuff!" By the third Saturday, I used my acting skills and pretended I was a hardened and experienced soft-drink seller. It seemed to work. I wouldn't even watch the football games; I'd work my ass off selling everything in my pail and then refilling it.

Once I saw an announcement asking students if they wanted to exercise polo ponies; in Brooklyn the only horses I knew pulled ice, milk, and fruit wagons. I went over to the university stables near the football stadium and met the manager of the polo team and asked if I could help exercise the ponies.

"Do you ride?" he asked.

"No, but I'm willing to learn," I said.

"All right, you're hired," he said. "There's no salary, though."

For a whole semester, before selling soda pop at the football games, I learned to work with the ponies—brushing them, mounting, dismounting, galloping. I really enjoyed it. Little did I know how handy these skills would come in when I would start to act in Western films.

The best job I had in college was as an usher at the State, which was the only legitimate theater in downtown Austin. Not only did I get paid for ushering, but I got a chance to see the touring road plays that came in from Broadway. I had never been in a Broadway theater, and the State looked nothing like the little school playhouses or the Yiddish theater in Brooklyn; it looked like an Arabian palace. My ushering uniform consisted of black pants with a green stripe down the side, a red jacket with fancy gold epaulets, and a very powerful flashlight.

The city of Austin in the 1930s was strictly segregated and so was the university. Blacks were only permitted to attend the plays in a roped-off section in the balcony, quaintly named "Nigger-Heaven." After I checked their tickets, I would turn down their seats for them. One night the manager made a rare visit to my post, the balcony. He saw me hand an elderly black couple their programs and turn down their seats. The manager pointed at me. "Come over here! Come over here!" His voice was full of irritation and anger. "Don't ever let me see you do that again!" he said.

"Do what?" I asked.

He turned the flashlight into my face. "Don't play dumb!" he growled. "You're not to turn down seats for any niggers. Never! Never!"

When I was growing up in Red Hook, I had never seen any blacks. I had heard about Harlem but had never been there. The only time I had ever been to Manhattan was when I went with my pop to buy toys for our store.

"They showed me their tickets," I told the manager. "I was just doing my job."

"Never mind about your damn job," he said. "You don't turn down seats for any of those people."

I looked over at the couple; their heads were buried in their programs. They didn't want to get involved.

"You understand what I'm saying?" the manager asked.

My answer was a meek "Yes, sir." The manager left me standing there, my face all red, my eyes tearing. "I'll quit this job," I thought. "The hell with him and his theater and his 'Nigger-Heaven' too." I was going to walk right down to the manager's office, hand in my goddamn red jacket with the goddamn gold braid, but the play that week was *Dodsworth*, adapted from Sinclair Lewis's book, which was one of the books that Sam had assigned me to read. The play starred Walter Huston, father of the famed director John Huston, who would later direct me in *The Misfits* and who was a distinguished actor in his own right.

During the intermission of the final performance, I went back to the alley in the rear of the theater looking for Walter Huston. He was standing on the landing platform, smoking a cigarette.

"Mr. Huston," I said timidly, "I'm a student at the university, but I'm from New York and I've got my heart set on being an actor. I want to get into the theater."

"We all do, kid," he said. "We all do." He flipped away his cigarette and was gone. I couldn't figure out his answer. Years later, while acting in *The Misfits*, I told John Huston of my meeting with his father. "Yep!" He smiled. "Yep! That's my pop!"

For the rest of the year, I continued ushering at the State, and after checking to see that the manager was nowhere to be found, I cheerfully handed ticket holders their programs and turned down their seats.

"All's fine in 'Nigger-Heaven,'" I would say to myself.

◎ ◎ ◎

When I was growing up in Brooklyn, I had nothing to do with girls. I never dated, never went to a prom, hated everything about high school. In Texas all the girls looked beautiful to me, and at the beginning of my sophomore year in Austin, my roommate Charley Young, who was three years older than me and the chief Romeo in our boardinghouse, caught me masturbating in the bathroom, at which point he decided to lead me out of my desperate straits.

"You need to get laid," he said. "On Thursday we're going over to the whorehouse on State Street. You can go to bed with a girl for only $2."

"I can't afford that," I said. "No, no, no, it's way out of my price range and, besides, I don't think it's legal."

"Don't worry about the law; the police have all been paid off," he said. "And don't worry about the price. I'll handle all the money matters."

On Thursday Charley and I entered the whorehouse on State Street. We climbed some rickety steps and were greeted by a bright red sign on the door: ALL GOOD MEN ARE WELCOME. ENTER AND ENJOY.

"Are you sure we're doing the right thing?" I asked.

"Leave it to me," said Charley. "Go on, ring the bell!"

The madam, a tall, elegantly dressed woman, opened the door. She reminded me of Margaret Dumont, the lady from the Marx Brothers movies. She asked us to come in and led us into a room that smelled like a florist's shop. The linoleum on the floor was all curled up and yellowing. Gray-and-red drapes hung off the windows. There was a scent of sweet perfume. What caught my eye at first was the huge jukebox with tiny blinking lights and a glass-enclosed cage through which I could see all the records. The cage held many records.

The madam smiled. "Take your pick," she said in a deep voice, and pointed to four girls sitting on the couch near the jukebox, all wearing short-shorts and brassieres.

"Which one do you like?" Charley whispered. I pointed a shaking finger in the direction of the girl sitting second from the left. "Here's some quarters," Charley said. "She'll tell you what to do."

The girl rose slowly and walked toward me. It seemed to take an eternity. "Hi," she said. The "hi" was soothing and soft. "I'm Edna May and we're going to have some fun." She was just about my height and had brown curly hair cut short and a tiny beauty spot near her left eye. I also noticed that her nipples seemed to be ready to thrust through her brassiere. The coin in my hand felt hot. "Let's go over to the jukebox, pop the quarter in, and dance," she said.

I started to press a number on the jukebox for a Duke Ellington jazz piece, thinking I'd use some of the fancy New York dance steps my sister had taught me, but Edna May pushed my hand aside and pressed another number. The record dropped down and the needle descended slowly onto the record; it was a slow, dreamy blues song.

"That's better," she said, pressing her body close to mine. She whispered in my ear, "This is what we call the belly rub. Is this your first visit?"

"No, I've been around," I assured her.

We kept dancing so close that one particular part of my anatomy began to grow. When the music stopped, she smiled. "Ready to come in?" she asked.

"No, sorry, I can't." I said, "I've got an exam in the morning. I'll see you next week."

Charley, who had watched the whole scene, ushered me out of the room. "You did well," he said. "The girl seemed to like you. You've now entered the 'man's world.'" I didn't know what the hell he was talking about; I thought I had entered the "man's world" when I was bar mitzvahed. Still, I enjoyed the belly rub, even if it was a poor substitute for the real thing.

◎ ◎ ◎

With my sister no longer in Austin, I grew homesick and lonely, particularly around the holidays. Homesickness is a painful illness.

I had felt it several times when I was a young kid going to camp. At Christmas during my sophomore year, 90 percent of the students had gone home while I was still in Austin, mopping up the student union. Leaning on my mop, I noticed an intriguing Christmas invitation on the bulletin board of the student union building. It read, "If you're too far from home, come spend the Christmas holidays with us." There was a phone number listed for the "Johnson Sisters" in Houston, a pair of kind elderly ladies who took in boarders during the holidays. I called the number and was greeted by the sweet voice of one of the ladies.

"Come soon," she said. "We look forward to your arrival."

Houston was the largest city in Texas and was not too far from Austin. I hitchhiked the whole way there and bought some flowers for my hosts.

The Johnson house was quite a sight to a young man from Brooklyn. It was set back from a well-tended lawn, the windows were all twinkling, and there were Christmas lights and a huge wreath hanging from the front door. Before I could press the bell, the door swept open.

"Oh, we're so happy you're here," said a petite elderly lady. "Thank you for the lovely flowers." She turned and looked behind her. "Mabel, come down and meet our Christmas guest." The two looked so much alike I assumed they were twins. They were even dressed identically. "Come in, come in," Mabel said. "Welcome."

The sisters seemed very excited by my presence. I walked into the living room, which was full of sturdy furniture. In a corner there was a large Christmas tree, and the room was filled with the smell of pine. On the limbs of the tree, there were colorful tiny balls, little cherubs, silver strings strung over the branches. There was a large star stuck at the top. A phonograph was playing Christmas carols.

We never celebrated Christmas back in Brooklyn. I remember when I first learned that there was no Santa Claus. Lilly Mangano, the brains of our gang, said, "That's a lot of crap. Santa is supposed to come down the chimney? What about all of us on Union Street. We don't have no chimneys. If we had, he'd be too fat to come down." And there was I—poor, lonely, and homesick. But I didn't dare tell the Johnson sisters that I didn't believe in celebrating the birth of Christ, especially after that time in Brooklyn when my gang accused me of killing him. As a matter of fact, when I was a boy in public school, whenever Christmas carols were sung and Jesus's name was mentioned, I'd hum because I didn't want him to think I was Catholic.

"Would you like some eggnog before we have dinner?" one of the sisters asked me.

"Oh, yes," I said. I had no idea what they were offering me, but it tasted sweet and delicious. I asked for another.

"Certainly," they chirped in unison, seemingly delighted to have me as their drinking partner. But after three or four eggnogs, my brain stopped giving orders to my tongue. My head hit the table and I was out.

I awoke the next morning in a four-poster bed in their guest room. "Did I ever have dinner?" I thought. "How the hell did I get upstairs? Did they undress me?" I felt ashamed that I'd passed out. When I found the bathroom, there was a towel spread over a table with a new toothbrush, toothpaste, a comb, and shaving utensils. After getting dressed, I closed the door quietly and started to tiptoe down the steps, but then I heard the sisters laughing. There they were, greeting me at the foot of the stairs. The beautiful Christmas tree lights were still blinking.

"There's a present for you," one of them said. "It's the one in the green wrapper."

My eyes got teary as I opened the gift: a bright red tie. "How can I thank you?" I asked.

"You can thank us by sitting down and having breakfast with us."

For more than an hour, we talked about the university and my Brooklyn background. They made me promise that I'd return next Christmas if I didn't get to go home. They stood in the doorway, waving me a fond good-bye, and I was more convinced than ever that they were twins. I hitchhiked back to Austin. I never saw the Johnson sisters again, but I always sent them a big colorful picture of Santa at Christmastime.

@ @ @

After the holidays I continued to carry a full schedule of classes, odd jobs, book reports for Sam, and extracurricular activities—I was on the fencing and water polo teams and even rode horses on weekends—but I never had the opportunity to study drama; the university did not have a fine arts department. But Austin did have a theatrical group called the Little Theater, where local dentists, lawyers, accountants, and doctors were able to realize their hidden desires to become actors. The Little Theater would put on plays that had previously been performed in New York or that they found in the Samuel French catalog.

I went down to their theater and asked if I could join. "Sorry," the artistic director said. "We've got a full quota of local Austinites." He suggested that I try the Curtain Club at the university. I had never heard of it.

The bulletin board at the university's student union building, where I was still a lowly janitor, was my major source of information. There, I found a large poster announcing the Curtain Club's next production, *The Second Man,* a play by S. N. Behrman. I found the club's office and asked if I could join the group. I was willing to cut back on all of my other extracurricular activities if I could get a chance to be onstage again. I auditioned using a poem I had learned in high school, Robert Service's "On the Wire." As I recited the poem about the plight of a wounded soldier, tears came easily to my eyes. It was corny as hell, but I was accepted into the club. At first, I didn't get to act much. I painted scenery, ran errands, gathered props, typed up scripts, all the while waiting for the chance to show the established actors of the club that they had an acting genius in their midst.

At long last, toward the end of sophomore year, I got to act in a play called *The Ninth Guest,* a murder mystery. A young journalism student from Missouri named Walter Cronkite played the doctor. Carrying his little black bag, he walked onstage and asked a distraught wife, "Where's the body?" She pointed to the closet, Cronkite opened the door, and I fell out. I made as much as I could of this brief moment; figuring that rigor mortis hadn't quite set in, I bent my knees slightly and slid slowly to the floor. The audience gasped. None of the critics mentioned me, but I thought I had supplied an exciting moment onstage. I was sure now that the Curtain Club would offer me more substantial roles.

The next year I appeared in two more shows, including Noël Coward's *Private Lives*; most of the Curtain Club's shows were drawing-room comedies. I played tiny parts and shared the stage with fellow students Zachary Scott, the first actor I ever met who wore an earring; Zachary's wife at the time, Elaine Scott, who later became an officer at the Theater Guild and married John Steinbeck; and future Texas governor John Connally, who would be critically wounded while he was a passenger in the car during JFK's assassination; and Walter Cronkite—the doctor who found my body—who later became a great journalist. I rarely had time to socialize with any of my fellow actors; I was still selling soda at football games, working as a janitor at the student union, and ushering at the State Theater.

Toward the end of my junior year in Austin, I wrote to various summer camps in New York applying for a position as a counselor. My credentials were pretty good by now; I could teach swimming, horseback riding, and drama. The camp that accepted me informed me that I was to report and meet the staff of the camp at Grand Central Station on the mezzanine at 8:30 A.M. on July 1 before we were to head off to upstate New York. The camp's colors were orange and white, the same as the University of Texas. With the money I'd make as a counselor, I could spend more time at the Curtain Club when I got back to Austin and maybe even get to direct some plays too. I hitchhiked back to New York, spent a week with my family, and kept my appointment at Grand Central.

On board the train, I sat next to a very pretty girl. She had jet-black hair, bangs that just about covered her big brown eyes, and a body like silk.

"Strange," I thought. "This is an all-boys camp. What's she doing here?"

We struck up a conversation, and she asked me what I would be doing at the camp.

"Well," I told her, "I have several jobs." I showed her my big Texas longhorn belt buckle, mentioned my swimming and horseback riding skills, and deepened my Texas accent, all with the intention of impressing her. "And what will you be doing?" I asked.

"I'm going to medical school," she said, "but this summer I'll be helping the doctor at the clinic in the girls' camp just down the road from you."

"A doctor?" I thought. That really impressed me.

Each night at the camp after taps was played and the kids were tucked away in their beds, the two of us would meet at the flagpole and take long walks by the lake, and we slowly began to obey that mysterious magnetic force that brings young people together. I would talk about my hopes for a theatrical career, and she would speak of her love for medicine. This was my first real romance, and we pledged to continue our new friendship after the summer.

At the end of the summer, we met in the city, had a late supper in an inexpensive restaurant, and renewed our pledge to continue seeing one another. I told her about how I was going to make it on Broadway, and she told me that she would soon be finishing medical school. After supper I walked her home; her parting kiss was long and heartfelt. "This is it," I thought as I rode the subway home to Brooklyn. "This is the woman for me."

My last year at the university was filled with writing letters to my doctor with ardent declarations of love. I cut back on my extracurricular jobs and spent more time at the Curtain Club. James Park, the director of the club, was determined to introduce a new sort of theater to Austin; he drifted away from drawing-room comedies and the Samuel French catalog and searched for new plays. He became my mentor, encouraging me to read Chekhov and Shakespeare and assuring me that I had talent. He cast me in the title role in Ferenc Molnár's play *Liliom,* which would later serve as the book for the Rodgers and Hammerstein musical *Carousel.* Liliom was a tough drifter who worked on the carousel, got involved in a robbery, and was ultimately killed. Mr. Park felt that even though my Brooklyn accent had survived three years of Texas, I was just right for the role. I felt strong and secure in this part, and all my fantasies, dreams, and yearnings about acting came to fruition. Audiences were most generous in their response, and the review in the university paper, *The Texan,* was quite complimentary. I knew then and there that this was to be my life's work. Nothing—*nothing*—would deter me.

I graduated from UT Austin in 1936. Dressed in caps and gowns, we sat on little folding chairs on a sloping green hill. It was exceedingly hot outside. The tassel on my cap kept tickling my nose, and the black gown was covered with sweat. There was not a breath of air. The speaker, the lieutenant governor of Texas, droned on, serving up the usual heartfelt platitudes, telling us that our odyssey was just about to begin and that we were now ready to face what was out there.

"Out there," I thought, "there's nothing out there." Most of the graduates would wind up as lawyers, politicians, or doctors. Not me.

After graduation several of my Curtain Club friends gathered for a late supper and to say good-bye. At one point, John Connally took me aside. "Why not stay down here in Texas?" he asked. "Work in the oil fields and you'll become a millionaire in no time."

"I don't think so," I said. "I'm going back to New York; I've got my heart set on the theater."

John shook his head. "I feel for you," he said. "But I promise to come see you in your first play. Keep in touch."

"And what are you going to do?" I asked.

"Politics," he said.

"Politics? Now that's something," I said. "You remember Governor Hogg? He had two daughters and named them Ima and Ura." I thought that was a cruel joke to play on his daughters. The first year I had been in Texas, the governor was a woman, Ma Ferguson; her husband, Pa Ferguson, had been impeached. She ran in his stead and was elected. All he did was move his chair right next to hers and continue to run the state. "That's Texas politics," I thought; it would make a great play. Later John would become governor of Texas and secretary of the navy and even ran for president. But he never came to see me on Broadway.

This time when I returned to New York, I took a Greyhound bus. No hitchhiking; now I could afford the trip. I was sad about leaving my Texas friends, but as we approached New York, I felt refreshed. I was now ready to swim upstream, climb the highest mountain, jump out of airplanes, anything, I thought, anything just to get into the theater. And then I recalled Walter Huston's tart reply to me about that: "We all do, kid. We all do."

Well, that "we" was now "me." I got off the bus in the middle of Manhattan. The lights of Broadway were twinkling. I walked past a theatre, and I imagined the marquee had my name in lights. At that very moment, a poem popped into my head: "My heart leapt up as I beheld my name in big, bold letters . . . A great big star is newly born, on this momentous morn."

"God," I thought, "it rhymes."

3

Before the War

AFTER I'D BEEN BACK in Brooklyn for three days, my Texas accent faded away, but my acting hopes ran into a big problem. At a tense family dinner, I began to discuss my plans about theater, but all my siblings had settled on teaching careers. Sam was already a high school teacher.

"Yes," I said, "I got a liberal arts degree, but you can throw all the courses in history, economics, chemistry, and English lit into the garbage bin. I want to be an actor."

Pop looked at me sternly. "From this you can make a living?" he asked. "It's the Depression, my boy. Even the Yiddish theater is dying."

I was not inspired by my father's remark, I reminded him of one of the times he had taken me and my sisters to the Yiddish theater on Second Avenue and how affected I had been by one of the scenes I saw being performed. In it, a hero was saying good-bye to a rich girl to whom he was engaged; the poor girl who loved him watched as he kissed the rich girl and went off to war. In the second act of the play, the whole neighborhood lined the street to welcome the hero home; he wore many medals, but no hand showed from his right sleeve. The rich girl screamed, "I don't want him; he's a cripple. I can't marry such a man! He's not the same man I was engaged to." The poor girl addressed the crowd. "I love him and I'll take him as he is," she said, "whole or not whole." At that point, the hero pushed his hand out from the sleeve, where he'd been hiding it all the while. "Haaaah!" he cried. I remembered being so startled that I almost jumped out of my seat. This just reinforced my decision to go into the theater.

"I don't care," I told my father. "I'm not giving up. I want to become an actor."

Sam now took the floor. "Look, Eli," he said. "You must look at the hard facts. Teaching is a proud profession and you'll make a good salary and get a pension."

I fought back. "Every damn lawyer, dentist, or doctor, and— yes—teacher, and even my friend Walter Cronkite all want to be actors."

Mom interceded. "Darling," she said gently, "just try to see what we all want, that you should have a life of financial security. Listen to Sam; he only wants what's best for you."

"But what do I have to do?" I asked. "I can't just go down to the Board of Education and say, 'I want to teach.'"

Sam explained that in order to teach in New York, one needed a master's degree. City College was offering free tuition in order to encourage teachers to join the school system. My sisters seemed to agree, and so it went.

Slowly, ever so slowly, I could see my boat the SS *Actor* pulling up anchor and drifting away from shore. I gave in. "I'll try, all right, I'll try," I said.

The week after that meeting, I called my doctor/girlfriend. "Oh, you seem so sad," she said. "Why?" I told her in detail about the discussion I had had with my family.

"I can't go up against the will of the family," I said. "So I'll stay in New York and get my master's in education and become a teacher."

"A teacher you shall be," she assured me, "and a doctor I'll be, and we'll be together." This seemed to ease the gnawing pain I felt.

I plunged into my studies at City College, and she went down to Richmond, Virginia, to attend medical school. We alternated weekends—one in New York, one in Richmond. We'd read poetry, take long walks, and make love. "This is it! This is it!" I said to myself. "I found the woman for me."

For months I studied for the teachers' exam; a written thesis was not required for a master's. The exam was based on four books. In Brooklyn, on the fateful day of the exam, I walked into the run-down Board of Education building on Livingston Street and sat down in a room with about a hundred other people. We each received a thick sheaf of pages. The words seemed to move around, and my sweat dropped onto the printed page. None of the questions made sense to me; they didn't seem to have anything to do with the four books I had studied so carefully. "Was I in the wrong room?" I wondered. "Had I read the wrong four books? Was this the exam for firefighters?" I didn't know what the hell it was. The proctor walked up and down the aisles. She stopped, looked at me, and smiled, seeming to take on the role of an executioner. I stupidly smiled back and my mind went blank.

A month later I opened the envelope from the Board of Education. "We regret to inform you," the letter began. My eyes narrowed; the word *failed* leapt off the page. At the next family gathering, I broke the news about the exam and my failure. Sam shook his head. "Well, that's not good news," he said, upset and disappointed. But as we walked out of the room, Sylvia whispered to me, "My new boyfriend is a conductor in a symphony orchestra, and he knows the head acting teacher at the Neighborhood Playhouse theater school. I'll try to get you an appointment. The path is clear, go for it!" Now Sylvia was my ally and co-conspirator.

Sylvia kept her promise and I got the audition. Secretly, I was delighted. I was sure that, aside from Sylvia, someone up there was on my side. On the day of the audition, full of confidence, I walked into the administrative office of the Neighborhood Playhouse. A secretary told me that I could get a scholarship contingent on being accepted by the acting teacher. She told me that my audition would take place in one of the classrooms. The classroom looked exactly like one I'd occupied in junior high school. Seated at a desk was a handsome, well-dressed man, wearing stylish glasses and a beautiful suit. He was smoking a cigarette. "All right," he said. "Let's hear your audition material."

I took a rickety chair, set it in the center of the room, bent over it, and launched into my surefire piece "On the Wire." I got down on my knees and bent my arms over the back of the chair. "O God, take the sun from the sky," I sobbed. "It's burning me, scorching me up. God, can't you hear my cry? Water—a poor little cup." While gasping for breath on the barbed wire, I caught a glimpse of the well-dressed examiner. He removed his stylish glasses and wiped them. "That'll do," he said, and stubbed out his cigarette. "I'll accept you as a scholarship student, but I think it'll take you about twenty years to become an actor."

"Twenty years," I thought. "What the hell is he talking about?" Didn't he know I'd done *Liliom* at the Curtain Club in Texas and my college newspaper had said I was great?

At home in Brooklyn, my family gathered to hear the result of the audition. When I told them of my acceptance, my mother smiled, Sylvia blew me a kiss, and Shirley nodded her approval. "Well," Sam said grudgingly, "I'm glad you're going to get a chance to try to make it in the theater."

My pop just shook his head. "From this you make a living?" he asked once more.

"I'll try," I said. "I'll try."

The Neighborhood Playhouse had a strenuous two-year course with a balanced curriculum: voice training, acting classes, movement, dance. The faculty was impressive: Sanford Meisner, acting coach; modern dance pioneer Martha Graham; and Laura Elliott, a famous voice coach who would take care that we'd speak trippingly on the tongue. Rita Morgenthau and Irene Lewisohn, two ladies who loved the theater, ran the school. Both had been social workers on the Lower East Side and believed strongly in an acting school that would train students and thus enrich the acting pool of the theater. My scholarship was $5 a week, which took care of my subway fare, cigarettes, and lunches.

The first morning of school, I rode the BMT train from Brooklyn to Forty-second Street and walked to the school playhouse on Forty-sixth Street. There were seven men and six women in my class; each of us stood up and introduced ourselves, after which Paul Morrison, the school administrator, spoke. "This is a school with no fancy frills," he said. "You'll all work hard; lateness is inexcusable. At the end of the first year, about half of you will not return. Those of you who make it through the second year and finish the course will be well trained."

The fancy, well-dressed acting teacher with the stylish spectacles was sitting at his desk. I labeled him my "twenty-year doubter."

"I'll show him," I thought. "He, Sam, and my pop will all get the surprise of their lives."

The teacher, as it turned out, was Sanford Meisner, who was already well-known throughout the theatrical profession. He'd been one of the original actors in the Group Theatre, along with Franchot Tone, Bobby Lewis, Morris Carnovsky, Stella Adler, John Garfield, and Elia Kazan. The Group Theatre had brought new life to Broadway. Founded in 1931 by Lee Strasberg, Harold Clurman, and Cheryl Crawford, it was the first American theater company to employ the teachings of Konstantin Stanislavsky and the so-called Method school of acting. The Group Theatre revolted against the staid, slick drawing-room comedies that were popular during the 1930s, opting instead for a new sense of realism and truth. In the summers the members of the Group would travel to upstate New York to work on new plays by writers such as Sidney Kingsley and Clifford Odets, who started out as an actor in the Group's ensemble.

For the first year at the Neighborhood Playhouse, we concentrated on acting exercises. For one of them, we had to pretend to sneak into a room through an imaginary window, tiptoe about, and search for valuables, all the while listening for sounds. Suddenly, Meisner would bang the table to watch our reaction. "I don't know about this," I thought. "This is probably a school for thieves."

Though following his years with the Group Meisner had grown somewhat disillusioned with some of Stanislavsky's methods, he had devoted his life to developing a method of acting that grounded the actor in reality, ridding us of our bad habits and our singsong vocal deliveries. "Why do you look up when you say the line 'I remember'?" he asked me once. "Can't you remember without looking up?"

For one month we moved about like animals, not using words but speaking gibberish. We made animal sounds instead of delivering lines. I wondered when we'd ever get to do a scene. Slowly, he would reconstruct us. With Meisner, we learned to listen and to talk. Simple talking, I learned, is one of the hardest things to do onstage.

Although I was doing very well as a student at the playhouse, I felt I was doing even better with my lady doctor. One weekend I went down to visit her in Richmond and found her in the anatomy lab. I peeked through the window in her lab. "Come in, come in," she beckoned—she was the only one in the lab and she was standing over a man's body on a slab. The room smelled like it had been washed down with Clorox. "Don't stand there," she said, "come closer." As I did, I felt like my whole breakfast had come to revisit my throat.

The man on the slab looked to be middle-aged. There was a big gash from his chest to his groin, and a blue tag was attached to his big toe.

"Let's go to lunch," she said, as she flipped a sheet over his body. I gulped.

"Lunch? What lunch?" I asked. "I'll watch you eat."

In the cafeteria I watched as she studied the menu and ordered a three-course meal. I couldn't believe it. "I'll just have tea," I said to the waitress. Halfway through lunch, my doctor began to regale me with tricks the teaching doctors played on their students. They would secretly run a wire up the leg of a male corpse, insert it in the penis, and as the unsuspecting anatomy class bent over to look at the body, the teacher would yank the wire, up rose the penis, and the ladies in the class would scream.

"That's not funny," I said. "I don't see anything funny about that."

Still, now we were really going steady, and for the next year, the future looked wonderful. I'd come up from Brooklyn regularly to have dinner with her family. Her mother and father were Russian immigrants; they were also doctors. I told them of my admiration for Chekhov, Dostoyevsky, and Tolstoy, and boasted about riding in an ambulance with their daughter while she was doing an internship at Harlem Hospital. Someday, I told them, I'd be appearing on Broadway, and I would set aside special seats for them.

But one evening while we were sitting on a bench overlooking the Hudson River in Riverside Park, my young doctor said to me, "I have a terrible thing to tell you."

"What?" I asked.

"I've met someone else," she said. My body went rigid. At that moment I heard the siren of a fire engine. I had a sudden urge to throw myself in its path—that would show her. "What could my girl see in any other man?" I wondered. I went home to Brooklyn, called my brother, and told him what had happened.

"Get on the subway and come over to our house," Sam said—by now, he was married to a teacher named Lottie Tannenbaum. "She'll make you some tea—and we'll talk."

"Listen," Sam said. "It's better that this happened now. There are thousands of girls in this city who would be happy to find you." He led me over to the public tennis courts near his building.

"Pick up that racket and get on the other side of the net," he ordered, and proceeded to smack tennis balls at me for the whole afternoon. That remedy didn't work. For days I moped around the house. Finally, I wrote a letter to my doctor.

"Dear Doctor," I wrote. "Until now, I was too stunned to pick up a pen. To put it mildly, it's taken me weeks to have this heart mended. Without any flowery language, I have a simple proposal for a remedy. I will send you a card on your birthday. You may send me one on mine. If, at the end of a year, you're still seeing someone else, I'll understand and you'll never hear from me again, Eli."

A month later she called. "This is strange," I thought. "She's not sticking to the contractual agreement."

"I was a fool," she said. "More than anything, I want to come back to you." Eagerly, I accepted. And for the next year, our relationship grew even stronger. Often she would watch me perform at acting class demonstrations. And I would make rounds with her at the hospital. Slowly, the aching void I once felt disappeared.

I went back to the Neighborhood Playhouse for a second and final year, having survived the elimination process; I didn't quite understand how the process worked but was confident that I would be asked back and was proved right. I felt secure and happy in my relationship with my doctor and looked forward to sharpening my skills as an actor.

Among the new students were two of the handsomest men I had ever met: Efrem Zimbalist Jr. and Gregory Peck. Peck was tall, slim, almost regal, and very shy. I knew instantly that he would wind up a movie star.

In the second year of training, once Meisner felt that we had mastered his exercises, he allowed us to do scenes. Martha Graham, happy with our grasp of her technique, allowed us to create and choreograph dance pieces that combined acting and movement.

The dictionary defines the word *mentor* as a "wise teacher or counselor," and in Martha Graham, I found such a person—petite with long black hair and piercing eyes, she was an exacting taskmaster who taught me the meaning of movement. I must confess that before I met Graham, I equated ballet with ice-skating—do three leaps, turn, and the audience would burst into applause. But when I saw her perform onstage, I found that she was able to make me laugh and cry, all with movement. She could choreograph

Emily Dickinson poems, any of the Greek legends. In her choreography, she encapsulated all of our longings, fears, dreams, and nightmares.

Initially, I was physically tortured by her techniques of contractions and releases. But during one of her dance classes, I chose to play an arthritic old black man sitting in a wheelchair. Another actor wheeled me down to an imaginary river that had miraculous restorative powers. I was no sooner set down in the water than I jumped back onshore, completely cured. I let out a joyful whoop and performed a dance that was a combination of a tango, gavotte, and Lindy Hop. "Fine, that was fine," said Miss Graham. "I'm pleased with your imaginative choreography." My heart swelled—I had proven my skills to the master.

"However," she said, and looked at me a long time. That *however* hovered in the air. "You're like a peasant tied to the earth. I want you to walk as though you 'carried the seed.'" I never doubted that I was a seed carrier—my doctor/girlfriend could testify to that—but Miss Graham's remark did help me to improve my posture and walk.

While we were at the Playhouse, we actors-in-training were always eager to watch the professionals at work. David Stewart or Tony Randall and I would wander over to Broadway with an old theater program in hand. We would join the paying customers as they marched back to their seats after intermission and slide into an empty seat, usually at the rear of the orchestra. My heart would pound while I waited for the houselights to go down; it always seemed to take an eternity. Sometimes an eager usher—evidently raised as a detective—would spot one of us. Shining a flashlight in our eyes, he'd ask, "Where's your ticket stub?" We'd pretend to search our pockets, and the paying customers would laugh as we were marched out of the theater. Still, that wouldn't deter me from trying the same trick the next night.

Today the Theatre Development Fund in New York serves as a sort of clearinghouse where one can purchase cut-rate tickets for that day's matinee or evening performance. In my time in the late 1930s, Broadway producers turned their unsold tickets over to Gray's Drugstore on the corner of Forty-seventh Street and Broadway. A large space was cleared in the basement of the store for avid theatergoers. About an hour before curtain time, an auctioneer would mount a platform and begin his spiel in a raucous voice: "At the Royale Theatre tonight, a roaring comedy. I have eight seats in the orchestra, eight!" The bidding would be brisk and fervent. I became a sharp and shrewd observer, always waiting for the second before the auctioneer would bang his gavel. Then up went my hand. "Sold!" shouted the auctioneer. "Sold— to that young man in the red sweater." That was me. And now I could trot over to the theater with my cut-rate ticket. I'd sit in style and see a Broadway show from the beginning.

With my cut-rate theater tickets, I was able to sample a lot of the current plays. One night Tony, David, and I went to see Sanford Meisner in *Awake and Sing!* by Clifford Odets. I guess we were trying to check up and see whether he could do what he was teaching us. He played a shy man who was tricked into marrying a neighbor's daughter. We were duly impressed and proud of his work; he seemed so in control, so at ease, so vital. But we were too frightened to go backstage afterward to compliment him.

One evening I went to the Belasco Theatre to watch Odets's new play *Waiting for Lefty,* which dealt with a taxi strike. I sat next to a man who looked like a taxi driver and who seemed to get more and more agitated as scene after scene unfolded. Finally, a small bushy-haired taxi driver stepped to the footlights. "Let's not live like slaves," he shouted. "Let's strike! Strike!" The man sitting next to me jumped to his feet and started yelling, "Strike! Strike!" Carried away, I joined him. "Strike!" I shouted. "Strike!" The man looked at me approvingly and smiled. By now, half the audience was on its feet.

"Oh god," I thought, "I'd love to be up there on that stage."

For our final demonstration at school before graduation, we did a scene from Henrik Ibsen's *Peer Gynt* under Meisner's direction. For Martha Graham's dance class, we were to prepare a movement piece using her techniques. Tony Randall met me in the hall. "Listen," he said. "I've got a great idea. Let's do something based on Thomas Wolfe's *Look Homeward, Angel.*"

I glared at him. Tony was a huge fan of Wolfe's book and had already read it three times, but I had tried to read the book and couldn't get through it. One critic had even said, "Mr. Wolfe has diarrhea with ink," and I had agreed.

"The book is over seven hundred and fifty pages long," I told Tony. "How in the hell can we dance that?"

"Don't worry," Tony assured me. "I'll cut it down to size. It'll be my responsibility." And using his edited version, which continually repeated Wolfe's phrase "A stone, a leaf, an unfound door," he choreographed the piece.

On the night of the final demonstration, the junior students—

including Gregory Peck and Efrem Zimbalist—the faculty, and the founders and their friends jammed the tiny theater. We got through *Peer Gynt* effortlessly. Meisner's teaching and direction had helped us show the audience that we were ready for the professional theater. Then came Randall's gem of a dance version of *Look Homeward, Angel*.

Tony danced his role as though he were Nijinsky. Remembering Miss Graham's instruction to "carry the seed," I leapt around the stage like a kangaroo or, even better, a gazelle in heat.

At one point, one of the dancers acting as a narrator stood on a stool, pointed at me, and said, "Uncle Sam wants you!" The audience—although realizing we'd never be good enough to become members of Miss Graham's dance company—gave us a rousing ovation.

Riding home that evening on the subway, I kept repeating over and over again, "Broadway, here I come!" But Tony Randall's dance was prophetic because Uncle Sam patted his beard, smiled, and said, "Not yet, not yet! You've got a job to do for me."

4

The War Years

DESPITE THE FACT that the war had engulfed all of Europe and that Hitler's armies were scooping up one country after another, the United States was still at peace. But Congress, in order to prepare for the possibility of war, passed the Selective Service Act on September 16, 1940, to strengthen the army; under the act, 900,000 men would be drafted into the army every year. Every physically able male between the ages of eighteen and twenty-eight was given a number; the lower the number, the quicker you were drafted.

One afternoon after a particularly miserable audition for a play, I walked into a newsreel theater on Broadway. I would often attend the newsreel theaters—for a quarter, you could see the news and kill time while waiting for your next audition. I sat in the theater and watched the screen as Secretary of War Henry Stimson, on film, reached into a bowl and drew out numbers. Suddenly, he seemed to look directly at me. Using the same gesture as Uncle Sam, he said, "You, yes, you sitting there so smugly in this movie house. You've got one of the lowest numbers I drew out of this bowl. You'd better get your affairs in order."

The movie screen went white and the lights came on in the movie house while I sat there sweating. "Did he really point at me?" I asked myself. "Was I dreaming? Do I have to go into the army?" Not long afterward, a letter arrived from Selective Service informing me that I was to report for a physical in December 1940.

After I got that letter, I had dinner with my doctor/girlfriend and explained my new status to her—1A, the lowest category in the draft. After a long pause, she told me that she could find a way to keep me out of the army.

My head popped up. "How can you do that?" I asked, thinking that she was my savior.

"I'll do an artificial pneumothorax," she said.

"What does that mean?"

"I'll inject some air into your back to collapse your lung," she said. "Don't worry; it's just a procedure doctors use to rest a lung when a patient has TB. A collapsed lung will make you ineligible to serve and no one will know."

I looked at her in disbelief. Did she really mean that? Did she love me that much that she was willing to risk her whole career to keep me out of the army? Or did she secretly want to kill me?

I said nothing. "Collapse my lung? How the hell do you get along with just one lung?" I thought. "No, not me; I'm going into the army."

At the end of 1940, I was summoned to the army medical center, where I, along with a long line of other civilians, was asked to strip before being examined by a doctor. The fellow directly in front of me was rejected. "Get your eyes and ears checked," the doctor said. "You can't hear or see too well. Next!"

Now I stood naked before the doctor; his stethoscope was icy cold as he passed it over my back. "Breathe deeply," he said. "Now again."

"Sir," I interrupted, "I have flat feet."

"So do I," the doctor said. "You're in good shape. You're in the army. Next!"

The night before I was to report, after saying good-bye to my family over dinner, I had a strange dream. In it, I was about to be executed, but I didn't know what crime I had committed. All my friends walked in front of the governor's office pleading for him to save me. But the governor looked out the window at all of them, sneered, and shook his head. The sentence was to be carried out. Right before I woke up, I was being led to the electric chair.

Before dawn I tried to tiptoe out the door before anyone else woke up, but my mother was standing there waiting for me. She handed me a package. "It's a lunch," she said, "and you've got a white shirt and some underwear. Take care of yourself!"

I was sent to Camp Upton in Yaphank, Long Island. It was there that Irving Berlin had written the song "Oh, How I Hate to Get Up in the Morning." What a title. After all the paperwork had been completed, I was assigned to the Twenty-third Station Hospital. I had no idea why; I was an actor—what was I doing in a hospital unit? Was I supposed to entertain the troops? It briefly occurred to me that the army experts who put together these units must have done a lot of research; how else could they have known that I was going with a doctor who wanted to puncture my lung?

I received my uniform; it was old, itchy, and left over from World War I. "Why don't your clothes fit?" my mother asked when she visited me at Camp Upton. "That coat is too long. Are you warm enough?"

After basic training at Camp Upton, we were driven to Grand Central Station, where we took a four-day ride on a dirty train, arriving finally at Camp Hulen in east Texas. We were marched to our barracks, where we received sheets and blankets and learned how to make our beds. Each morning the sergeant would conduct an inspection. One day he stopped at the bed next to mine, ripped off the blankets, and growled, "How in hell can you sleep in that mess? Do it over." When he approached me, I gave him an innocent look, and after a long stare, he passed me by and went down the line ripping blankets, cursing loudly. I could never understand why sergeants were always so damned angry.

For the next three months, we took courses in ward management, first aid, and hospital administration. I wrote long letters to my love, embellishing them with poems. They must have been effective because she wrote to tell me that she was coming to visit me.

I got a three-day pass and met her at the train station, and we settled in at a local motel. After each meal, we would have intense discussions about our future. "Why don't we get married?" she asked me.

"Marry?" I asked. "How can we do that? The army has me; I don't know for how long. We may all go off to war."

She gave me a painful stare. "You've missed the boat with me," she said.

"I can't commit," I told her. "I just can't." This may have been an automatic response on my part, and I have never completely understood why I said those words. Had I ever really forgiven her for having met someone else? Was this retribution on my part? As the train pulled out of the station, I saw her face pasted against the window. I waved a weak good-bye, but inside I was relieved.

One night not long afterward, I was on duty at Camp Hulen as sergeant of the day when the telephone rang. It was the operator; she wanted to talk to her boyfriend.

"Is Fred there?" she asked.

"He's in town on a pass," I told her.

"You tell him Muriel called," the operator said; in exchange, she told me that she'd connect me at no charge to anyone I wanted. "Who would you like to talk to?" she asked.

"My pop," I said. "It's my birthday today."

The operator put me through and Pop's voice came through clearly. "Eli, have you heard?" he asked.

"Heard what?" I asked.

"The Japanese attacked Pearl Harbor," he said.

"Pearl Harbor?" I thought. "Where the hell is that?" My head pounded; my heart skipped a dozen beats. I remembered while I was a boy attending school at Nathan Hale Junior High, I was taught that Hale, after being caught by the British and accused of being a spy, stood tall as the hangman's noose was slipped over his neck. "I only regret that I have but one life to give for my country!" he declared.

"Oh my god," I thought. "Is the army now asking me to do the same?" The next day, December 8, 1941, President Franklin D. Roosevelt in a famous radio speech before a joint session of Congress declared that December seventh was a date that would live in infamy. On the following morning, our unit received orders to go overseas. Our first stop was the Presidio in San Francisco. After living in tents for two weeks, we were marched aboard a camouflaged troop ship. And as the San Francisco skyline slowly disappeared, we headed west. "Well," I thought, "my love told me that I missed the boat; now I'm catching one." Days later we arrived at one of the most beautiful islands in the Hawaiian chain: Maui.

We set up a hospital in an elementary school at the base of Haleakala, an extinct volcano. My job as staff sergeant was to assist the officer in charge of admissions and dispositions. The day after opening, we suddenly got an overflow of soldier patients suffering from acute infectious hepatitis. None of our doctors could figure out where the hepatitis had come from. Strangely, none of us were affected. But we were wary about Japanese subs, which were reportedly encircling the island; as a result, the unit was put on alert and guards were posted around the hospital.

While I was in Hawaii, my faithful confidante and correspondent was my sister Sylvia. But the one letter of hers I remember most vividly was incredibly short. "This will explain it all" was all it said. She had enclosed a newspaper clipping with a simple wedding announcement: The love of my life, my doctor, had married. My stomach churned and all my rationalizing about not committing and missing the boat was gone—she was gone too. So I puzzled, "Should I have married her? And how could she have married a doctor and done it so quickly?" It was a deep pain and I wondered briefly if I would ever recover. "No," I said to myself, "I won't be defeated by such a turn of events."

At one of the free evening dances in Wailuku, Maui's biggest city, I met a young Hawaiian girl with deep brown eyes, cascading black hair, a dark complexion, and a body that caused heads to turn as we spun around the floor. Her name was Anita and she had lost her husband, a sailor, in the Pearl Harbor bombing. I told her of the loss I had experienced with my former doctor/girlfriend. As we consoled each other, I asked her if she was free on Sunday. "I'd love to take you to dinner," I said.

"Yes," she said, "yes, we need each other. I'll arrange things." And she sure did. She called me at the hospital and told me to meet her at the Wailuku Hotel. I arranged for my ambulance unit to pick me up there at 5:00 P.M. on Sunday.

Shortly after I arrived at the small hotel room she had booked, we fell into bed and made love, made love, and made love. For me, this was a wonderful consolation dance. At 5:00 P.M. promptly, my unit's ambulance arrived. My buddies trotted past the lobby, knocked on my door, laid me out on a stretcher, covered me up with a blanket, rolled me past the goggle-eyed hotel clerk, and loaded me into the ambulance. I went back to the hospital, and I vowed not to come back to the hotel in Wailuku again. But by the following Saturday, my yearning reached a peak. "To hell with my doctor/girlfriend in the States," I thought, and I wound up in that hotel again. I sure needed Anita, and Anita seemed to need me.

Two and a half months into my stint in Hawaii, I walked into the office of the colonel, who told me that he liked my attitude and the work I'd done in the clerical office. He said that he was going to send me to Officer Candidate School in Abilene, Texas, where I would be trained to be a medical administrative officer. I was a good candidate for administrative work, he said. I wasn't particularly keen about leaving Hawaii. It was a beautiful place and the weather was sublime; every morning at 10:00 A.M. the rain fell down and watered all the beautiful plants. I knew that I would miss Anita, too, but I would never see her again.

In Abilene I took a three-month intensive training course where we studied how to set up and run hospitals, allowing doctors a free hand to tend to the sick and wounded. I was so steeped in learning a whole new skill relating to the world of medicine and hospitals that I had little time to think of the theater. "Who the hell knows when I'll ever get to Broadway," I thought. "There's a war on and my first allegiance is to the army."

Graduation from Officer Candidate School was a colorful affair; there was a parade and a marching band. As the music faded away, we all rushed over to the headquarters building, where we were greeted by a colonel who handed us our diploma, a gold-plated bar to be worn at each tab on our collar, and one bar for our cap. Our assignments were listed alphabetically on a bulletin board in the headquarters building. My name begins with the letter W, so it took a hell of a long time to approach the board.

Finally, I looked up and there it was: "Wallach, Second Lieutenant. Assignment: Madison Barracks, New York."

"Finally, I'll be stationed in New York," I thought. "I'll be close enough to get home often."

Madison Barracks had been built during World War I. It was located near Watertown, New York, hundreds of miles from New York City in one of the coldest regions of the state. The barracks were located on the edge of Lake Ontario. Here, our new unit, the Sixty-ninth Station Hospital, was assembled comprising doctors, nurses, and enlisted men.

Army tradition decrees that after you become an officer, you give a dollar to the first soldier who salutes you. Walking across the campus of Madison Barracks, I felt my heart stop beating as I saw a soldier approach me. I wondered if he would salute; I already had the dollar in my left hand. The soldier gave me a snappy salute and I returned it. I felt great. As he started to walk away, I said, "Just a minute there, soldier. Here's your dollar!" I don't know if he knew about the tradition, and I imagine he thought all officers were crazy. Still, he took the bill, gave me another salute, and walked away.

It was not long before we received our travel orders; soon, we were told, we would embark upon a mission to deliver medical services to soldiers overseas. "Overseas?" I thought. "God! Here we go again."

I had not had the opportunity to visit my family yet, so before we shipped out, I received a three-day pass and went home to visit them in Brooklyn. My mother seemed so proud of her young officer. Pop—who had come to America from Poland in the early

1900s in order to escape serving in the Austro-Hungarian army—saluted me. "You'll come back," he said. "I know you'll come back. Where are you going now?"

"I can't say, Pop," I told him. "It's a military secret." Secret or not, I actually had no idea where we were going.

"Can't they keep you in one place?" he asked. "Why don't they make up their minds?"

We sailed out of New York Harbor. It was a slow journey aboard our troop ship. We met the nurses and enlisted men on the first day of our journey to an unknown destination. My eye caught sight of a beautiful nurse. We kept staring at each other. She introduced herself—"Call me Betty," she said. "Call me attracted," I said. Each evening after dinner we walked around the deck. She was a trained pediatric nurse and, unlike me, had enlisted in the army. She was tall and blond and had a beguiling smile. I was excited by the thought that we'd be together when we got to wherever we were bound. Eventually we arrived in Casablanca, North Africa, where we took over a maternity hospital on a lovely tree-shaded street. A big new sign was posted above the front door: THE 69TH STATION HOSPITAL. It took us a few days, but everything seemed to fit in place and we were up and running.

Second lieutenants such as myself had to perform many jobs: registrar, responsible for admission and disposition of patients; company commander, in charge of enlisted personnel; adjutant aide to the commanding officer. I got all three jobs at once. I just hoped that I could handle them.

I had only just settled into the job of registrar when Staff Sergeant Watkins, who had taught me the duties that administrative work required, walked in one day, saluted me, and said, "Lieutenant, there's an ambulance driver who wants to see you." We walked out the front door of the hospital; there was an ambulance outside with its motor running.

The driver saluted me. "I've got a body in the back of the ambulance," he said. "My captain told me to deliver it to this hospital."

He walked us around to the rear door, opened it, and said simply, "There he is." Lying on the floor of the ambulance were body parts; only some of them were covered by a blanket. I could barely get a word out. "What, what happened?" I asked.

"He was a flyer," the driver said. "He crashed near the airport in Casablanca."

Sergeant Watkins, recognizing that I was shaken, said, "I'll sign the papers; we'll take him to the morgue." As I was still shaking, Watkins put his arm around me and led me back to my office. "That was a tough way to start your job," he said, "but you'll get used to it."

Our commanding officer in Casablanca was a colonel and a proctologist (or an "ass doctor," as we would have said in Brooklyn). He was a crusty, demanding old-timer with penetrating eyes who wore rimless half-glasses. One day at 7:00 A.M. on the dot, I entered his office and saluted him. He looked up at me, smiled, and said, "Well, how is President Rosenfeld this morning?"

All my digestive juices congregated at the back of my throat. "Sir," I said, "he's our commander in chief. I don't think that's funny." The colonel smiled. "Come on, Wallach," he said. "Lighten up. Some of my best friends are Jews."

Some months later in my job as registrar, I admitted a large number of British sailors who had been severely burned after their ship had been attacked by Nazi planes flying out of Spain. Our colonel was suffering from hearing loss, and one of my jobs was to repeat any question addressed to him in a loud voice. The commanding general for the North African area dropped by to check on the British burn cases. I stood close to the colonel as he escorted the general around the wards.

"How often are the sheets changed on the burn patients?" the general asked. Before I had a chance to repeat the question, the colonel responded, "The food here is well prepared, three meals a day." The general's eyes narrowed; each time he asked a question, the colonel would offer another inane or disconnected response.

A month later I was happy to place a Teletype wire from base headquarters on the colonel's desk. I had read it before I put it there and eagerly awaited his reaction—he was being relieved of his command and shipped back to the States. The colonel put the paper down on the desk and stared at me for a long time. I think he was trying to figure out if I had a hand in this. "Just salute and get the hell out," he said. I shut the door slowly. Retribution? Perhaps. But I think that President "Rosenfeld" would have been pleased.

As I worked at the hospital in Casablanca, Sylvia continued to be an avid correspondent. In one letter she wrote to tell me that David Stewart, my classmate and closest friend from the Neighborhood Playhouse, had enlisted in The Eighty-first Airborne, Parachute Division. One of my jobs as registrar was to greet army units arriving at the airport, and on one particular morning, I noticed on a sheet that the incoming unit that day would be the

Eighty-first Airborne. I drove out to the airport, and once I was there, sent word to the captain on duty that if David was in the unit, I wanted to meet him.

"Yes," said the captain, "he's here. I'll send him over. Wait by the car."

David heard that I was waiting for him. He started running toward me and I ran toward him. Then he stopped, spreading his arms out as if to hug me. I started to salute, then he started to salute, and I held my arms out as though to hug him. We went back and forth like this and then started laughing. I then threw my arms around him and hugged him. All the soldiers on the tarmac started to whistle. "Why don't you guys hold hands?" one of them shouted. I gave them a stern officer's look and the shouting died down. We spent the next two days talking about the theater and what we would do after we got out of the army.

"Why in hell did you enlist in a parachute unit?" I asked. "That's the most dangerous job in the army."

David smiled and said, "I just wanted to prove that a Jew could face that danger."

It was a wonderful reunion, but soon after, the Eighty-first Airborne had to depart. Later David would jump on D-day in Europe—and survive.

Several weeks later the entire personnel of the Sixty-ninth Station Hospital stood at attention as we were introduced to our new colonel. "At ease," he said. He was short, stocky, and a natty dresser. His voice was soft and he spoke with a southern accent. "I'm happy to join y'all," he said. "My orders are to take this unit out of Morocco and go on to Algeria. If y'all go along, we'll all get along and this hospital will do a great job; dismissed!"

We packed up and crossed the Atlas Mountains by train, setting up a tent hospital just outside the city of Oran off the coast of the Mediterranean. We used Quonset huts as our operating rooms, x-ray labs, and mess halls. All doctors and enlisted personnel were housed in tents.

Early one morning in Oran, the chief of surgery asked me to transfer an unruly patient to a general hospital. The patient, a soldier, had tried to jump off a two-story building. "He's threatened to kill me if I don't let him see the nurse on duty. He says he's in love with her," the chief said.

The soldier was brought over to my office. He was a tall, blond-haired giant, and he stood before me in a hospital robe and glared.

"I'm a paratrooper and I could have jumped off that goddamned building with ease," he told me. "Where are you taking me?"

"Well," I said meekly, "there's a hospital near here that can take better care of you. We need to get you well quickly, so you can go back to your unit. I'll personally escort you over there."

"No tricks," he warned me. "I can kill you in two seconds."

"No, no tricks," I assured him.

"I kind of trust you," he said, and put his arm around me. As we sat down in the ambulance, he pulled out a pack of letters. "See these?" he asked. "These are letters from home. I haven't opened any of them, not one. I don't need them. I love the nurse. She's like a mother to me." He rested his head on my shoulder and began to cry.

"Oh god!" I thought. "What have I gotten myself into?"

As the ambulance pulled up to the general hospital, my paratrooper friend looked through the rounded windows in the rear door. He could see two armed guards waiting for him. I watched them drag him away as he kept shouting at me, "You traitor! You bastard! You son of a bitch! I should have killed you."

Two weeks later he showed up at my office and saluted me.

"Sorry I scared you," he said. "The nurse and I are finished. I'm going back to my unit now. Hey! Next time I jump, I'll think of you."

Many miles east of us, our soldiers were locked in battle with General Erwin Rommel's vaunted Afrika Korps, and we treated many of the wounded. Strangely, few of our patients had physical wounds; most had suffered mental breakdowns, and some had been struck mute in battle. The doctor injected some of the wounded with sodium pentothal, also known as truth serum. One time I saw a soldier lying on a cot in the receiving office; he seemed to be sleeping. A doctor invited me to sit beside him as he leaned over and said to the patient, "Why don't you tell me what happened to you, soldier?"

No answer from the soldier.

"Where are you from?" the doctor asked.

Still no answer.

"I'm going to give you a little injection," the doctor said. "It'll make you feel better."

A few minutes later the soldier stirred, sat bolt upright, and began shouting. "I'm standing next to my buddy," he said. "We're caught in a cross fire. I tell him, 'Goddamn it, get down! Get down!' I turn to him. He's lying there and his head is gone. His head is gone." Suddenly, the soldier stopped talking and stared at both of us. "I don't like you fucking doctors," he said. "I want out! I want out!"

My mouth went dry, my fists were tight, and I was crying.

"Lie back," the doctor told the soldier, "just lie back."

The soldier relaxed and seemed to go to sleep again.

Years later I auditioned for the role of Coney in Arthur Laurents's play *Home of the Brave.* One scene in that play was exactly like what I remembered happening to that soldier when he got the injection of sodium pentothal.

"You're not right for the role," said Laurents, a future Tony Award winner who would go on to write the books for *West Side Story, Gypsy,* and *La Cage Aux Folles.*

"Not right?" I said to myself. Then, since I was in my early insufferable sure-of-myself phase as an actor, I said, "You're making the greatest mistake of your playwriting career," then stormed out of the room. However, my remark didn't seem to deter Laurents from going on to make a major contribution to the theater and film.

In August 1944 the Sixty-ninth Station Hospital boarded a hospital ship: destination unknown. As we were crossing the Mediterranean, we found ourselves in the midst of a huge armada. Every ship was blacked out or camouflaged except ours. Our smokestacks were brightly lit with neon lights arranged in the shape of a red cross.

"Why do we have to be all lit up?" I wondered. It seemed like an open invitation to German planes. Still, we arrived without incident in Marseilles, the largest port city in the South of France, where we set up quarters in a deserted bread factory. The German army had used hand grenades to destroy most of the machinery. On one wall, I found a large oil painting of Hitler that I kept as a souvenir.

One evening our hospital unit was invited to see a USO production of *The Barretts of Wimpole Street* starring the celebrated actress Katharine Cornell. I was excited—this was my first chance to see a play since I joined the army. After the show was over and Cornell and the cast had received a standing ovation, I nudged my nurse who was seated beside me.

"I'm going backstage," I told her.

"Are you crazy?" she asked. "Do you know anybody in the show?"

"Oh, yes," I lied. "I met Miss Cornell several times. She was on the board of the Neighborhood Playhouse when I was a student there."

I had brought a large package with me and took it backstage. The doorman introduced me to a maid, who ushered me to Miss Cornell's door. She knocked on the door, then whispered to me, "Don't stay too long. Miss Cornell and the company are leaving for another performance in another city early tomorrow morning."

The door opened and I stood there and stared. Miss Cornell was seated at her makeup table. She looked beautiful. "Yes?" she said—her voice was musical. "Do come in."

I took two or three steps and continued to stare at her.

"Yes?" she repeated.

Finally, I stammered, "I'm a graduate of the Neighborhood Playhouse, and I hope to get to Broadway after the war. I'd like to thank you for bringing the theater to all of us here in Marseilles. Today I got a promotion to first lieutenant, but your performance was my best present. In return, I'd like you to have this painting."

I handed her the portrait of Hitler. She thanked me, set the

painting aside, then surprised me by saluting. My nurse was impressed not by the play but by the courage I had shown in going
backstage.

Several weeks later we moved on to Nice, a lush paradise on
the French Riviera. We took over the Hôpital Pasteur, a newly
built salmon-pink facility that stood six stories high. Outside, it
was nippy, and the colonel ordered me to have the heat turned
on. In my fractured French, I explained to the concierge of the
hospital that our wounded soldiers would be arriving soon.

"Please, monsieur," I said, "could you turn on the heat?"

"Impossible," he said with a shrug. He explained that the furnace needed to be repaired and walked away.

It was at this point I learned that my soft-spoken southern
colonel was truly a hard, no-nonsense man. "All right," he said.
"Tell messieur"—he said the word *monsieur* very slowly—"that I
want you to install kerosene stoves on all the wards and let the
chimneys stick out the windows."

I delivered this message to monsieur, whose face turned white,
and voilà!, in two hours the furnace was turning out heat.

Officers and nurses were quartered in villas that had been
abandoned by the Vichy French, most of whom had been sympathetic to the Nazis. My eyes just about popped when I saw the
elegant villa that the colonel had reserved for himself.

"You'll have the garage," he told me, then pointed to a two-
story building with six doors.

"Thanks a lot," I thought, "a garage—he must be joking."

I wasn't prepared for the wonderful layout that I would be in-
heriting. The garage became a wonderful meeting place for Betty

and me. There were no cars on the premises; the French land-owner had already driven them away to nearby Italy. On the grounds were manicured gardens, topiary, and life-size statues, many of them nudes.

My colonel was known to consume large quantities of liquor, and one day while I was on duty, I received an urgent call from one of the officers: "Wallach, get your ass over to the colonel's villa!" I sped over, jumped out of my jeep, and there was the colonel, paintbrush in hand, busily covering breasts and penises with black paint. He sang as he painted.

"Sir," I said, "can we go back to the house?"

"Yes, we can; of course we can," he said, then handed me the brush and the paint can. "Finish covering those ladies and gentlemen over there," he said, then wobbled over to the house, knocked on the door, and went in. I didn't comply with his order, assuming that he'd never remember the episode when he sobered up.

In order to run our hospital, we needed additional personnel, so base headquarters sent us about fifty German POWs who performed heavy manual labor, cleaning the wards and doing KP, dish washing, and grounds-keeping work. The colonel assigned me to command the POW detail, and I sent a half-dozen German prisoners to scrub and wash off all the black paint from my colonel's artistic work with the nudes in the garden. I'm sure they were puzzled, but they performed their jobs eagerly. After all, they were out of the war and got three meals a day and a clean bed.

Over time, I did develop a good relationship with the colonel. He looked through my records and discovered that I had studied to be an actor. He asked me to assemble a group of enlisted men from our unit and put on a show for the patients. Inspired by the touring USO show *This Is the Army,* created by Irving Berlin in 1942, I helped to develop a show that we called *Is This the Army?* Some of my men fancied themselves playwrights and wrote several very funny sketches. One actor played Mussolini, Leo Yanowitz played Emperor Hirohito, and I played Hitler. We sang, danced, and clowned around, and the patients loved it.

After the show the colonel came backstage and congratulated me. He was so enthusiastic that he arranged to book the show into several other area hospitals. This was the first time that I'd been onstage since I'd been in the army, and it felt and tasted good. I loved hearing the sound of the applause again. We played for hospital units in Cannes and Juan-les-Pins. The colonel was so pleased with our touring company that he promoted me to captain.

"Well," I thought, "doing what I love doing and being promoted is better than winning an Oscar or a Tony."

Shortly after the attack on Pearl Harbor, our government, in a fit of anger and fear, passed a law setting up concentration camps in Arizona, California, Nevada, and Utah. Whole families of Japanese American citizens and noncitizens alike were rounded up and interned for the duration of the war. This action was approved by Congress, President Roosevelt, and the Supreme Court. One exception was the 442nd Battalion, a unit made up entirely of Japanese American soldiers who were shipped to the European Theater of Operations and fought on the Franco-Italian border. Our hospital was responsible for providing all medical service to them. I'd ride a fast train past Monte Carlo to the border, where we would pick up the wounded and bring them back to Nice. I was also assigned to issue Purple Hearts, and the 442nd won more of these awards than any other unit in the army, though whenever I issued those Purple Hearts, I would always think of Bill Mauldin's famous cartoon in *Yank*, the army newspaper. Seated at a desk piled high with Purple Hearts was an officer, just like me. An unshaven and unkempt soldier stared at the proffered Purple Heart. "No, no thanks," the soldier said. "I just want some aspirin."

In 1945, with the war in the west coming to a fast close, General Dwight Eisenhower gave the Red Army the honor of crushing the Nazi defenders in Berlin, which they did with great speed. In August I received a three-day pass and flew into Berlin, where I landed at Tempelhof Airport. The entire city looked devastated; only a few buildings were still standing.

I was met at the airport by a young Russian major. She was built like a halfback and her blond curly hair peeked out from under her helmet. A big pistol was strapped to her hip. "Comrade," she said in broken English, "I have been ordered to escort you on a tour of the city."

The Ministry of Propaganda was our first stop. One of the rooms was knee-deep in official photographs from the German army. I asked the Russian major if I could take some of the pictures.

"Da! Da!" she said. "Take all you want."

I swooped up about fifty pictures; among them were photos of Mussolini being rescued by Nazi glider troops in northern Italy, where he had been a prisoner. Later, when I returned home from the army, I didn't have much money, so I wound up selling ten of the photographs to *Life* magazine for $300.

Back in Nice, our medical unit was disbanded, and I was subsequently transferred to another medical unit. The army had made plans for medical units to leave the European Theater of Operations and proceed to the Far East to set up facilities for the potential invasion. I was sent to a new unit in Marseilles, where I was to await passage to the Far East. While I was there, I heard the radio crackle with news of the atomic bomb being dropped on Hiroshima, and then two weeks later on Nagasaki, thus ending the war with Japan.

"Good," I thought when I heard the news. "Good! Now I'll be able to return to civilian life. I'll be out of the army. I can go back home, see my family, and get to Broadway."

Years later when I was on Broadway appearing as an Okinawan in *The Teahouse of the August Moon,* Norman Cousins, the editor of the magazine *Saturday Review,* arranged for a small group of severely burned Japanese women from Hiroshima to come to America for plastic and reconstructive surgery. After the play they came backstage to say hello to the cast. I was still in my costume, and the women tittered and grinned as we were introduced. They bowed to me and I bowed in exchange. This went on for a minute or two. "This is getting to be a real routine," I thought. But each time I looked at their faces, I felt that their plastic surgery didn't do a good job. Each time I bowed, I lowered my eyes. It was hard to look at them. And then I remembered my initial reaction to the bombings at Nagasaki and Hiroshima—"Good, good! At last I'll get to go home"—and I felt ashamed.

Before returning to the United States for eventual discharge, I was named a finance officer of another medical unit. I was issued a .45-caliber pistol; it was the first and only time I carried a weapon in almost five years. Two armed sergeants carrying a safe accompanied me on board. I was to make final salary payments to my unit. While packing to go home, I found copies of two letters that I'd written to the ladies who founded the Neighborhood Playhouse.

March 22, 1944

Dear, Dear Ladies,

Word has reached me that Miss Lewisohn is ill. I would be deeply grateful if you would write me as soon as possible letting me know how she is. I'm not a sentimentalist nor a highly excitable guy, but you both are a strong part of me. To you both, I owe the unrepayable, for you were patient with me and your hands were of molding force. Miss Lewisohn's home was where I first ate shrimp during a costume party. Mrs. Morgenthau was the first lady who asked me if I wanted to be an actor and didn't try to tell me to become a dentist or a stock clerk or a teacher. I've been away for many years and will probably be gone for many more. But the Playhouse was a landmark I could touch in a New York that was cold. I could pray for Miss Lewisohn but I want to put it on paper. Just know that all the way from Africa I send my earnest hope that she will recover happily.

The second letter I wrote was dated May 2, 1944, and was addressed to the Neighborhood Playhouse.

I feel so helpless, so crushed. I read the news of Miss Lewisohn's death. I read it alone and then walked out of the office, and away from the hospital. She's gone but I know deep inside me that she

*wants the school to continue. She was a stalwart opponent of intoler-
ance. She is what the war is being fought over. I'm sorry she couldn't
be here to see the last remnants of hatred and fascism wiped off the
earth. To me, and others, it is a challenge, a chance to keep Irene
Lewisohn and her ideas and ideals alive. In this, we shall not fail.
You can carry on, I know it. And when your Playhouse boys get back,
we'll pitch in too.*

Those two letters represented a transition for me. Yes, I was
fearful of what I would face when I came back. But I was proud
of the adjustment I had made to army life, putting my acting career in cold storage. I had always planned to become one of the
Playhouse boys who made it back. Now I intended to make the
school proud of me and finally, finally be able to say, "Broadway,
here I come!"

All through my time in the service, I had corresponded with
my family via V-Mail (express delivery), with the producer Her-
man Shumlin and the director Elia Kazan, whom I'd met before
I left for the army—I considered them my lifeline back to the
theater.

We set sail from Marseilles—the crossing was to take six days,
we were told. We boarded the troop ship, which was still painted
in green-and-black camouflage colors. I carried out my finance
officer duties on the second day at sea, paying off the men in my
unit in time for them to enjoy playing craps and poker. I dutifully turned in my .45-caliber pistol to the commanding officer.
After lunch each day, I'd go up to the stern of the ship and stare
out at the wake.

"Good-bye, Europe," I thought. "Good-bye army!" I wondered if I would be able to wash away the five years I had spent in uniform.

During my time in the army, I had developed a deep sense of discipline. Each day was clearly charted. I learned about hospital administration, the world of medicine and doctors, and the meaning of death. I jumped over many hurdles in trying to make my dream of being an actor come true: my family's resistance, college, teacher exams, acting school, the army, the war. I was nearing my thirtieth birthday. I wondered if I was already past my prime; most actors start their careers quite young.

Right on schedule, on the sixth day, our ship was gently nudged into place in New York Harbor by tugboats; each little boat proudly flew the American flag. On land a band was playing "Stars and Stripes Forever." The New York skyline was ablaze with lights; this was quite a change from the blackouts we had experienced in Europe.

We entrained to Fort Dix, New Jersey. Two days of paperwork and I was handed my discharge papers. "Welcome back," said a lady from the Red Cross. She handed me a doughnut and a cup of hot coffee. "We're happy you're home."

"Yes," I thought. "I'm happy to be home."

Betty, my nurse, and I met again after we were discharged. She was now doing pediatric nursing duty at Presbyterian Hospital in New York and was happy that we'd be together again.

A taxi deposited me on Bedford Avenue in Flatbush. The house that had looked like a mansion when we had moved from Little Italy now seemed so small and run-down. Thomas Wolfe wrote a novel called *You Can't Go Home Again*. Well, we'll see about that.

5

Broadway,
Here I Come

UPON MY RETURN to Brooklyn, just as I was about to ring the doorbell, suddenly all of the upstairs windows popped open. My sisters, Shirley and Sylvia, leaned out and shouted, "Welcome! Welcome!" And then the door opened and I saw Mom and Pop. Pop saluted me; his hair was all gray now.

"We'll go see a baseball game," he said, "my treat."

There were tears in my mom's eyes as she gave me a lovely smile. "We'll have a great dinner; it's all prepared," she said. She seemed shorter than I remembered. As I entered the house, I saw Sam walking across the room toward me. He gave me an extra hug.

"Welcome back," he whispered. To me, Sam's hug seemed to

say, "The family believes in you, and you're about to cross the finish line after a long race."

Dinner brought back old memories: Friday nights, chicken soup. But this time, I didn't reach across to pull the wishbone with my little sister, Shirley. I sat there in my uniform as my family began to ask me questions.

"No, no, no," I told them, "I don't want to talk about the army. I want to know about you."

"Can you at least take the uniform off now?" Mom asked.

"No, not yet," I said. "I'm on 'terminal leave'—I have to continue to wear it for a few months." Actually, I enjoyed wearing the uniform; it gave me a feeling of importance.

I settled back into life at home with no bugles, taps, or reveilles. But one night I had a vivid dream. I was seated in a dingy court in Brooklyn. The judge, beetle-browed and taciturn, brought his gavel down. "You may now begin your opening statement," he said. The prosecutor rose, turned to the jury, and said, "I've come to present the state's case against this defendant. I intend to show him as a self-centered, hubristic charlatan. He intends to delude you into thinking that he can contribute something to the theater. He cannot. And I repeat, *cannot!*"

On and on he droned. The jury shifted in their seats, their eyelids slowly coming down like a final curtain. The attorney for the defense rose, cleared his throat, and stated, "I intend to paint a completely different picture. This actor's only crime is his desire to open his heart to the truth, to enrich your lives, to turn the mirror, as it were, up to nature. He wants to bring you joy, pleasure." The jury sat upright, their eyes glistening. One began to clap and then the others joined in. Finally, they all stood and cheered. "Silence! Silence in this courtroom," the judge growled. "Silence! I want silence!"

Suddenly, I woke up, refreshed, renewed, determined now more than ever to get into the theater.

Broadway was thriving now. Many, many plays were put on. I'd come into the city from Brooklyn. Sometimes I would go to auditions proudly displaying my captain's bars, but it didn't help much. I met up again with many of my classmates from the Neighborhood Playhouse. David Stewart had survived jumping out of planes, and Tony Randall had also overcome the years of service. At Walgreens Drugstore on Forty-fourth Street and Broadway, a hangout for actors, we'd discuss honing the skills we learned at the Playhouse to get to Broadway and some of the many dilemmas facing actors. One such dilemma had to do with the union, Actors' Equity: You couldn't get a job in the theater unless you were a member of the union, and you couldn't get into the union if you didn't have a job.

As I pursued auditions, I often thought of myself as an unlucky fisherman sitting in a tiny boat, staring out at the water, waiting. Then the rod was almost pulled out of my hand completely—a strike. That's what happened the day I walked past the Belasco Theatre on Forty-fourth Street. Six guys were standing in line.

"Are they casting?" I asked.

"Yeah," one of them said. "Believe it or not, we're the last batch. Hop on line!"

The play, written by Harry Kleiner, who would later go to Hollywood to become a screenwriter, was called *Skydrift*, and it concerned a group of dead soldiers returning from the war to their families as ghosts. Not a pleasant subject for a play. I happened to be wearing my uniform at the time of the audition, and the director, Roy Hargrave, asked what branch of the service I was in. I told him I had been a medic, and he gave me some lines to read. Once I had read the lines, he told me that he would cast me in the role of the dead soldiers' crew chief. Maybe the uniform helped this time. Finally, I would have my Broadway debut.

The set for the play was a huge plane that had been cut in half so that the audience could see us moving about inside. In my role as crew chief, I was to issue orders to the other characters, telling them where to sit, but my voice was barely strong enough to rise above the noisy sound effect of the airplane motors. Throughout rehearsals I kept watching the producer, the stage manager, and the director whispering. I knew they were staring at me, and I was doubly sure I was going to be fired. At the time, Equity rules stated that if you were fired before five days of rehearsal, you would be paid only for the days you rehearsed. After the five-day period, you were entitled to at least two weeks' pay.

There's an old apocryphal theater story about an actor who is handed a telegram after the fifth day of rehearsal. "The bastards don't even have the courage to tell me to my face; they have to send me a wire," the actor says as he opens the telegram. But then, as he reads the telegram, his facial expression turns calmer. "It's okay," he says. "My mother just died."

A few days before our opening, I was still worrying about being fired. While supervising the lighting of the set, Roy Hargrave stepped back too far and fell into the orchestra pit. After the doctors got through with him, he returned to rehearsals thumping around the stage wearing a heavy cast. Relying on my army medical training, I was able to maneuver his broken leg so he wouldn't be in pain. In this way, I managed to stay on in my original role.

Skydrift opened at the Belasco on November 13, 1945. On opening night, I recalled all the great Group Theatre plays I'd seen there—*Waiting for Lefty, Awake and Sing!, Johnny Johnson, Golden Boy*. And now I was thrilled to be on that same stage. On opening nights, actors would always get telegrams or flowers. James Park, my mentor from the Curtain Club, sent me a telegram. Sam and my sisters sent flowers. Sam wrote me a note, too—"You did it, dear brother; I'm proud of you"—which made my heart jump. I remember standing in the wings, listening to the audience as they filed in to take their seats. "Breathe deeply," I thought. "You're a crew chief; go act like one!" The curtain rose and I'd made it; Broadway, here I am.

But all the New York critics seemed to have banded together; they sneered at the premise of the play, hated the set, the direction, and the actors. Our play was shot down, and four days later we closed. Happily for me, my name was nowhere to be found in the scathing reviews. And I was able to start off fresh without the taint of a visible failure.

For weeks in the early mornings, I would wander around to agents' offices. "Too short," they'd say, "not a leading-man type." Tony Randall always told one joke about going to an audition. A casting agent would look at him for a long time. "Say something," he would order.

In a rich baritone, Tony would say, "My name is Randall; I'm from Oklahoma."

The agent would shake his head: "The voice is too deep, your hair is too short; you've got the beginning of a beard. Actually, we're looking for a girl."

At the time, I didn't think Tony's joke was all that funny because I kept hearing this same damn refrain day in and day out. Agents would shake their heads. "Drop by again next week," they'd say. "Try us again."

Still, I managed to keep my spirits up. I had heard a story about a wealthy actor named Conrad Kenson who left a quarter of a million dollars in his will to the Actors' Fund to pay for shoes for unemployed actors. According to his will, any actor who needed shoes could go to a Thom McCann shoe store and the Actors' Fund would pay for the shoes. Kenson used to say, "An actor cannot hold his head up if his heels are run-down."

"Not me," I remember thinking, "I'll never have to take advantage of that gentleman's offer."

After weeks of wandering, I did manage to get an interview with an important agent: Maynard Morris of the William Morris Agency. Morris asked me to tell him about my acting experiences.

"Well," I began, "I've been in the army for a long time."

Just then the phone rang and he picked it up. While he was talking, my eyes wandered about the room. There on the walls were huge pictures of famous actors. They all looked so handsome. I thought, "Will my picture ever be up on that wall?"

Morris hung up the phone. "Now," he said again, "tell me about your background, your experiences."

"Well," I started again, "I just closed in a play called *Skydrift*."

"Oh," he said. "Well, the critics shot that one down pretty quick. Come back in a month or so and we'll talk again."

After early morning casting rejections, I'd usually have a whole day to kill before riding the subway back to Brooklyn. Often I would wander into the film houses on Forty-second Street, and for a quarter, I would watch movies starring great French actors— Harry Baur, Jean Gabin, Louis Jouvet, Jean-Louis Barrault, Raimu. "God, that was beautiful, brilliant acting," I would think, and try to find something in their performances to take as my own.

Before the war, I had met a dynamic, creative southern girl named Terry Hayden. She was devoted to the theater and asked me to keep in touch with her after I got out of the army. In February 1946, still wearing my uniform, I walked up the steps of her apartment on West Fifty-fourth Street, wondering if she would remember me, if she had given up her plans for the theater.

After we had talked for a while, she told me about a plan she was developing to produce plays in New York branch libraries. It turned out that many libraries had tiny, barely used theaters in their basements. Terry had already gotten the cooperation of Actors' Equity and the head of the New York Public Library to start her theater company, which she was calling Equity Library Theater.

"We'll put on play revivals," she said, "and producers, directors, and especially agents can come see the actors display their wares."

She told me that she would be directing Tennessee Williams's two-character, one-act play *This Property Is Condemned* and that she wanted me to act in it.

"Read the script, come back next week, and I'll have you read with a young actress who I think can play the other role," Terry said.

The following week I showed up at Terry's apartment, and she asked me to take my script and have a seat by the window. I was thumbing through the script when the door opened and in came a pretty redhead with beautiful blue eyes. Terry introduced us, but in my nervousness I instantly forgot the girl's name. She regarded me coolly. I sensed that she was not sure about what I was doing there. Terry took the girl aside and said, "Listen, he's going to play the role of Tom with you."

The girl looked surprised and her voice, soft and sweet like a viola, traveled across the room.

"He's a soldier, Terry," she said. "He's too old. He's too old for a fifteen-year-old boy. And what's he doing in a uniform?"

"Just act with him," Terry said. "You'll enjoy it."

Williams's play takes place on a set of railroad tracks. A young boy is flying a kite, a girl comes by, and they begin to play the scene. As we read, I kept trying to shave years off my age.

"I'm nearly thirty," I thought as I heard the girl's voice echoing in my ear—"too old, too old." Still, I read the part and I got it. Little did I realize that I would spend the rest of my life with that red-headed girl whose name I couldn't remember: *Anne Jackson*.

We rehearsed the play in the basement of the Hudson Guild Library in Greenwich Village. Terry was an excellent guide, putting us through our paces. While Anne's coolness disappeared, my temperature went up. Some strange chemical process was taking over. Slowly, her "too old" statement no longer mattered. As we talked before and after rehearsals, she revealed that she, too, had studied at the Neighborhood Playhouse. Though she was only twenty years old, she had already toured America as the ingenue in Chekhov's *The Cherry Orchard* with Eva Le Gallienne and Joseph Schildkraut.

Our play was very well received, and Anne and I really enjoyed performing together. And meanwhile, our romantic relationship began to grow. We'd often eat at the Golden Peacock on West Ninth Street in Greenwich Village, where a complete dinner for two cost $4. We spent a lot of time talking and listening to each other and staring at one another across the table. I talked a lot about my army career and hospitals and the war, tending to enlarge the dangers I had faced.

Now I had to make a difficult decision. My army nurse—and companion for more than two years—had to be told that I'd found someone else. That jolted me, for those were the exact words that my doctor had used years before in our talk at the park on Riverside Drive.

Betty and I sat in the nurses' lunchroom at Presbyterian Hospital. I felt miserable all through the meal. I finally got up the courage to say that I had met someone else. "Are you telling me we're through?" she asked. I couldn't find the words to answer her question. "It's all right," she said as she patted my hand. I droned on about how much I treasured our time together in Africa and France. "It's all right," she repeated as she walked away. The waiter came over, tapped me on the shoulder, and said, "The lunchroom is now closed."

I felt like a bastard on the long subway ride home to Brooklyn. But I realized that I'd been involved in medicine in my two previous relationships. It was a time for me to shed all that and settle on my acting career. I'd found an actress who shared my hopes and dreams and who understood what the life of an actor meant.

Anne always dressed beautifully; her speech gave no clue as to her background or upbringing. Frankly, I'd always thought she was a wealthy socialite who had abandoned her family to become an actress, until she asked me to come meet her father. I imagined us driving up a winding, tree-lined road into posh Locust Valley, Long Island. We would arrive at a huge mansion, where three servants would greet us on the front porch. Instead, we took the subway to Astoria, Queens.

"He's a barber," Anne said of her father, adding that he was a Croat and a Bolshevik who had changed his name to Citizen John Jackson when he came to America.

"He's very radical, but you'll like him," Anne said.

After we had entered the barbershop, Citizen John looked me over and I suddenly remembered the cool look Anne had given me when we first met at Terry Hayden's apartment. "Either it's in their genes," I thought, "or else he's had to interview a legion of suitors that Anne's brought to the shop."

With a flourish, he put a CLOSED sign in the window. "What is your outlook politically?" he asked me.

"Well, I'm quite liberal," I said, after which I discussed my career in the army, all of which he seemed to consider carefully.

"All right," he said when he was done. "Take off tie." He snapped an apron, then tied it around my neck. "I give you trim. You want shave?"

"No thanks," I said.

"All right," he said, "now we talk and then I play for you my concertina."

And sure enough, he soon whipped out the concertina and began to play while I smiled appreciatively.

"I see you soon again, I hope," he said. As we left, he turned the CLOSED sign around to OPEN, gave me a smile, and waved good-bye. "I must have passed inspection," I said. Anne squeezed my arm and gave me a smile that weakened my knees. "Let's go eat at the Golden Peacock," I said. "Dinner's on me."

Greenwich Village in the late 1940s was a garden nourished by the artistic blood of painters, actors, artists, poets. Fifth Avenue was always crowded with double-decker open-air buses; the fare was five cents. Anne had a furnished one-room flat on lower Fifth Avenue with maid service; her monthly rent was $35. Every morning I left Brooklyn early, and Anne and I would meet for breakfast and then go off to auditions, interviews, lunches, and dinner. Then came the long trip back home.

At the same time, we both came to a decision; we'd room together. There was no discussion, no wavering; it just seemed right. After all, we were in the heart of Bohemia, so it seemed the proper thing to do. The only drawback for me was the single bed she had. It seemed to have been designed for people who had dieted for years.

One day in Brooklyn, I rented a truck and loaded my twin bed on it.

"Where are you going with the bed?" my mother asked.

"Mom," I said earnestly, "I always have auditions, meetings, and business to take care of. I found a little room in Manhattan, so I'll sleep there."

She gave me a pained look. Sam and Sylvia and Shirley all had married and moved on. Sam had married a teacher, as had Shirley.

Sylvia had married a physical education instructor and had moved to El Paso, Texas.

"Come back, come back when you want," my mom said tearfully. "We'll always have room for you."

As I was leaving, I felt I had burned my bridges behind me—all three of them: the Manhattan, the Willamsburg, and the Brooklyn. At the same time, I recalled the title of Thomas Wolfe's short story "Only the Dead Know Brooklyn."

"Well, I'm not dead," I thought. "I'm going off to the world of theater. I'm alive, healthy. I have my bed, I'm in love, and who could ask for anything more?"

6

A Life
in the Theater

ANNE AND I SETTLED into her one-room apartment at 43 Fifth Avenue. The apartment was located on the ground floor, and it had a single window that looked onto an alley. The bathroom was outside the front door of the apartment, and Anne had placed a big white refrigerator against one of the bathroom walls. I purchased a little two-burner stove for cooking.

One morning, after we'd been living together for a few months, we heard a loud knock on the door. Anne stared at me. "Who is it?" she asked politely.

Then came the response: "It's your father—Citizen John."

I leapt out of bed, dressed quickly, and jumped out the window. Later Anne told me that Citizen John had called her older sister Katherine and said, "I did not go into the Anna's apartment [he always called Anne 'the Anna']. I walked out the front door of the building and saw a young man running down the street combing his hair. I do not think the Anna was alone."

Nevertheless, my professional and romantic relationship with the Anna continued to grow. After the brief run of *This Property Is Condemned* with Equity Library Theater, Terry Hayden decided to preserve our performances on film. None of us had any money, but we managed to raise $200. We found some railroad tracks out in Weehawken, New Jersey, to serve as our location. And once the trains had passed, Anne walked along the tracks, I flew my kite, and our cameraman Tom Palumbo began filming the one-act play. We played the scene just as we had onstage, except now we could hear train whistles in the background. This was my first taste of acting on film and another chance to act with my beloved.

Soon Anne and I would go on to act with the American Repertory Theatre (ART), which was formed in 1946 by three great ladies of the American theater: Eva Le Gallienne, who had had great success with a repertory company on Fourteenth Street in the late 1930s; Cheryl Crawford, who was a founding member of the Group Theatre; and Margaret Webster, a lovely English director. I had an opportunity to audition for ART—at the time, Actors' Equity held open auditions for actors hoping to give newcomers a chance to win roles in plays that were scheduled to open on Broadway.

For the audition, I prepared a scene from Maxwell Anderson's *Winterset,* which was loosely based on the Sacco-Vanzetti case. The play had starred Burgess Meredith and had been a big hit when it was performed on Broadway. Knowing that Anne had already toured in *The Cherry Orchard* with Miss Le Gallienne, I figured that having her onstage with me would give me an advantage. I asked her to play the role of Miriamne in *Winterset*. It wasn't a very difficult role for her to memorize; all she had to do was say, "Yes, Mio," and "No, Mio."

As Mio, I had to deliver long speeches, pouring my heart out in anger over my father's execution. My heart throbbing, I walked onstage and began to act, with a capital A-C-T. Meanwhile, Anne quietly said her lines: "Yes, Mio. No, Mio. Yes, Mio."

Worn out from my emotional outbursts, I awaited the judgment of the three ladies watching my audition.

"Thank you," said Miss Webster. "That was very nice."

That evening they phoned Anne and offered her a two-year contract with the company that paid $85 a week. While I, heartbroken, went off to Washington, D.C., to appear in a new play by Horton Foote called *People in the Show;* the salary was $5 per week, plus room and board. I had been acting in the show for a few weeks when a telegram appeared on my dressing-room table. It was from the three ladies of ART. I tore it open and read: "One of our actors has dropped out. Stop. We're offering you a place in the company. Stop."

As soon as I was through with Horton Foote's play, I raced back to New York, eager to become a member of ART and, more important, to be with Anne in a Broadway company. Le Gallienne, Crawford, and Webster had assembled a wonderful company, a mixture of old pros and young hopefuls. The veterans included Walter Hampden, best known for his brilliant performance as Cyrano de Bergerac; Victor Jory, a famous screen actor; Ernest

Truex; and Philip Bourneuf. The young hopefuls included William Windom, June Duprez, Richard Waring, Anne, and me. Our first production was to be *Henry VIII*, starring Jory as Henry in a fiery performance, marrying and leaving wives with abandon. I would play Cromwell, faithful aide to Cardinal Wolsey. David Ffolkes, who only two years before had been sitting in a Japanese prisoner-of-war camp, designed our opulent sets and costumes. The rest of the season included *What Every Woman Knows*, by James Barrie; *John Gabriel Borkman*, by Henrik Ibsen; *A Pound on Demand*, by Sean O'Casey; *Androcles and the Lion*, by George Bernard Shaw; and *Yellow Jack*, by Sidney Howard. I acted in every play save for the Ibsen. We performed at the International Theater, an elegant house on Columbus Circle. The International was later torn down and replaced by The Coliseum—where trade shows displayed their wares. And now it has become a huge complex owned by AOL-Time Warner.

Set in ancient Rome, Shaw's play *Androcles* concerns a mild-mannered little man who comes upon a groaning lion in the jungle and removes a thorn from the lion's paw. Years later Androcles and a group of fellow Christians are being forced into the Forum to be fed to the lions; one of the lions dashes out of his cage snarling, then stops, suddenly recognizing his old friend who removed his thorn. The lion stands erect, licks his friend's face, and after wrapping his tail around his paw, bows to Androcles, and they both dance out of the arena. The part that caught my eye, though, was Spintho, who was a flashy character—mean, sneaky, devious, and the only one who finally gets eaten by one of the other hungry lions. Frequently, in the dressing room, I would talk about how I wanted to play Spintho; night after night, I would complain about the roles in which I was cast, always putting in my two cents about how the company was being run—why wasn't I getting better parts; it was about time they woke up to who I was.

One evening Miss Le Gallienne requested to see me in her dressing room. She politely asked me to sit down. "I hear you're interested in playing Spintho. True?" she asked.

Ahh, I thought, at long last I had been recognized as a valuable member of the company.

"Yes," I said modestly, "I'd love to do the part."

"The walls have ears," she said. And now her polite tone took on another aspect. "What you complain about in your dressing room has been reported back to me," she said. What did she mean by that? Oh god! Then the hairs stood up on the back of my neck. She stared at me and smiled. Evidently, she read my mind. "You're a malcontent," she said, "a rebel and a force for spreading unhappiness in our company, and that won't do. I was going to cast you as Spintho. It's a strong and vital role, but you'll not get the part. You're not even going to play one of the Christians."

I backed out of the dressing room like a whipped dog. "Not even a Christian?" I thought. "Why didn't I keep my mouth shut?" Still, I was determined to get that role. I would think about what Miss Le Gallienne said about my being a malcontent and a troublemaker. I felt I was admirably equipped to play Spintho, who had similar personal characteristics. True, he was also an alcoholic and an all-around no-good character, but I figured I could act that.

A week later Miss Le Gallienne called me into her dressing room again. "We decided that the actor who was going to play Spintho isn't right for the role," she said. "I want you to play the part, and I want no comments from you, either." Now I went back to rehearsals feeling vindicated and triumphant—I knew I had all the right qualities for the role; one touch I was especially proud of was drawing varicose veins on my legs. Anne was upset about the varicose veins and didn't believe I would actually go onstage with blue veins and red arteries drawn on my legs, but I insisted that Spintho was a drinker, and instead of having broken veins on his nose, I decided he'd have varicose veins on his legs.

The varicose vein dispute underlined the differences in how we worked on our roles. I'd always work quickly and give my characters physical qualities, harking back to all the animals that Sanford Meisner had made us play at the Neighborhood Playhouse, like a sly fox or a wily weasel. Anne would always take her time, learning her lines before rehearsals, then developing her role. Over the years, I'd steal some of her methodology, she'd pick up mine, and peace would reign at home.

During rehearsals, as we Christians were being forced into the arena for the lions' dinner, Miss Webster, the director, asked us to ad-lib: "Say some lines; make some sounds," she said. I'll never forget Anne's classic ad-lib. The gates opened and the Roman soldiers threatened us with their spears: "Move in, move into the lions' den, hurry up!" they said. Then, in one moment of silence, Anne's voice came through loud and clear: "Don't push, brother," she said.

@ @ @

In addition to performing myriad jobs with ART, Cheryl Crawford was a producer; one of her biggest hits was the musical *Brigadoon* with music and lyrics by Lerner and Loewe. For the musical, she had hired Group Theatre cofounder Lee Strasberg to give the dancers and singers free acting lessons. She also invited Anne, myself, and two other actors from ART to attend Strasberg's classes and participate in scene-study work. Following the demise of the Group Theatre, Strasberg was struggling to make a living and Crawford had come to his rescue.

Each Tuesday morning we'd all gather on the stage of the Ziegfeld Theatre, where *Brigadoon* was being performed, and listen to Strasberg talk on and on about the great actors of the world: Eleanora Duse, Salvini, Sarah Bernhardt, Laurette Taylor, and Ruth Gordon. Then he'd tell more long stories about Konstantin Stanislavsky and the new concept of Method acting he had brought to the Moscow Art Theater.

At first, the classes were full, but after several weeks, there was a noticeable lack of attendance. The dancers went off to exercise, and the singers went off to strengthen their vocal chords with their singing coaches. At the end, the only members of the class who remained were the four actors from the American Repertory Theatre. But Strasberg didn't seem to notice or care. He continued discussing the Method and Stanislavsky. And the four of us enjoyed working with Lee, particularly when he taught us about "emotional memory," which was a technique of transplanting emotional moments from our own lives into what a particular script required.

◎ ◎ ◎

The next play in repertory was *Yellow Jack*, by Sidney Howard. The play dealt with the yellow fever plague in the Caribbean and called for an all-male cast, except for Anne, who played a nurse. The Samuel French catalog noted that if *Yellow Jack* was done at a boys' school, the nurse could be performed by a boy. That didn't amuse Anne. During this production, I first noticed signs of difficulty with ART. Costs involving actors, stagehands, royalties, rent, and advertising were taking their toll. Plus, critics were not enamored of *Yellow Jack*. All the discipline seemed to be slipping away from the company, and I was becoming moody and depressed, fearing that the theater company would soon be shutting down.

The day after *Yellow Jack* closed, Le Gallienne, Webster, and Crawford called a meeting of the ART company; all of us expected the dreaded announcement. Instead, Miss Le Gallienne seemed cheerful as she rose to address us, informing us that she would be reviving her classic production of *Alice in Wonderland*.

"There'll be parts for all of you," she said enthusiastically, "and we feel sure that we will continue to bring vital theater to New York."

That announcement revived our spirits. Anne and I were excited to read the printed version of the play; it was filled with exotic characters—Humpty Dumpty, the March Hare, the Red Queen, the White Queen, and all sorts of animals. Anne was the youngest member of the company, and it seemed obvious that she'd get to play Alice. Miss Le Gallienne phoned Anne and asked her to drop by for a meeting at her Tenth Street apartment in the Village.

When Anne came home afterward and opened the door, she looked like there had been a death in the family. "The ladies," she said, giving special emphasis to the word *ladies,* "have decided to cast Bambi Lynn as Alice." Bambi Lynn had really made a name for herself in the musical *Oklahoma!*

"I gave in my notice," Anne said, which was the polite theatrical term for "I quit!"

I was stunned by the three ladies' decision and awed and impressed by Anne's decision to leave the company. For a short while, I thought I'd join Anne in walking out, but such a courageous act didn't make sense when I realized that I would be the sole source of income for us. So, I stayed on at ART.

At supper that night, our dear friend David Stewart, who had now appeared onstage in several productions with Katharine Cornell, comforted Anne. "It's not the end of the world," he said, telling her that Cornell was producing a road tour revival of *The Barretts of Wimpole Street* and that the part of the ingenue still had not been cast.

Several days later Anne walked into our apartment, radiantly happy.

"I've got the part!" she said.

"How long is the tour?" I asked.

"Three months," she said. "We rehearse in New York for three weeks and then go cross-country."

I didn't know what the hell to feel. On the one hand, I was happy that she'd be acting in a major production, but I was miserable that she'd be leaving me for a long tour. I also would have to be moving back to Brooklyn for the three months that Anne would be on tour; she had decided to sublet the apartment to another actor—Marlon Brando.

"I told him that you'd come by the first of every month to collect the rent," Anne said.

That bit of news deepened my pain. Not only was Anne leaving me for three months, but I was going to be a rent collector. Well, at least my mom would be delighted to have me home. "You'll take the room Sam used to have before he married," Mom told me when she heard the news.

Dutifully, on the first of every month, I would troop over to 43 Fifth Avenue. Marlon, ever the teaser, would always stall about paying the rent. "Sorry, Eli; I'm broke," he'd say. Or, "My motorcycle needs new tires." Once he said, "I'm behind on payments to my analyst."

Brando did his poverty act for three months, but after stalling, he would always pay me the $35 rent he owed for Anne's apartment.

Moody and unhappy about being alone in New York, I returned to ART for rehearsals for *Alice in Wonderland*. I was to play a duck and several other small roles, and I would also be the understudy for the role of the caterpillar. I spent a lot of time researching how a duck moves and found that Burgess Meredith, the original duck in Miss Le Gallienne's production, had strapped roller skates onto his knees, propelling himself around the stage with his arms. I asked the prop man for a pair of roller skates, and he suggested that I talk to Miss Le Gallienne about it. She said I wouldn't need them.

"I remember your skill at dancing," she said, recalling a cast party where I had danced a Russian *kazatsky*. "You'll be able to charm us all doing the 'duck walk.'"

The "duck walk," as any army veteran knows, puts a particular stress on the legs. I wondered whether this was her revenge for my chatter in the dressing room, where I was accused of sabotaging morale and upsetting the company.

"All right, I'll do the damn duck walk," I thought. "I'll suffer for the good of the play."

On one night, during the caucus race—an elegant dance in which all the animals compete for the attention of the Red and White Queens—I glanced offstage and there was Miss Le Gallienne in her Red Queen outfit waving to me.

"Come off, come offstage," she whispered. Despite being encased in my duck outfit, I could hear her clearly.

"I'm out here," I thought. "I'm out here and, damn it, I'm gonna stay."

I gave her an extra loud quack in reply and continued running around the stage. Again, Le Gallienne signaled me; this time, her Red Queen face had gotten even redder.

Fearing the worst, I gave my fellow animals a loud quack and walked offstage.

"What happened?" I asked.

"The actor who plays the caterpillar never showed up," she said. She whispered to the stage manager, who forcefully stripped me out of my duck outfit and pushed me into the caterpillar costume, then hoisted me onto a tall wooden structure on wheels that was painted to look like a mushroom. Miss Le Gallienne's parting words were, "Go out and play that caterpillar!"

I had never rehearsed the part. I had no makeup on; I couldn't even catch my breath. I hoped I could remember some of the lines. My platform was pushed onstage. Alice gaily danced around the mushroom, looked up at me, and almost fainted. When I came off, I felt triumphant I'd gotten through the lines. But Miss Le Gallienne never congratulated me on my courageous performance.

On the day before Anne was to take off on her long tour in *The*

Barretts of Wimpole Street, I walked over to Shubert Alley to pick her up for a final lunch. A man stumbled out of the stage door. He was obviously intoxicated. He kept trying to light a cigarette in the heavy rain. I whipped out my Zippo lighter and lit it for him. "Thank you," he muttered. "Thank you very much. And what do you do, young man?"

"I'm an actor," I said.

"Oh, really," he said. "What are you currently appearing in?"

"Currently, I'm appearing as the duck in *Alice in Wonderland*," I said, "also the leg of mutton, the voice in the railroad carriage, and I understudy the caterpillar."

"Oh, yes, yes," he muttered. "Miss Le Gallienne's company. She invited me to come to America to join you in repertory. I was to play Cardinal Wolsey in *Henry VIII*."

"Really?" I said. "I just finished playing Cromwell."

"You played Cromwell?" he asked. He stretched the *you* as if it were an unbelievable and improbable boast.

"Yes, I did."

As we stood out in the rain in Shubert Alley, the man put his arm around me and, with a wet cigarette dangling from his mouth, launched into one of the most famous soliloquies in all of Shakespeare.

"So farewell…farewell, a long farewell, to all my greatness," he declared.

And as we kept walking up and down the alley, he continued: "This is the state of man: today he puts forth the tender leaves of hopes; tomorrow blossoms, and bears his blushing honors thick upon him. The third day comes a frost, a killing frost. And, when he thinks, good easy man, full surely his greatness is a-ripening, nips his root, and then he falls, as I do."

Tears streamed down his face as he leaned heavily against me. His voice rose in an anguished cry. "O Cromwell, Cromwell! Had I but served my God with half the zeal I served my king, he would not in mine age have left me naked to mine enemies."

Suddenly, the stage manager stuck his head out of a stage door and said urgently, "Please, sir, please come in. It's time to continue rehearsing."

The man looked at me and flipped the cigarette away. "Farewell, Cromwell, farewell," he said, and disappeared through the stage door.

The man's name, as it turned out, was Wilfrid Lawson. He had become famous for playing Eliza Doolittle's father in the film *Pygmalion*. Laurence Olivier, John Gielgud, Ralph Richardson, and Alec Guinness, at one time or another, would all reverently tip their hats to him. Lawson was noted for his drinking prowess. In one perhaps apocryphal story about Lawson, he was starring in a new play in London's West End. One day during intermission, one of his drinking buddies came backstage. Off they went to a nearby pub, lifted a glass or two or three, walked back into the theater, and took their seats in the rear of the orchestra. After a bit, Lawson poked his friend and, in a voice that could be heard all over the theater, said, "This is where I usually make my entrance." And they both sat back and roared with laughter.

7

My Method

THE AMERICAN REPERTORY THEATRE lasted only one year. Shortly after it was disbanded, Cheryl Crawford, Bobby Lewis, and Elia Kazan formed the Actors Studio; it was a workplace, almost a gym for professional actors, where they could do scenes and work on exercises. Usually, life in the theater took one of two paths: being cast in a play that would flop after a short amount of time or settling down to a long, successful run, which offered the actor financial security but came with a Faustian punishment: boredom. The Studio allowed actors to do character work they might not be hired to do otherwise. And they would also receive training in the Method, which theoretically served as an antidote to the conventional clichéd, hammy emoting that was the standard for most of what was currently seen on the stage. No one had to pay dues to the Studio, and once admitted, actors could stay on for life.

Kazan and Lewis formed two groups. Kazan taught the younger actors. Among them were Steve Hill, Julie Harris, Jocelyn Brando, and Don Hamner. The older group came under Bobby Lewis's guidance: Tom Ewell, Marlon Brando, David Wayne, John Forsythe, Karl Malden, Maureen Stapleton, Patricia Neal, Joan Copeland, Anne, and myself. All of us became charter members, and over the years, new members were added to the roster—Montgomery Clift, Barbara Bel Geddes, Paul Newman, Joanne Woodward, Lee Remick, Shelley Winters, Rod Steiger, Kim Stanley.

We'd meet on Tuesdays and Fridays from 11:00 A.M. to 1:00 P.M., perform scenes, and comment upon the work of other actors. Kazan and Lewis would analyze and criticize our work. The Actors Studio was my third encounter with the Method. The first time had been while I was training at the Neighborhood Playhouse with Sanford Meisner; then, later on with Lee Strasberg at the Ziegfeld Theatre. And now, finally, with Kazan and Lewis.

I discovered there was no one "Method"—the teachers made their own refinements of Stanislavsky's writings and teachings, inserting their own subjective slant. Nevertheless, we became almost evangelical actors, reborn as it were, setting out like Crusaders eager to bring fresh new energy to the theater. We must have seemed rather smug and difficult at the time.

◎ ◎ ◎

Years later I participated in a debate about the Actors Studio on British television. Kim Stanley, who was also a member of the

Actors Studio, and I were to speak in support of the Method. Opposing us were English actors Wendy Hiller, Robert Morley, and Rex Harrison. Orson Welles was the moderator. The program had been devised by Kenneth Tynan, a well-known critic in London and America and a dramaturge for the National Theatre that Laurence Olivier was forming at the time.

Tynan showed a film clip that he had made while he'd been in New York visiting the Actors Studio. In it, Lee Strasberg described certain acting exercises. Then Tynan showed a clip of English actor Kenneth Haigh, who complimented our school of acting at the expense of the English.

"I like the discussion of 'the Method,'" Haigh said. "Of course, my fellow English actors will say, 'Oh, nonsense, old chap! Just get on with it!' My question is, 'Get on with what?'"

Haigh's remarks caused quite a sensation. Robert Morley said, "Lee Strasberg uses fifty words where one word will do." At one point, Rex Harrison turned red, feeling that Haigh's film clip had been used with the sole intention of making fun of the English actors. After the show, when we were milling about the green room drinking tea and eating sandwiches, Harrison cornered Tynan and said, "You bastard! You wrote that script for that young actor to make those nasty remarks about us and the English theater."

Kenneth, who stuttered, said, "No, no, no! I did n-n-no such thing!"

Rex Harrison's wife Kay Kendall came over to me during the dispute and said, "Don't pay any attention to Rex. We English are so square, we have to smuggle our tits past customs."

One particular member of the Actors Studio, of course, created a sensation. In plays like *Truckline Café, A Flag Is Born, Candida,* and finally *A Streetcar Named Desire,* Marlon Brando seemed to have synthesized all the teachings of the Method. His pained cry "Stella!" in *Streetcar* became a set piece for TV and radio comics. They jeered at the methods used by these Studio actors. "Make like a tree!" they yelled. "Be like a snake!" "Don't bathe!" "Mumble your lines!" "Wear torn T-shirts!"

That bothered me at first, but I felt that all pioneers must be willing to withstand the caustic comments leveled against them. After all, we were embarking on a voyage into the mysteries of what makes an actor, and there were conflicts.

Once I had to improvise a scene with Brando at the Studio. Just before we were to perform, I said to him, "Listen, I'm going to be playing an FBI man and I'll be going through your apartment looking for drugs. Give me a few minutes, then come on and we'll do the scene." I began tiptoeing around the apartment, carefully opening and closing drawers. Suddenly, the door burst open and there stood Marlon.

"What are you doing here?" he asked.

"Well, the super told me the apartment is for rent, so I was looking around," I said.

"Liar! That's a damn lie!" he hollered. "The super's crazy and I want you out of my fucking room."

"Watch your language," I said. FBI men never cursed, I thought. Marlon then spewed forth with a hailstorm of curses— some I'd never even heard before.

"Watch your language," I repeated. Marlon shoved me. "Don't push," I said.

At this point, Marlon picked me up bodily and threw me out of the room. I charged back in, furious, forgetting all about the improvisation while Marlon stood there and laughed. I was criticized for not completing my action, that is, finding the drugs. Meanwhile, Brando was delighted with his performance.

Some exercises in the Studio drove me crazy—digging up painful childhood experiences, for example. I wondered how older professionals had given great performances without ever having seen, read, or heard about the Method.

I once saw Alfred Lunt in Friedrich Dürrenmatt's play *The Visit.* In one scene he was surrounded by a group of villagers who had been hired by a mysterious visitor to murder him. As they formed a circle and closed in on him, he stretched out his arms, stood on one leg, and sank from view. I went backstage after the performance, and the doorman kindly ushered me to his dressing room.

"Yes?" Lunt asked.

"Sir," I said, "I'm an actor at the Studio. I was so moved by the scene where you stood on one leg as the villagers surrounded you. How did you find that?"

Lunt looked at me. "I don't know," he said. "I may have had to go to the bathroom." Well, I added that bit to my arsenal of special things to do in creating a character.

Ultimately, I just decided to excerpt and extract what I could use from each of my Method teachers in creating my characters. And what I learned from the world of music, dance, and painting I put to use in the laboratory of my mind. I never felt guilty about using great moments I saw in other performances.

I'd analyze, take apart, and study what they did, and then I'd just make it my own.

One of the most important acting lessons I learned came on the opening night of *Androcles and the Lion* at ART. I was walking offstage with Ernest Truex, who was the star of the play.

"I sure get a great laugh on my last line out there," I said.

Truex was an old pro, a tiny man with a voice twice his size. He looked at me, shook his head sadly, and said, "You did?"

"Yes," I answered, "didn't you hear the audience's response?"

At the very next performance, I delivered my line as usual and waited for the gratifying thrill one gets when one captivates the audience. There was no laughter, no response at all, nothing. I couldn't understand it. After the show that night, Truex tapped on my dressing-room door.

"Wallach," Truex told me, "you're not the only one onstage when you get your laugh." He stressed the word *your*. "Your laugh came about because there are other actors skillfully setting up the situation for you."

I ate my humble pie after that lesson from the old pro. "Well, yeah," I said, "I do find that there are other actors acting with me, and I should listen to them."

◎ ◎ ◎

Once Anne had completed three months on the road with *The Barretts*, we were able to move back into our apartment, and we began making plans for plays that we could do together. David Stewart helped to arrange an audition for me in Katharine Cornell's next production: Shakespeare's *Antony and Cleopatra*.

"Are you trying to keep us apart?" I asked David. "Anne just finished her long tour, and I don't want to be separated again. I'm not going on the road."

"Go in and audition," he said. "It's for New York."

Cornell's husband, Guthrie McClintic, was a successful Broadway director and producer and a witty raconteur. Most recently, he had directed Burgess Meredith and Maureen Stapleton in *The Playboy of the Western World* and Marlon Brando in George Bernard Shaw's *Candida*. I met him in his office. He handed me a script, then told me to appear at the Martin Beck Theatre at 11:00 A.M. sharp the following day.

The next morning at 11:00, I walked onto an empty stage with two chairs lit with only one bare bulb. When McClintic walked in, we shook hands and he told me he wanted me to read for the part of Diomedes, the soothsayer.

"Did you say soothsayer?" I asked.

"Yes," he said. "It's a very interesting role."

I began to read using my deepest voice because I felt soothsayers should have deep voices. I barely got out six lines when McClintic interrupted. "I'll read the part of Antony," he said. I stood there and listened to him deliver a long soliloquy, after which he stopped, wiped his brow, and said, "That was a wonderful scene. Good! That was good. Yep, you've got the part!"

"It pays to listen," I thought.

The first day of rehearsal of a play is sometimes gut-wrenching, but the read-through went well. After we were done, I got up the courage to approach Katharine Cornell, whom I hadn't seen since the war when she'd performed for the USO.

"Do you remember getting an oil portrait of Hitler in Marseilles in 1944?" I asked her.

"Oh, yes," she said. "Yes, I do remember."

"Well, I was the officer who gave you the painting," I said. "Whatever happened to it?"

"Oh, I feel so guilty," she said. "I did tote the painting all over Europe during the tour. But I left it at the dock as we sailed back to the United States.

"You're a soothsayer," she added with a smile. "You should have predicted what would happen."

Miss Cornell had a strict rule about her performances; if she appeared in the opening scene of any play, no latecomers were to be seated. The soothsayer and his predictions didn't come on until scene 2. On opening night, I entered for scene 2. Wearing a heavy beard and a long black robe, I walked to the edge of the stage and began using all my oracular powers to make my predictions. I had barely gotten four words out when the latecomers cascaded down the aisles as ushers used their flashlights to direct them into their seats. I stopped and glared at the miscreants. Didn't they realize that by missing my opening remarks, the whole story would become an unfocused mess, I wondered. Apparently not. The audience settled in, the play picked up speed, and my soothsaying was not missed.

After we opened, David Stewart, who was playing the meaty role of the messenger, became ill and I had to replace him. When David returned to the show he replaced me as the soothsayer, and taught me a valuable lesson in acting. When he played the soothsayer, he walked to the edge of the stage and the latecomers stopped and stared at his tall, regal, black-bearded presence. He had sewn glittering beads in his beard, and as he turned his head from side to side, the beads picked up the light. His beard looked like the moving luminous globe at the Roseland Ballroom. He stood there patiently and waited for silence; even the ushers tiptoed up the aisle. Finally, he spoke and his predictions seemed to register for everyone in the audience, even the latecomers, because he had managed the trick of being the focus of everyone's attention.

Charlton Heston was in the cast; he played Proculeius, a Roman general in Caesar's army. Heston was six feet tall, handsome, with a deep and powerful voice. For the role, he wore a gray-blue leather uniform, a short skirt revealing his brawny legs of which he was very proud, and greenish-brown boots. During one of the scenes, he would walk out in front of the curtain, salute by slapping his right arm across his chest, and say, "Caesar, I come!" Caesar would then greet his general with a return salute and hand him a scroll and declare, "You will attack by sea!" Proculeius would then repeat his chest-thumping salute and say, "Caesar, I go!" On one particular performance, however, Caesar was nowhere to be found; it turned out he was in the bathroom under the stage. Heston stared offstage. He waited. And waited. Then, shading his eyes from the sun and remembering that he must attack by sea, he pretended to see Caesar's ship in the distance, "Ahoy, Caesar!" he shouted, at which point the stage manager signaled for a blackout. I imagined that the Shakespeare lovers in the audience who would have open books on their laps, following the dialogue in the play, must have been puzzled that night; there was no "Ahoy" in their copies of the play.

In 1923 eight-year-old Eli Wallach mounts up for the camera for the first of many times.

Eli Wallach's parents, Bertha and Abraham Wallach.

Eli Wallach (left), who is wearing his Texas Longhorn belt buckle, and his brother, Sam.

Eli Wallach (first row, third from right) was a member of the Curtain Club at the University of Texas in 1935.

In 1944 Eli Wallach played Hitler in *Is This the Army?* while he was stationed in Nice, France.

Eli Wallach and Anne Jackson first appeared together on stage in an Equity Library Theatre production of Tennessee Williams's *This Property Is Condemned* in 1946. They were married two years later.

Eli Wallach bares his chest
to Maureen Stapleton
in Tennessee Williams's
The Rose Tattoo at the
Martin Beck Theatre
in 1953.
Photograph by George Karger

The *Camino Real* cast: Eli Wallach, author Tennessee Williams, director Elia Kazan,
Jo Van Fleet, and Joseph Anthony backstage at the Billy Rose Theatre in 1953.

Anne, Eli, and Peter Wallach
in the dressing room during
The Teahouse of the August Moon,
April 1955.

Carroll Baker and Eli Wallach
in *Baby Doll*, 1956.
AFP/Getty Images

Eli Wallach and Anne Jackson
in George Bernard Shaw's
Major Barbara, directed by
Charles Laughton, March 1957.

Eli Wallach dances with Marilyn Monroe as Clark Gable looks on in *The Misfits*, 1960.
Photograph by Inge Morath/Magnum

On the set of
The Misfits (1960):
(from top, left
to right) Arthur
Miller, Eli Wallach,
John Huston,
Montgomery Clift,
Marilyn Monroe,
and Clark Gable.
*Photograph by Elliott
Erwitt/Magnum*

Eli Wallach as the bandit Calvera
in *The Magnificent Seven*, 1960.
United Artists/The Kobal Collection

Eli Wallach and Anne Jackson
in *The Typists and The Tiger*,
the Orpheum Theatre, 1962.

Eli Wallach and
Peter O'Toole in
Lord Jim, filmed in
Cambodia in 1964.

Eli Wallach and Audrey Hepburn in *How to Steal a Million*, 1966.

Eli Wallach about to get strung up while Clint Eastwood fires a gun in the background in *The Good, the Bad and the Ugly*, 1967. *P.E.A./The Kobal Collection*

Eli Wallach and Clint Eastwood survey the scene in *The Good, the Bad and the Ugly*, 1967.

Eli Wallach and Anne Jackson with their grown children (from left) Roberta, Katherine, and Peter. *Photograph by Richard Corman*

One day before a performance, I listened to a lecture by Lee Strasberg at the Ziegfeld Theatre. He was trying to explain the technical acting term *action.*

"What is it you're trying to do onstage?" he asked. "Do you want to seduce the leading lady? Are you trying to overthrow the government? In completing your action, you're carrying out your task as the actor."

"Oh, that is a pearl of wisdom I can use," I thought. "I'll use it; I'll use it."

At the theater that night, I could hardly contain myself. "Messenger, messenger," I kept saying to myself as I pulled on my boots, jumped into my Egyptian skirt, girded on my dagger, and rushed onstage. Remembering Strasberg's lecture, I was determined to complete my action, to deliver the message: "Antony had married! Antony had married!"

Katharine Cornell, playing Cleopatra, was onstage when I made my entrance.

"Madam! Madam!" I cried.

Cleopatra held up her hand. "Antonius is dead," she said. "If thou say so, villain, thou kill'st thy mistress...."

"First, madam, he is well," I said.

Now, Shakespeare wrote long speeches for Cleopatra. But with great urgency, I kept saying, "But, madam, but, madam." Another long speech from the impatient Cleopatra. Finally, I shouted, "Will it please you hear me?" There was silence. Miss Cornell glared at me; her look was homicidal. I had cut fourteen of her lines. As I slunk offstage, the stage manager gave me a thumbs-down.

Next day after class, I went up to Strasberg. "What is this

Method?" I asked. "I rushed onstage, eager and anxious. I started to carry out my action as you suggested. I was about to give her the message, but in my excitment I cut fourteen of her lines."

Strasberg cleared his throat, his usual sign of irritation.

"So," he said quietly, "wait for your cue."

8

Husband and Actor and Director and Father

AFTER DELIVERING MESSAGES of Antony's marriage eight times a week at the Martin Beck Theatre, Anne and I decided that we should do likewise. On March 5, 1948, we took our blood tests, went to City Hall, got a license, and without ever changing her name we became a married couple. Before the performance of *Antony and Cleopatra* that night, Anne's agent Peter Witt held a reception at his home for our immediate families. Mom and Pop and my brother and sisters welcomed Anne into the Wallach clan. Anne's father, Citizen John, and her sisters, Katherine and Beatrice, and their husbands, Boris and Emil, were delighted that the youngest of Citizen John's girls had found me. The champagne flowed.

That night I ran onstage and played the scene with Miss Cornell, making sure not to step on any of her lines. When the messenger tells Cleopatra of Antony's marriage, she goes berserk, and during this performance, screaming in anger, Miss Cornell chased me about the stage, caught me, and hit me extra hard on the side of the head—this was a new bit of business on her part. With my ears ringing, I ran offstage to my dressing room. There, I found a wedding gift from Miss Cornell, a set of elegant Czech cut-glass perfume bottles. "How," I wondered, "had she found out about our marriage?" It turned out that Maureen Stapleton, who was also in the cast, had spilled the beans.

Anne and I had a late supper at Sardi's, where Maureen kissed both of us and tearfully wished us a long marriage. Across the street from our play, Sid Caesar was doing a musical called *Make Mine Manhattan,* and "Mo," as we called Maureen, had tipped off the cast about our rash, impulsive act—they didn't know we'd been living together ever since I brought the bed over from Brooklyn—and every member of the cast sent us Manhattans. Neither Anne nor I knew how to drink, but we kept on raising our glasses and nodding to all our generous friends as we downed drink after drink. We never knew how we got home, and we still don't remember our wedding night.

◎ ◎ ◎

At the Actors Studio, things were going fairly well, but we soon discovered that rifts had developed between Elia Kazan and Bobby Lewis. Kazan wanted to enlarge the Studio's activities. As teacher of the younger members, he decided to cast many of them in a production of *Sundown Beach,* which toured summer theaters but never came to Broadway. Lewis, on the other hand, felt such activities violated the original plan to train and stimulate actors without going outside of the Studio into the world of commercial theater. He left and began to teach private acting lessons.

After Lewis's departure, I continued to study at the Studio with guest moderators, who included Martin Ritt, Daniel Mann, Sanford Meisner, and at one point, the director Josh Logan, who suggested to the class that we try our hand at directing. I chose a Tennessee Williams one-act called *Hello from Bertha* about a prostitute who is being evicted and clings to her bed, defying her landlord and her pimp. I cast Maureen Stapleton as Bertha and Margaret Phillips and Anne Jackson as her coworkers.

After ten days of rehearsal, I felt I'd put the actresses through their paces. On the day of the performance, with our Studio members and our moderator in attendance, I stepped before the curtain. "I chose this play," I said, "because I'm interested in prostitution."

The class laughed.

"No, seriously," I said. "As a medical administrative officer during World War II, one of my jobs was raiding whorehouses all over North Africa. My main task was to protect and preserve the physical health of our troops, and I became an expert in venereal diseases. Now, the play."

"The hell with the play, " Logan called out. "Go on with the sex lecture."

"No, no, no," I said. "Let's go on with the play."

I was unaware that a revolt was taking place backstage; my three stars were so furious at the laughter in the audience and the fact that I had given such a lengthy introduction that they disregarded every one of my directions. The performance went well, but I was crushed and I never directed again.

Apparently, Logan felt sorry for me, because after class he asked me to audition for *South Pacific,* a new Rodgers and Hammerstein musical that he was going to direct. He asked me to read the character of Luther Billis, a sailor who has a ship tattooed on his belly.

"Am I going to have to sing?" I asked.

"No," Logan said. "We just want you to read."

That night at home, I told Anne about my audition. "Be careful, Eli," she warned. "They're going to ask you to sing."

"Nonsense," I said. "Logan knows I can't sing; I can't even carry a tune."

"They'll ask you to sing, you'll see," Anne said.

I spent days studying the role of Luther Billis before I walked out onstage. Sitting in the darkened orchestra were Rodgers and Hammerstein, producer Leland Hayward, and my new friend and mentor Josh Logan, who said in a soft, comforting southern voice, "Please read the role of Billis."

At home I had drawn a sailing ship on my belly with a black eyebrow pencil. As I inhaled and exhaled, the ship would seem to be riding the waves. I worked on that trick first in my apartment. Onstage, after my last exhalation, I felt a surge of power. My stomach went in and out; the ship rocked in the waves—I could do the ship stuff.

Again, Logan's soothing southern voice came out of the dark. "That was wonderful," he said. "Now, please sing!"

Little did these Broadway geniuses know that as a child, in

singing class at PS 46, my teacher would always point at me. "You," she'd say, "you're flat! Better for you not to sing."

The pianist ran over to me. "What key?" he asked.

Key? I didn't know what the hell he meant by that. But remembering Anne's warning to be prepared, I decided to act. I whispered to the pianist, and as he returned to the piano, I put an imaginary coin into an imaginary phone and dialed an imaginary number.

"Hello?" I said, and nodding to the pianist, I sang, "I'll be down to get you in a taxi, honey, you better be ready about half past eight. Now, honey, don't be late. I'm gonna be there when the band starts playing." Then I hung up the imaginary phone.

"I can't do it," I said. "I can't sing. I've got butterflies in my stomach."

"That's okay," Logan said in that reassuring voice. "We'll get you a real phone next time."

Feeling tricked and trapped, I walked out of the theater. I imagined that people on the street were staring at me. "Take some singing lessons," I thought I heard someone say. As soon as I opened the door at home, Anne sensed what happened. She never said, "I warned you," for which I was grateful.

That evening Logan called. An actor was leaving his Broadway production of *Mister Roberts* with Henry Fonda. "The part is yours," he said, "and you don't have to sing." So, as a result of my sex lecture and my failed singing audition, I would spend the next two years as a happy sailor at the Alvin Theatre: salary, $85 a week.

Joining the cast of a hit is never easy. For a newcomer, it's like trying to jump onto a fast-moving carousel. The other sailors in

Mister Roberts had settled into their roles after months of playing. They knew where the laughs were and all their moves. But the sailors tried to make me feel at home. Logan didn't want any of the cast to wear makeup; instead, he had the production install a phallus-shaped suntanning machine in the basement. Each evening all sailors were required to stand nude in a circle in front of it: three minutes front and three minutes back.

Near the suntanning machine was a large, round felt-covered poker table. Dangling directly over the table was a speaker through which we could hear the onstage dialogue. We learned how to time ourselves so that we could make it onstage just before our cues. One rule of the poker game: If your cue took you away from the table, someone else could play your hand. Upon returning to the game, if money was piled in front of your seat, you'd know you'd won the pot. One time I ran onstage thinking, "Oh boy! I've got three eights—nobody will beat that." I came back to the table, and there was a neat pile of money in front of my seat. Since we were only making $85 a week, the money was important.

I enjoyed working with Fonda. Many years later, Anne and I saw him perform on Broadway in a play called *First Monday in October*. He was in his seventies at the time and using a pacemaker. There was one scene in which he fainted, and Anne poked me and asked, "Is it real?" I'm sure he would have been pleased by that reaction.

Every night onstage in *Mister Roberts,* we would give Fonda a medal as he left his ship, and every night, his eyes would tear up. It reminded me of a story that Herbert Berghoff had told me about an old actor named Dudley Digges. Digges had been appearing in Eugene O'Neill's *The Iceman Cometh*. During each performance, he would open and read a letter from his son, and at exactly the same time each night, a tear would drop on the page. Berghoff was awed by this and had asked Digges, "How do you do it at exactly the same spot? How do you get that tear to drop?"

The old actor looked at him, smiled, and winked. That was his answer; it's still a mystery.

On most evenings when I was performing in *Mister Roberts*, Anne would drop by the Alvin Theatre at the curtain call. She loved to watch the sailors take their final bows. After the show we'd all go out to Downey's on Eighth Avenue, but one evening she said, "I don't want to go out for late supper; let's just go home."

As I turned the key in our apartment door, she tapped me on the back of my head. "Is something wrong?" I asked.

Anne gave me a *Mona Lisa* smile; her eyes were glistening. "Hold your breath," she said. "I'm pregnant."

I have always snorted in disgust at movie scenes when the wife says, "I'm pregnant." The husband always jumps to his feet with a grim look of surprise. "Sit down," he orders. "Get comfortable. Are you all right? When did this happen?" Happen? What the hell did he think they were doing in bed? Playing chess?

"What do we do? What do we do? When did it happen?" I asked.

Anne calmed me down. "I'm a navy wife," she said. "It happened while you had shore leave from *Mister Roberts*."

At her physical exam, Anne informed her obstetrician that she was Jean Arthur's understudy in the play *Peter Pan* and that she was supposed to fly, soaring over the stage and audience.

"No, no flying for you," the doctor said. "You're grounded."

We went shopping for maternity clothes. The salesladies would always give me knowing and sympathetic smiles. We began reading baby books, and I was frightened most of the time. "Suppose she miscarries," I'd wonder. "What happens if she dies?" I learned that pregnant women look even more beautiful as the mysterious process of baby-making goes on. Even though Anne's belly began to swell, she got many offers for theater work.

Our dear friend Terry Hayden came up with an idea to provide work for actors during the summer. In the 1950s, theaters were usually closed in the summer because there was no air-conditioning, so Terry decided to produce shows for summer theater tours and, after three or four weeks, bring them into empty Broadway theaters. The Alvin Theatre, where I was appearing in *Mr. Roberts,* was "air cooled." Three hundred–pound blocks of ice were unloaded in the theater each day, set up on tables in the basement, and fans would blow over the blocks of ice to circulate the cool air around the theater. Still, I got a week off from *Mister Roberts* to appear in one of Terry's productions: *The Lady from the Sea.* It was fun for me to leave my ship buddies from *Roberts* and spend time doing a different play. Meanwhile, in another production, Terry cast Anne in George Bernard Shaw's *Arms and the Man.* Though Anne was pregnant, Terry said that she could play the maid—"You'll just wear a loose apron," Terry said. Anne said that her leading man enjoyed feeling her baby kick as he embraced her in their scene. But I was always very squeamish about touching her belly.

———

One day at the Actors Studio, Elia Kazan asked if I'd work on a scene from one of Tennessee Williams's one-act plays, *Ten Blocks on the Camino Real*. He said it would sharpen his directorial skills for dealing with fantasy. Each evening I'd get out of my sailor outfit, then go over to the Studio and rehearse the scene until two in the morning. Weeks later we performed the scene before Tennessee, who laughed all the way through. "I'm going to expand *Camino* into a full play," he said with a slight lisp and a lilting singsong southern accent, adding that he thought I would be just right to play the part in his new play, *The Rose Tattoo*. "Cheryl Crawford is producing it. Give her a call," he said.

In *Tattoo*, Tennessee had written the star female role Serafina Delle Rose for the Italian film star Anna Magnani. But after months of interviews, letters, and telegrams, Magnani refused. "Sorry, I can't do Serafina," she wrote to Cheryl Crawford. "It is a wonderful role but my English is not strong enough. I wish you great success." Crawford then asked me to meet and read with another Italian stage and film actress, who, for reasons that will soon become obvious, I will refer to as Signora X. Evidently, the producers thought that the role had to be played by an Italian stage and screen star. I was to meet her at the Hotel Royale.

I arrived at the Royale one hour earlier than scheduled and called up to Signora X's room on the house phone. Her voice was low, rich, and sexy. "Come up, please, room 1438," she said. Her English was polished and assured. When I arrived at her room, I saw a pretty, tiny blond-haired, green-eyed lady. She wore black slacks and a beautifully embroidered vest. It was unbuttoned. My eyes naturally focused on her barely covered breasts.

"Welcome," she said. "We talk and then we read, okay? And Tennessee will be here soon." She pointed to some tiny dolls on a tray table near the sofa. "I made these dolls myself to show Tennessee how much I love the play. The costumes represent each character."

I noticed the Serafina Delle Rose doll; its vest was unbuttoned with tiny doll-like breasts peeking out. Signora X went on to describe each doll. Tennessee soon arrived, greeted Signora X, shook my hand, and sat down in an easy chair near the window. We began to read the script while seated on the couch.

As we read, Signora X became more and more animated until she stood up, leaving me sitting on the couch. "Here!" she cried. "Here! I have this feeling, here!" I watched with amazement as she started advancing on Tennessee. "Yes! Yes!" she continued with a sexy growl. "It is here, here, I have this feeling! I open my blouse." And this she did with great force. "And here is the rose tattoo of my dead husband."

Tennessee's eyes opened as wide as the lenses of his glasses. "Oh!" he said. "Oooh! Very good, very good, signora." I congratulated the actress on her impassioned reading. Just as we were about to say our good-byes, she handed me a tiny doll dressed in a truck driver's outfit.

"For you," she said. "I wish you *buona fortuna,* good luck." As Tennessee and I rode the elevator down together, he didn't say a word; he just shook my hand and winked. Later I learned that the producers decided to continue their search for a leading lady. I felt sorry for the actress; she had literally bared her breasts and it hadn't helped.

I read next with Maureen Stapleton. She was beautiful with

black hair, big blue eyes, a wicked sense of humor, and, I'm convinced, a touch of genius. It was clear that Maureen had given the best reading, but the producers were afraid to entrust a major playwright's work to two unknowns. Maureen and I were called back repeatedly to read, and both of us became impatient with the process.

"To hell with them," I said. "They don't know what they want. I'm not going back there again."

"I know you," Maureen said. "You'll go back there fifty times in order to get the part."

Finally, Miss Crawford and her backers, and I'm sure with the support of Tennessee, decided to take a gamble, and we were hired for the two major roles.

To prepare for the role of the truck driver Mangiacavallo, which means "eat a horse," I thought I should have bulging muscles. I told Cheryl Crawford that Abercrombie & Fitch was having a sale on chinning bars.

"I'll lend you mine," Cheryl said.

Elia Kazan had wanted to direct the play, but he had committed to go to Europe to direct the film *Man on a Tightrope* with Fredric March. Daniel Mann, who I knew from the Actors Studio, took over. Tennessee wanted the play to open in Chicago because Claudia Cassidy, the chief critic there, had given *The Glass Menagerie* a rave review.

Daniel Mann invited me to sit in the theater and watch the auditions for the minor roles. I was flattered by the invitation, but as a wounded veteran of the audition wars, I felt sorry for the actors and actresses who tried so hard to make an impression. However, my empathic feelings were jolted when I saw a three-hundred-pound lady come thundering onto the stage. I leaned forward to watch.

In a powerful voice with a thick Italian accent, the woman said, "My name is Augusta Merighi."

Daniel Mann said, "Thank you. Now will you please read?" Both of us were leaning forward now.

The lady shrugged her shoulders. "I don't read," she said. "My daughter—she reads for me." She motioned for a young girl to come onstage, handed her a script, and whispered, "Get behind me." Then smiling and turning to the director, the lady proudly said, "My Angelina, she read for me."

The girl stood behind her mother completely hidden and quietly prompted her mother's lines.

DAUGHTER: And what do you think happened?
MOTHER: (*loudly*) And what do you think happened?
DAUGHTER: She told me to get out the door.
MOTHER: (*angrily*) She told me to get out the door.
DAUGHTER: I told her she could jump in the lake.
MOTHER: (*pushing her hand under her chin in an Italian gesture of disgust*) I told her she could jump in the lake.

Daniel Mann leapt to his feet and in a voice as strong and powerful as that of the lady up onstage said, "Thank you, that was great, just great, thank you." The mother hugged and kissed her daughter and yelled *"Grazie! Grazie!"* to the people in the audience as she left. She ran offstage despite her three hundred pounds—and she got the part.

We rehearsed for four weeks, then performed our final run-through in an empty Broadway theater before we were to take off for the Erlanger Theater in Chicago. In attendance were Daniel Mann, Tennessee's agent Audrey Wood—who resembled a meek librarian but had a reputation for discovering new writing talent—and her husband, William Liebling, my agent at the time, who always wore stiff white collars and dark suits, and who looked like the tiny doll on the top of a wedding cake.

As I stood in the wings for the final run-through, the play seemed flat. Mangiacavallo, my character, didn't enter until nearly the end of the first act. I did twenty push-ups offstage, took a deep breath, and on cue came running on. I thought, "I'll show them; now the play will come alive." For the first ten minutes I was onstage, I thought I was in top form. But slowly, ever so slowly, the scenes started to unwind. The silence out front was deafening, and the curtain came down with a thud.

After the final curtain, I sat in my dressing room, weary, dripping sweat. "O god, what did I do out there? I don't understand," I said as Daniel Mann came into my dressing room. Referring to the few members of the audience, I said, "I thought I saw the panel of judges put their heads together, like the witches of *Macbeth* sealing my fate."

"No, no, no," Mann said, and patted me on the shoulder. "I asked you to apologize for every line you spoke. Forget all of my corrections. I want you to create your own Mangiacavallo." Just before he closed the door, he said, "I've canvassed that jury and they agreed with me; you'll play the part on Broadway."

Despite those assurances, I was still blue, morose, unsure. But

David Stewart, who was also in the play, spoke carefully and gently to me; he sounded like a wise psychiatrist.

"Go back to your roots," he said. "You grew up in Little Italy in Brooklyn. Mangiacavallo is buried in your brain, so let him come out; have fun!" And so I did. Our Chicago production, as Tennessee had predicted, opened to tremendous reviews. Although, perhaps, some of the audiences were not too enthusiastic.

In act I, Serafina tells Mangiacavallo about the rose tattoo on her dead husband's chest. In the second act, Mangiacavallo tries to impress her by having a rose tattooed on his own chest. During intermission I would go to my dressing room to paint on the tattoo; it took less than a minute using a black eyebrow pencil and red and green watercolors. One evening, while I was sitting in my dressing room and painting that rose on my chest, the door burst open and a big barrel-chested man entered. He was obviously intoxicated.

"I've seen this play four times," he shouted. "I'm here on a furniture convention, and I want you to know that I love this play. I love you; I love Maureen." By now, his voice had softened as he said tearfully, "But you're not the only one with a goddamned rose on his chest."

"What do you mean?" I asked.

"Look here," he said, and he ripped open his shirt. Popping out of his hairy chest was a big red rose, stuck on with Scotch tape. Just then, the stage manager came in. And as he was dragging the furniture dealer out, the man yelled, "I'll see you opening night in New York. I'll be there. Don't worry, I'll be there."

On February 3, 1951, I got to the theater early and stood across the street from the marquee of the Martin Beck Theatre on Broadway. There was the title of the play—*The Rose Tattoo*—and there was Maureen's name and mine. Fame, at last. Patience, guts, stamina, and faith had finally paid off. "My name is in lights," I thought. "How about that?"

On opening night, I was sitting in the dressing room reading congratulatory telegrams when the stage manager entered.

"There's a man outside who insists on seeing you," he said. "He says he's a good friend of yours. He says he's here on a furniture convention."

"Tell him I left," I said. "Tell him I'm gone. Tell him I'm dodging a subpoena. Tell him I jumped out the window and you can't find me."

Still, the performance went well and Maureen was radiant. After the show Anne, now in her ninth month of pregnancy, came backstage, glowing with excitement.

"I was so nervous," she said. "You've gone through a complete transformation from the performance I saw at the run-through. What happened in Chicago?"

"Well," I said, "I have David Stewart to thank for that. He restored my belief in myself."

Afterward the cast and friends gathered for the traditional party at Sardi's. At 1:30 in the morning, our press agent called for quiet and held up the early edition of the *New York Times*. "We're in! We're in!" he shouted. "*Tattoo* is a hit!" We hugged one another; a cheer went up. I felt like a runner who had just broken the tape after a twenty-six-mile marathon. "I'm a real actor now," I thought. "I made it!"

The next day our pediatrician Dr. Fraad called. "Congratulations!" he said. "Since the play is a hit, I've booked you into Le Roi Sanitarium." Le Roi was a posh fifty-bed hospital on the East Side of Manhattan where the elite used to go to dry out after a bout with alcohol. It also had several maternity suites.

Soon the excitement of our opening of *The Rose Tattoo* was topped by another opening. Late one evening in mid-February, Anne and I were working on a *New York Times* crossword puzzle when her eyes widened. I thought she had solved some difficult word.

"Hurry, Eli, hurry," she said. "It's time; let's go!"

Off we went in a cab.

"Let's go!" I told the driver. "My wife's pregnant."

The cabbie turned his head slowly. "I'll get her there," he yelled, "so relax. I've driven a lot of pregnant women in my cab. Some of them threw up. If your lady does likewise, you'll have to clean it up."

"I'll clean it up," I shouted, "but let's go."

We rushed into the waiting room at the sanitarium. "Nice to see you, Anne," the doctor said.

"Why the hell is he so calm?" I asked myself.

Anne kept looking at me; her red hair was all curly and she was perspiring.

"God, she's beautiful," I thought. "She's beautiful."

"Go home," the doctor said. "I'll call you when she delivers."

"Can't I stay here?" I asked. "Husbands usually stay. I'll be quiet."

"No, no, no," he said. "We don't need you."

At home I walked round and round the kitchen table. "Oh god," I kept thinking, "I hope she doesn't have any problems." All my army medical thoughts came rushing to my brain: cesarean sections, miscarriages, ectopic pregnancies. The phone rang. I banged my knee rushing to answer it.

"Congratulations!" Dr. Fraad said calmly. "You've got a healthy baby boy, a big healthy boy, and Annie is fine."

I rushed back to the hospital and tiptoed into her room. Again, she looked beautiful. And again, she smiled at me. One day later Anne escorted me to the nursery; there were three walls and a large glass panel. I looked through the glass panel and saw eight babies lying in a row.

"Which is ours?" I asked.

"That one on the left," she said. "He looks just like you."

"They all look alike," I thought. "How can she tell?"

The following day I was sitting beside Anne's bed when a nurse entered with a tray laden with food. "Breast of guinea hen under glass," she announced proudly. Anne's eyes turned toward the ceiling, and an odd gurgle came out of her mouth.

"Take it away, please, take it away," Anne said.

The nurse left the tray and tiptoed out. I kept staring at the breast of guinea hen under glass and, remembering my mother's admonition to never waste food and to think of the starving children in Africa and thinking also of dollar signs and the big bills I'd get from Le Roi Sanitarium, I said to hell with it and devoured the damn guinea hen without the glass. It was delicious.

We named our son Peter. I remember seeing Anne standing at the top of the hospital steps holding the baby. At home, I gave him his first bath. To get him ready for feeding, without planning it, I began to act. I always pretended I was Louis Pasteur in a white jacket in my laboratory, scrubbing bottles, carefully measuring out pasteurized milk, and tending to the needs of my son.

9

The First Taste of Hollywood

DURING THE RUN of *Tattoo*, I tried to understand the many complex sides of Maureen Stapleton. She was an actor's actor. She could curse like a sailor and dance like a Rockette. One night onstage, shortly after the show opened, I entered and Maureen turned her back to me and yawned. After the show that night, I banged on her door.

"What were you doing out there?" I asked.

"Acting," she said decisively. "I was acting."

"I come onstage and you yawn," I said. "What the hell kind of signal does that send to the audience?"

Maureen had a magnificent sense of composure. Quietly and in measured tones, she gave me her answer. "I'm onstage at the beginning of the play. For almost an hour, I fight with the neighbors, argue with my daughter, attack the priest, question the sailor, so when you come on fresh as a daisy yelling and shouting, I have two seconds to recover from my acting chores. So, I turn upstage and I decide to yawn. So fuck off!" She slammed the door.

Maureen and I received the 1951 Tony Awards for Best Featured Performances in *Tattoo*. That category surprised us since we had played the starring roles. But evidently, the powers that be decided that since we were young unknown actors, they would give the Best Actor and Actress awards to older performers. That year the Best Actor and Actress awards went to Claude Rains and Uta Hagen.

Unlike the elaborate televised coast-to-coast hoopla of today, our Tony Awards ceremony was held in a tiny hotel ballroom just behind the Martin Beck Theatre. Maureen gave a speech thanking her cast, the author, and producers. I was tongue-tied and stood before the audience for what seemed an eternity. I kept thinking, "I have to thank someone." Suddenly, I blurted out, "I want to thank my agent, Bill Liebling." The audience roared with laughter—back then, no one ever thought of thanking their agents. "No, seriously," I said. "I mean it."

After a long run on Broadway, we began a nationwide tour. We played Philadelphia, Pittsburgh, Detroit, Cleveland, St. Louis, and Los Angeles. We were a hit in Los Angeles, where the writer Ketti Frings and her husband Kurt Frings, a famous agent, threw a party in our honor in Beverly Hills. As we walked into the party, Maureen went goggle-eyed; there were Humphrey Bogart, Lauren Bacall, and Bette Davis, but I wasn't too happy. I wanted to go back to New York; I missed Anne and Peter very much.

One day during our run of *The Rose Tattoo* in Los Angeles, I got a call from the actor David Wayne, whom I knew from the Actors Studio. He was under contract to 20th Century Fox and was supposed to play the role of Sol Hurok—an entrepreneur agent who handled ballet dancers, opera stars, and concert musicians—in a film called *Tonight We Sing*. David didn't think he was right for the role and asked if I would do a screen test.

"I'll try," I said, "but I've never made a film."

The next day I met with the director, Jean Negulesco. He handed me two brief scenes—in one, I was to read opposite an actress playing Madame Pavlova; in the other, I was to play a scene with the actress playing Sol Hurok's wife.

"When do we rehearse?" I asked the director.

"No, no," he said. "Just learn the lines. You'll see."

The next day I walked onto a cavernous movie set on the 20th Century Fox lot. Negulesco walked me through the scene. "Now, you've just seen Pavlova dance on the stage," he said. "Wait till the red light at the top of the door goes out. Then burst into the room and there you'll see Madame Pavlova."

Someone shouted, "Quiet on the set," the red light went out, and I pushed open the door.

"Madame Pavlova," I said urgently, "I've just seen you dance; you're magical. I want to handle you. For your tour, I'll have a train built in the shape of a swan."

Sitting on a green velvet divan in front of her dressing-room mirror was Pavlova. The actress playing her was a big-bosomed blond wearing a pink tutu. She was doing her fingernails.

"Whaddaya want?" Pavlova asked with a thick Brooklyn accent. I froze; the camera must have caught what I wanted—"I want to get the hell out of here." I thought, "I've been on the road for months. I'd rather go home."

"Cut! Cut," said Negulesco. "That was fine."

He patted me on the back. "Now, let's do the next scene." He walked me over to another cavernous set where I met another actress.

"When I yell 'action,' you come in," Negulesco said. "You will be acting with your wife in this scene."

"What about the red light?" I asked.

"Oh yeah, yeah, yeah, you're right," he said. "Now, listen. In this scene you have forgotten to bring her a present. I want to see what happens to your face when she tells you it's your anniversary."

"Okay," I said.

"Action!" said Negulesco, and we did the scene.

"Good! Good! Cut!" he said. "That's fine, fine!"

Later my agent told me that Darryl F. Zanuck, head of the studio, had watched the screen test. "What's the deal on the guy?" he asked when he saw me. He was told I was auditioning for a two-picture deal spread over two years.

"Forget him," he said. "Sign the wife," meaning Anne Bancroft, who had played my lovely screen wife. She spent the next seven years at 20th Century Fox, and David Wayne wound up playing the role of Sol Hurok after all.

The last stop on the road tour of *The Rose Tattoo* was San Francisco. On closing night, our general manager, Max Allentuck, who was Maureen's husband, announced, "We're all flying back to New York tomorrow."

"Not me," said Maureen, stubborn as a mule. "I'll never get on a plane."

"You'll fly with us," said Max, using a tone that husbands adopt when their wives refuse to obey orders.

"No," she said. "Not until I talk to the captain of the plane."

Miraculously, Allentuck was able to get the captain on the phone.

"I need a parachute," Maureen told him. There was a long pause. Finally, the captain said, "Sorry, madam, I don't have a parachute. My copilot doesn't even have a parachute."

"That's crazy," Maureen said. "What if we crash?"

"I've been flying for fifteen years," the captain assured her. "We won't crash; I'll see to that."

On the plane Maureen refused to sit next to her husband, feeling he had shanghaied her onto the flight. Instead, she sat next to me. Every time the stewardess came up or down the aisle, Maureen would snare a drink. Once she was sufficiently anesthetized, she held my hand, closed her eyes, and seemed to pray. In those days, flying from the West Coast to New York took about ten hours. At one point, I shook Maureen gently. "Maureen, Maureen," I told her, "I have to go to the bathroom." She kept holding my hand. "Maureen, please," I said, "I have to go to the bathroom."

"All right," she said. "Let's go."

Maureen stood outside the bathroom door while I attended to my needs. As I came out, she grabbed my hand and led me back to my seat. "Buckle up," she ordered, "and no more bathroom privileges for you." I timidly obeyed for the rest of the flight.

Once I was back in New York, I'd decided that I had had

enough of my *Rose Tattoo* agent, Bill Liebling. Whenever I was rejected for a part in a play, he'd repeat his favorite line: "Well, that's life in the Balkans." So I decided to get the hell out of the Balkans. I signed up with Peter Witt, who represented a great list of prominent actors: Jason Robards, Lauren Bacall, and, most important, my wife. Witt was German born, an ex–tennis champ, and intensely loyal to his clients. I was to spend the next two decades with him.

During the tour of *Tattoo,* I had become very excited about the possibility of doing Tennessee Williams's next play, *Camino Real,* which he had enlarged from the scene that Elia Kazan had directed me in. But Cheryl Crawford was unable to immediately raise the money for the production, so it was temporarily shelved. Instead, Witt got me a movie audition with casting director Max Arno. I was to read for the role of a fiery Italian.

Arno and I met with Harry Cohn, the head of Columbia Pictures. Cohn looked like a balding ex-wrestler. When we entered his office, he was on the phone chatting away. He nodded at us, smiled, and said, "I'll be with you in a minute." His voice was a blend of Louis Armstrong and Lionel Stander. We kept waiting and waiting. Suddenly, Cohn looked up at me and said, "I don't know, he looks like a Hebe." And then he went back to his phone conversation. The muscles in my stomach tensed. Memories of my army colonel in Casablanca and his remarks about President "Rosenfeld" rattled around in my brain.

"What did he say?" I asked.

Arno looked at me and shrugged. "He said you look like a Hebe," he said.

"Well, you tell him I'm fucking well offended," I said.

Cohn put his hand over the phone. "I heard that. I heard what you said," he said with a smile.

"I'm fucking well offended," I repeated. "Your name is Harry Cohn. How can you make a remark like that?" Then, a bell rang in my head. "He's trying to upset me, so I'll behave like the fiery Italian in his film script," I thought. I turned up my anger volume and began to yell.

"Calm down," Cohn said. "I don't know; you just don't look Italian."

"I've been playing an Italian in *The Rose Tattoo* for a year and a half," I said. "I feel pretty Italian."

"Well," he croaked, "you'd have to do one picture a year for seven years."

"No," I said, feeling as if I'd finally pinned the balding wrestler to the mat. "I'll do one movie. If you like my work, you can hire me again. If you don't, don't!"

"You'll have to do a screen test," said Cohn.

"Fine with me," I said. "I'll be happy to on one condition. The director of the film must direct the test."

"It's done," said Cohn. He was still smiling at me.

I shot the test in a small studio in New York with director Fred Zinnemann, and the next day I got a call.

"You got the part," Peter Witt said.

But later that week, Cheryl Crawford called to tell me that she had raised the money for *Camino Real* with Elia Kazan set to direct. Now I had to choose between the movie and the play. I'd never made a film, but I thought, "Well, there's a lot of celluloid out in Hollywood. So, no coin tossing for me." I chose the play.

The movie, as it turned out, was *From Here to Eternity*, which would star Burt Lancaster, Deborah Kerr, and Montgomery Clift. Fred Zinnemann called and urged me to do the film, telling me that I was just right for the role of Maggio.

"I can't have two wives at the same time," I said. "I'll have to take my chances."

Frank Sinatra wound up getting the part I was to play and won an Academy Award for Best Supporting Actor. Over the years, I've read half a dozen books that discuss how Sinatra got the role. The press at the time also had a field day. They guessed that Sinatra got the role because of pressure from the Mafia. I've even read that Frank's then-wife Ava Gardner had indulged in various affairs in order to sway Harry Cohn to give Sinatra the role. Also, that I had demanded too much money—all fanciful fabrications.

Years later I was in Las Vegas, where I was to give a talk to the American Lung Association. As I got off the plane, I saw a huge billboard in bold letters: HE'S HERE, it said. My chest filled with pride. "How nice," I thought, "all for me." But there up on a corner of the billboard, I saw a drawing with two blue eyes. It was for Frank. I got a ticket for his concert at Caesars Palace and sat at his family's table beside his wife Barbara. In the middle of one of his songs, he stopped, leaned over the edge of the stage, and said, "Barbara, did Eli get here?"

"He's sitting right beside me," she said.

"Ladies and gentlemen," said Frank, "I'd like to introduce a friend. Our paths have often crossed, and he played a big part in my career." He paused, looked at me, and said, "Ah, the hell with that! It's an old story. I don't feel like telling it." I fell out of my seat laughing.

Every time Frank saw me after that, he'd say, "Hello, you crazy actor." And every time he came to New York, he'd send a limo for Anne and me. We'd sit in a box at the theater. He'd look up, smile at us, and afterward we'd have a late supper at 21.

◎ ◎ ◎

I wanted more than anything to do *Camino*, even though Kazan was and remains a controversial figure. After World War II, Winston Churchill gave a speech in Fulton, Missouri, decrying the Iron Curtain that had descended upon Europe, precipitating what would soon be known as the Cold War. In America during the 1950s, tensions grew as Congress began to investigate the loyalties of its citizens via Senator Joseph McCarthy and the House Un-American Activities Committee. People were ordered to name names of those whom they knew to be Communists or Communist sympathizers. To his credit, Elia Kazan initially refused to cooperate, but after pressure from the head of 20th Century Fox, he capitulated and gave names of actors from the Group Theatre. He even took out an ad in the *New York Times* explaining the reasons for his actions, saying that America was engaged in a worldwide struggle against Communism and that he felt it was his duty to cooperate.

Kazan's decision caused a tremendous rift in the Broadway community; some praised him, but many castigated him. Some members of the Actors Studio left in protest; the executive secretary turned in her notice. Many felt his career would not have been harmed if he'd refused to answer HUAC's questions.

I felt stuck in the middle. As a kid in Little Italy, I always knew that one did not squeal on his friends; if you did, you were considered a rat. I was torn between my career needs and my disapproval of Kazan's actions. Kazan was one of Broadway's great directors, and the chance to be in Williams's brilliant fantasy was tempting. At the same time, Arthur Miller and *Death of a Salesman* producer Kermit Bloomgarden had turned their backs on Kazan. Why not do the same thing they did and walk away?

"Coward," I remember thinking. "I'm a coward." But I stuck with my need to do the play. Kazan knew my feelings about what he had done, but we never discussed it then. Years later he was being honored by the Academy of Motion Picture Arts and Sciences in California; he was receiving a Lifetime Achievement award. This honor reawakened all of the old feelings. Rod Steiger, who had starred with Brando in *On the Waterfront*, was upset by the award. In New York Kazan spoke with me about what he should say before the Academy. "I know this is going to cause another tornado," he said. "All the old heated opinions will come to the fore." I told him that what he should do was to walk onstage at the award ceremony and simply say, "I've come three thousand miles to say thank you," then walk off. He was shaky about that advice; instead, he walked out onstage that night with Robert De Niro and Martin Scorsese at his side for security.

◎ ◎ ◎

Cheryl Crawford had fallen in love with *Camino* and was determined to bring it to Broadway, even though it seemed like quite a gamble. *Camino* was unlike any of Williams's other work. It was a fantasy set in a dirty plaza somewhere below the border. It was filled with gypsies, pimps, panderers, fascist police, and a host of legendary characters: Lord Byron, Marguerite Gautier from *Camille*, Casanova, the Baron de Charlus, Don Quixote. I was to play the role of Kilroy, an ex-boxer and ex-sailor who first appears at the top of a flight of stairs. On a crumbling wall, there is a message scrawled in chalk: "Kilroy is coming." Kilroy crosses out the word *coming* and replaces it with *here*.

I enjoyed working with Kazan; he often used sly means to build tension during rehearsal. One time during a rehearsal, he took me aside and told me to approach a group of strangers onstage. "You're alone and you're scared," he said, "so go on and make friends." Meanwhile, he told the actors playing a motley crowd of peasants, "Ignore this stranger; he's a gringo, and he has bad breath."

Kazan worked long and hard shaping Tennessee's play into a bold and startling fantastic extravaganza. Rehearsals were long and exhausting and yet strangely exhilarating. All of us in the cast felt we were embarking on a trip to a world we had never encountered before. Even though *Camino* was a fantasy, Kazan told us that the play would be stronger if each role was performed with a sense of truth.

For me, the play was very physically demanding. At one point, I had to jump offstage while police chased me, then run through the audience screaming, "Where the hell is the Greyhound bus depot?" I'd run up one aisle, then down another. People would have to stand to allow me to pass. Then I'd run up to the balcony, enter the box seats, climb over the rail, and jump directly back onstage, just like John Wilkes Booth did after he'd shot President

Lincoln. Once I was caught by the police, I was ordered to kneel onstage and a clown's hat was clapped over my head. Fastened to the hat were eyeglasses with a long string attached to them; the nose was a red Ping-Pong-ball-shaped bulb.

"Light your nose," the policeman would say, and I would press the button to light my nose, which kept blinking on and off as the theater lights went down.

Audiences were puzzled by some of the scenes. And in early previews, many walked out. The play was savagely attacked by the critics. Leading the charge was Walter Kerr, critic for the *New York Herald Tribune*, who ended his review with a terse sentence: "Williams is our greatest playwright. And this is his worst play."

After the reviews had come out, Tennessee sat down and wrote a letter to Cheryl Crawford, the producer:

Dear Cheryl,

Whenever I talk about you I say, "Cheryl is a great fighter. She's always there when you need her." In China, in the old days, they used to give an old man an opium pipe. I suppose now they just shoot him. I think we should show fight in this situation. I'm enclosing a letter I just wrote to that critic Walter Kerr.

Dear Mr. Kerr,

I'm feeling a little punch drunk from the feared, but not fully anticipated attack at your hands and a quorum of your colleagues. But I would like to attempt to get a few things off my chest in reply. What I would like to know is, don't you see that "Camino" is a concentrate, a distillation of the world and time we live in?

Mr. Kerr, I believe in your honesty. I believe you said what you honestly think and feel about this play. And I wouldn't have the nerve to question your verdict. But silence is only golden when you have nothing to say. And I still think I have a great deal to say.
Cordially,
Tennessee Williams

I don't believe Kerr ever answered Tennessee's letter. But there's one line in the play that affected Anne and myself so greatly that we decided to adopt it as our motto. "Lately," Lord Byron says, "I've been listening to hired musicians behind a row of artificial palm trees instead of the single pure stringed instrument of my heart. For what is the heart, but a sort of instrument that translates noise into music, chaos into order. Make voyages, attempt them, there's nothing else." Anne and I decided that we would always make voyages and attempt them.

Camino's end came quickly, with a crisp closing notice posted on the backstage bulletin board. We had just completed our fifty-sixth performance. The closing of a play is like a death in the family, and it leaves a deep scar on an actor's ego. I remember packing up all my belongings in the dressing room, then walking out into the rainy night. "Why me?" I thought. I loved the cast, the writing, the direction, but thankfully *Camino* didn't die. Over the years, many regional theaters have given Williams's fantasy a second chance.

I've never regretted the choice of doing *Camino Real* instead of *From Here to Eternity*. To me, *Camino* was the greatest experience I had in the theater.

10

From New York to
London and Back

ANNE AND I had two careers and one baby; somehow, we managed to sort out the household chores. I did the dishes and became an expert at the ironing board. Anne cooked and did the
shopping. Both of us learned how to parcel out our sleeping
hours. Then came job searching, auditions; always, we had to
make sacrifices. Our most joyful times came watching Peter take
his first steps, hearing him utter his first words. I invented a way
to keep his crib moving by tying a rope to the crib and the end of
it to my leg. Moving my leg up and down, I could sit in my chair
and read the *New York Times,* listen to the radio, and at the same
time soothe my colicky son.

The first play I did after *Camino Real* was Jean Anouilh's *Mademoiselle Colombe* starring Edna Best and Julie Harris. Harold Clur-

man, fresh from his production of *The Member of the Wedding,* would direct. After Peter Witt informed me that I got the part, he offered his standard joke: "Now you'll get 90 percent of what I deserve. How can I live on a mere 10 percent commission?" I enjoyed that remark about as much as my previous agent Bill Liebling's line, "Well, that's life in the Balkans."

Harold Clurman was a fancy dresser with two roving eyes for the women. He was also famous for the warm-up speeches he gave on the first day of rehearsal. He was like the football coach Knute Rockne, urging his cast on with pep talks to "Go out and defeat the enemy." In this case, the enemy was the audience.

Clurman was worried that one section of Anouilh's play would be too scandalous for American audiences. I was cast as Julien, who was going off to do his military service, leaving his wife and child in the care of his mother, a glamorous actress based on the stage star Sarah Bernhardt. Julien was a jealous, possessive, unyielding, and unforgiving husband. While away, he receives a letter stating that his wife is having an affair with someone in her theater company. Bristling with anger, he confronts his wife in her dressing room. "Who is it?" he screams, at which point the door opens and his brother enters carrying a bouquet of flowers.

"Ah, it's you," Julien says, and proceeds to berate his brother, then finally demands, "Kiss me."

"You forgive me?" the brother asks.

"No," Julien growls. "Kiss me, kiss me the way you kiss her." Julien chases him around the room, corners him, then, just before the final curtain falls, kisses him full on the lips. "Very French," I thought, as we began rehearsing.

We were to open in Boston, but Clurman was so terrified that the kissing sequence would startle and alienate the audience that he cut it out. My brother, played by William Windom, appeared in the doorway, I said melodramatically, "It's you," and the curtain fell.

When we were set to open in New York, Windom and I strenuously objected to Clurman's cautious approach. "We won't go on unless the kiss is restored," I told him. "It's ironic and funny and true."

Finally, Clurman gave in. "All right," he said. "Go ahead, but I don't know if I can watch."

On opening night, I chased Windom around the stage, kissed him right on the mouth, wiped my lips, said, "I don't understand," and the audience roared. Both Windom and I felt vindicated, and Harold, bless him, wiped his brow and smiled.

Julie Harris was the best gift I took away from *Colombe*. I'll never forget an incident during the run of the play. Julie was going through a messy divorce yet she never revealed her problems at home during rehearsals or the previews. But one afternoon we were waiting for the play to begin; and as the music faded away and the house lights came down just before the curtain was to go up, she tearfully took my hand and said, "I wish I was dead." "Julie," I whispered. "Julie, listen, we have a matinee, we'll talk about your death later."

Winner of numerous Tonys and devoted to the theater, Julie believed in taking shows on the road because she felt that the rest of America deserved the chance to see a Broadway production. No tour for us, though, because *Colombe* met the same fate as *Camino*.

With two flops in a row, I was biding my time and going to see lots of French movies when I got a call from Bobby Lewis, who was going to direct the play *The Teahouse of the August Moon* in London. I had heard that John Mills, who was currently starring in *Charley's Aunt* there, would be playing the role of Sakini. Bobby told me that the producer H. M. Tennant wouldn't release Mills from his commitment and would I be interested in coming to London to play the role?

Would I? Damn right. I'd seen the play in New York starring David Wayne and loved it. I almost didn't get the role at first because British Equity refused to give permission for an American to appear in the London production. But Bobby Lewis was adamant: "If Wallach isn't allowed to play Sakini, I'll drop the whole project and a lot of your English actors will be out of work." So they finally agreed and I had the part.

The famous acting couple Alfred Lunt and Lynn Fontanne decided when they got married that they would only work in plays where they appeared together, but both Anne and I felt that that would limit our choice of plays. Anne was performing in a hit show on Broadway: Edward Chodorov's *Oh, Men! Oh, Women!* But she also understood my need to undertake the lead role in *Teahouse.*

"If the play closes in London, I'll come right home," I told her.

"If my play closes in New York, I'll join you in London," Anne said.

Both of us wondered who would make the first transatlantic trip.

Upon arriving at Heathrow Airport, I was greeted by an official holding a sign with my name on it. "Welcome to London," he said. "I'm from Inland Revenue. You realize, of course, that you are liable for British taxes. Please sign this form."

"Well, that's a nice greeting," I thought. "I've just arrived and they're already dunning me for taxes."

Luckily, Peter Witt had with great foresight hired a wily Scotsman to serve as my accountant. As I sat in his office, he got Inland Revenue on the phone and asked if I was required to pay British taxes.

"Oh yes," he was told, "the same as any English actor."

"Good," the accountant told me. "We've got them."

"What does that mean?" I asked.

"British taxes are based on your income from the previous year," he told me. "Did you do well last year?"

"No," I said wearily, "I was in two flops in New York."

"Great," he said. "Just do your job here but don't come back for a year after you leave."

That took care of my tax situation.

At the time of my arrival in early 1954, London was still struggling from the effects of World War II. I remember the city as being cold and wet. The Brits were still burning soft coal, which made London the smog capital of the world. I settled in at a freezing rooming house just off Piccadilly. At night I'd pop a shilling into a little electric stove to warm my numbing feet. After six minutes the glowing coals would slowly fade, I'd make a run for the bed, and with script in hand, I'd study my lines.

One night I was walking along Shaftesbury Avenue when I espied a blinking marquee on the Globe Theatre: MARTHA GRAHAM IN CONCERT. I bought a ticket and sat down in the mezzanine section, where I could get a good view of the dancers. After the performance I walked backstage and asked if I could see

Graham, whom I hadn't seen since I was a student at the Actors Studio.

The doorman squinted at me. "American, are you?" he asked.

"I studied with her in New York," I said. "I'd like to surprise her."

"Follow me," he said, knocked on her dressing room door, and announced, "You have a visitor, ma'am."

Martha opened the door, and when she saw me, her eyes widened. "What a surprise," she said. "What are you doing in London?"

"I've decided to follow you all over the world," I said. "Tonight is my first stop."

After I had expressed my thrill at her ability to capture an emotion with one simple movement, she ordered her maid to set the teakettle boiling. Over a pot of tea, I told her the story of the artist James McNeill Whistler and how he had always signed his name in bold letters across the top of each painting. Initially, no one wanted to buy any of his work; they saw the big signature and thought he was on a huge ego trip. At first, he decided never to paint again. But after a year, he picked up his brush once more, but now, instead of signing his name, he drew a tiny butterfly somewhere on the canvas.

"From now on," I told Martha, "I intend to use a pure Graham movement in any stage role I perform. No one will know where it is, but it will always be there."

Years later Ms. Graham came backstage to see me after a play. "Where was the Graham movement?" she asked.

"I can't tell you; that's my secret," I told her. "Whistler had his butterfly and I have my Graham movement."

In preparation to play the role of Sakini in *Teahouse,* Bobby Lewis and I had several prerehearsal sessions. "I haven't the slightest idea of how to play an Asian," I told him. "How do I do it?"

"Okinawan," he corrected me. "Half your part is in Japanese.

"I've played Asians in half a dozen films, including one with Charlie Chaplin," he reassured me. He was short, plump, and bald. "Now, here's the secret: I used to ride in the open rumble seat of a car. When the wind blew in my face, I'd squint my eyes, and as I inhaled, I'd suck in the air and make a whooshing sound; *whoosh*—voilà! There's your Asian."

Bobby's explanation wasn't that helpful. I remembered that when I was a kid my nickname was "Chink" because my eyes got very narrow when I smiled. So as I worked on the role, I tried to do a lot of smiling. That would make me look Asian, I figured. Rehearsals were held in the Drury Lane Theatre near Covent Garden, and following Bobby's direction, I walked around sucking up all the dirt and dust of the stage. The result: a serious bout with bronchitis.

To transform myself into an Okinawan, I covered my eyebrows with soap. When the soap dried, I'd paint new eyebrows above the old ones and draw a little line in the inner corner of each eye. Then I'd slick my black hair back with sticky goo. A quick glance in the mirror and soon the transformation was complete.

I grew more anxious as we approached our opening night. In the London newspapers, there were always stories about the antics of the so-called Gallery Gods, a rowdy group that occupied the top seats of the theater. Their chief victims were American plays. If a show displeased them, they would boo and stomp their feet. *Pal Joey* had recently suffered such a fate.

On opening night at Her Majesty's Theatre, I stepped in front of the bamboo curtain and delivered my first lines, wondering when those bastards up in the balcony would start their attack. "Lovely ladies, kind gentlemen," I said, stressing the words *kind gentlemen,* hoping that would get through to the Gods, "Please to introduce myself: Sakini by name, interpreter by profession, education by ancient dictionary, Okinawan by whim of Gods."

There was no booing; no one stomped their feet—all in all, a wonderfully warm reception. The reviews were glowing and I was even accepted as an Asian. We settled into a long run. It took me awhile, but I figured out why the English liked the show so much. The show dealt with Americans trying to teach the Okinawan natives the principles of democracy. Of course, the wily natives ended up teaching the Americans a thing or two, something that British audiences seemed to find amusing.

One night, however, I was frightened to find that a number of Japanese were attending the show. I peeked through the bamboo curtain and, before my entrance, caught a glimpse of several of them in the front row. My heart sank. I wondered if the Gallery Gods had given them free tickets to harass me. As I stepped out onstage, all the Japanese words I had learned for the show went right out of my head. At one point, the army captain said to me, "Tell the natives there'll be rice for everyone." But rather than translating that line, I responded with the only line I could remember in Japanese, which translated roughly to "The school will have five sides like the Pentagon." Onstage, the cast started giggling, and the Japanese in the front row laughed so hard they almost fell out of their seats.

During our run in London, we had numerous famous spectators. One night the queen and Prince Philip attended; their only request was that no one sit directly in front of them so that they could have a clear view of the stage. Special commemorative programs honoring the queen and the prince were printed.

Another night the stage manager took me aside right as I was about to enter.

"Look in the front row," he said. "You have a famous guest."

Out I came and started to deliver my "Lovely ladies, kind gentlemen" line. I bowed to the left, then to the right, then directly to the front row, and then I stopped. There sat Winston Churchill. He was wearing a hearing aid. Just as I started my second line, he reached into his coat jacket and fiddled with something. For the rest of the play, I kept watching him. He sat like a bulldog throughout and never changed his expression. So I never knew if he turned the damn hearing aid off or on.

Toward the end of the play, a teahouse was erected onstage. Since the theater didn't have a lot of stagehands, the management would occasionally bring in students from the Royal Academy of Dramatic Art and pay them one pound per performance. They would stand in the wings and hand the actors pieces of scenery in order to build the teahouse. At one performance, three students from the Royal Academy of Dramatic Arts showed up to do the job: Alan Bates, Peter O'Toole, and Albert Finney. That was quite a trio.

Two months into the run, Anne called and told me that Cheryl

Crawford had finally agreed to let her leave the play *Oh, Men! Oh, Women!* At first, Cheryl had been reluctant, saying that Anne might well win a Tony if she stayed with the production, but Anne insisted on leaving.

"But I just had to come to see you, and I'm bringing Peter," she said.

I hadn't seen Anne or Peter since I'd left New York to do *Teahouse*. I scurried around London with a half a dozen real estate agents and finally found a lovely house on Chester Row in Chelsea. Before Anne and Peter arrived, I signed a three-month lease, then boarded a train to Southhampton, where I waited anxiously at dockside for the ship to come in. The publicity agent for *Teahouse* had arranged for some reporters to greet the ship. The reunion was delicious. I remember Anne standing on Deck A, waving to me, then Peter raising his hand and shaking it. The next day the papers were filled with headlines such as HAPPY RE-UNION OF AMERICAN FAMILY—*TEAHOUSE* STAR MEETS HIS LADY. After the train ride from Southhampton to London, we rode in a fancy taxi straight into Chelsea, where we settled in as a family once again.

Peter was four years old now, and he soon joined in with the neighborhood kids. He was something of an oddity with his cowboy hat and a toy pistol dangling from his belt. In a short time, however, he developed a strange Cockney accent. Each evening when I went off to the theater, Annie played housewife and I would feel guilty leaving her and Peter alone.

While *Teahouse* was selling out at Her Majesty's Theatre, Anne and I took in the riches of London: the museums, art galleries, antique markets, and theaters. Then the producers of the New York production of *Teahouse* wired to inform me that David Wayne was leaving the Broadway production; would I be able to come back to New York and replace him?

"Yes, be happy to," I wired right back. "Will arrive soon."

We sailed out of Southhampton on a ship called the *Ile de France*. Peter put away his cowboy outfit, hat, and gun and donned a sailor suit. Anne and I were looking forward to coming home. But in the middle of the ocean, I got a shore-to-ship phone call. As soon as I heard my brother Sam's voice, I knew the news was bad. My mother, Bertha, had died from a cerebral hemorrhage. It was quick and painless, Sam assured me. She died with the queen and Prince Philip's special *Teahouse* program at her bedside.

I asked Anne to leave me alone in our stateroom. For the next few hours, I sat and thought about my mother—her warm smile, the sacrifices she made for all of us, how beautiful she looked whenever she lit the candles and prayed on Friday nights.

After dinner Anne and I took a long walk around the deck, and she mentioned an incident with my mother that brought more tears from me.

"Bertha came to visit us when Peter was a baby," Anne said.

"I'll be happy to do anything you want me to do," Mom had said, "but only if you say it is all right."

And Anne was so moved by her offer that even when she was repeating the story to me, she still burst into tears.

11

The Dirtiest American Film Ever Made

ANNE, PETER, AND I arrived safely back in New York, where David Stewart had found us a new apartment in Greenwich Village on MacDougal Street. As it turned out, our bedroom was located directly over a nightclub. The blaring music kept us awake, but at least it seemed to soothe Peter.

Bobby Lewis put me through rehearsals for the Broadway production of *Teahouse* at the Martin Beck Theatre. Joining the New York cast went smoothly. I only made one change when I joined the company. The actor I was replacing, David Wayne, had had his dressing room made over as a little teahouse. He'd sit cross-legged on the floor and put on his makeup.

"Not for me," I thought, and asked for a regular-sized table; I saw no need to sit on the floor.

During one performance of *Teahouse* in New York, I faced an extraordinary and frightening experience. As the houselights went down, I took my place at stage right. Gino, an old stagehand, stood at the ready, about to raise the curtain. He gave me a thumbs-up and a quick wink. Suddenly, his hand slipped off the rope and he slid to the floor. I knelt down, but he had no pulse and I knew he was gone. The stage manager whispered to me, "We can't move him till the coroner comes. So, I'll raise the curtain; step over the body and go on."

My opening speech was always a cheerful greeting to the audience, but all I could think of was the stagehand lying there. But some mysterious force took over and I was able to get through the play.

@ @ @

By now, Anne was pregnant with our second child. In the 1950s, medical science was ill-equipped to reveal the sex of a fetus. But we tried an old trick we found in the *Farmers' Almanac*. Hold a key on a string and place it in front of the mother's belly, the almanac ordered. If the key dangles from side to side, it's a boy. If it moves in a circle, it's a girl. The key swung from side to side. Anne smiled at me: another boy. Okay, that was fine with me.

Our pediatrician told us that Anne would give birth at the end of July. I said, "Please, because the baby was conceived while we were in London with *Teahouse of the August Moon* and *Teahouse* was important to me for many reasons, could you hold off till August?"

"I'll try, I'll try," Anne said, and she did, giving birth on August

2, 1955. When the nurse handed the bundle to Anne, it was a beautiful girl. We named her Roberta in honor of my mother, Bertha. So much for the *Farmers' Almanac*. When she was born, Roberta had a mild case of hepatitis and looked a trifle jaundiced, but the nurse told us there was nothing to worry about. When Anne first saw Roberta, her eyes filled with tears. "Look at her," she said, "her black hair, her straight black eyebrows. She looks just like Merle Oberon." Once we got home, I again donned my white jacket and became Louis Pasteur, cleaning bottles and making formula.

Anne had interviewed a dozen young women to work around the house and to look after the children. One day Nell Counsel, a tall thin black lady, arrived and Anne interviewed her. Instead of going to baby Roberta, as all the previous interviewees had, Nell knelt down beside our son, Peter, and asked, "How does it feel to have a little sister?"

Peter shrugged his shoulders and said, "I don't know."

Anne was immediately taken with Nell; she was not just a nanny but a child psychologist as well. Once we hired Nell, Peter appreciated how much time she spent with him.

Nell became an integral part of our lives. We never could have managed our careers without her.

Several months later Josh Logan cast Anne in Paddy Chayefsky's play *Middle of the Night* with Edward G. Robinson, Gena Rowlands, and Martin Balsam. And while Anne was in rehearsal and I was still in *Teahouse*, Elia Kazan called me.

"I think it's time for you to get out of that *Teahouse*," he said, then asked me if I would consider playing a Sicilian American cotton gin manager in *Baby Doll,* a film that he was directing from a script by Tennessee Williams. This, I thought, was my reward for choosing to do *Camino Real* instead of *From Here to Eternity;* this was my reward for loyalty to Williams and the theater.

That night at home, I gave Anne a hug and started to make myself a cup of tea.

"I'm gonna make my first movie. We're gonna make piles of money," I told her. "Would you like a cup of tea?"

"No, no," Anne said. "Keep on with the story. What happened?"

I tossed the tea bag into the wastebasket and continued.

"Well," I said, "he offered me the role. It's going to be shot in Mississippi." I explained that Tennessee had adapted two of his one-act plays, *27 Wagons Full of Cotton* and *The Unsatisfactory Supper,* and made them into a great screenplay.

"I'll make a fortune," I told her.

Anne interrupted. "I think I will have some tea," she said.

Without pausing, I went right back to the wastebasket and took out the tea bag.

"Listen," Anne said, "now that we're rich, do you mind if I have my own tea bag?"

The next day I approached our *Teahouse* producer, Maurice Evans, who was also a wonderful Shakespearean actor. I told him about Kazan's offer.

"No, no, no," said Evans. "The author, John Patrick, will never let you go. You're under contract with us till November."

"Look," I said, "I've been in the play for over a year and a half in London and here, and this is a fantastic opportunity."

"Well," he said, "how long will the movie take?"

Not knowing anything about film, I closed my eyes and the number eight popped into my head.

"Eight weeks," I said.

"Only eight weeks? All right," he said. "For each week you're in the movie, you'll have to extend your *Teahouse* contract by two weeks."

But no sooner had I signed my contract for *Baby Doll* than I began to have misgivings. From the time I left the army, I had concentrated on stage work. I had really faced the cameras only twice before: first, when I missed out on *Tonight We Sing* and, second, when I turned down the offer for Maggio in *From Here to Eternity*. The only other time was when Anne and I had filmed our Tennessee Williams one-act in New Jersey. This was to be one of my greatest tests—how does one act in film? And how do I go from a two-year stint as an Okinawan onstage to a cotton gin manager on film?

Once again, I went to see another batch of French films to get a sense of what film acting meant. I noticed that French actors listened well. They shrugged their shoulders a lot and actually seemed to think. "I'll try that," I thought. Once again I would be separated from my family. Anne was going on tour with Edward G. Robinson in a new play—*Middle of the Night*—and I was off to run a cotton gin in Mississippi. Well, the Lunts had made their pact and we'd made ours, so off we went.

At the time *Baby Doll* was filmed, Mississippi was still completely segregated. A month or two before we began filming, a young black boy had been lynched, supposedly for whistling as a pretty white girl walked by. Tensions were high. Local authorities received assurances that Tennessee Williams was a true-blue southerner and that this would not be a smug, sneering film about the "po' South."

We settled in Greenville, Mississippi. The set was a big white antebellum mansion in nearby Benoit. It had seen better days: Its paint was peeling; some windows were missing; the front porch was sagging. It was exactly what we had been looking for. An old rusting Pierce-Arrow automobile was needed to sit in the front yard in order to complete the picture of decrepitude. The props department found a Pierce-Arrow near Detroit; it had been kept in mint condition by its proud owner, who named an outrageous price to lend it to the production.

"It must be returned to me as you received it, no ifs, ands, or buts," he said.

"Agreed, oh yes, certainly," the producers said.

The ink was hardly dry on the deal when the Pierce-Arrow was driven into a garage and the car was transformed from an antique showpiece into a rusting hulk. The car received a rubber coating; rust spots were painted all over the entire body, the motor was removed, the headlights dangled. After the film was finished, the car was restored to its former pristine state—no ifs, ands, or buts. I'm sure the owner, after seeing the film, must have wondered why no one had seen fit to use his Pierce-Arrow after paying him all that money.

Kazan cast the film with Actors Studio veterans: Karl Malden, Lonny Chapman, Carroll Baker, Mildred Dunnock, Rip Torn, and myself. For the smaller roles, he used a good number of local non-actors interspersed with the rest of us to add a sense of authenticity to the film. The film was supposed to take place in early summer, but the usual delays pushed our start into late October.

In the film Malden, whose cotton gin is consistently losing money to the syndicate company, decides to burn theirs down. I played Silva Vacarro, a manager for the syndicate who suspects that Malden is the arsonist. After the fire, Vacarro decides to spend time with Baby Doll (Carroll Baker), Malden's virginal young wife, and nearly seduces her, in an attempt to trap her into signing a confession about her husband's involvement in the fire.

One scene taught me a great deal about how to act on film. After the syndicate's cotton gin was burned down, I was supposed to stand on a pile of burning embers, turn, and look into the camera filled with hate and anger. But I couldn't find a way to play those emotions. "All the cotton gins in Mississippi could burn down and I wouldn't give a damn," I thought.

But Kazan was a very patient director. "Listen," he told me, "in movies it always takes a long time to light the scene, to get the set ready. There's very little rehearsal. And when all the technical aspects are ready—the sound, the lighting, the set—they nod to the director and he shouts out, 'Action!' I don't work that way. I want you to turn with your back to the camera, and take all the time you want, and look at the burning embers. When you're ready and you turn, I'll have the cameras going."

So, now that I had the time to prepare myself for a scene, I was able to find ways to sense those emotions. Standing on the embers, I turned my back to the camera and thought, "What if?" *What if?* The magical *What if?* always helps actors a great deal.

"What if a friend burned down my house with my wife and children inside?" I asked myself. Then I slowly turned, my eyes were tearing up, and I was filled with hate.

"Cut!" said Kazan. "That was very good; now let's move on!"

Kazan allowed us a certain amount of freedom in developing our characters' motivations. At one moment in a scene before I was supposed to seduce Baby Doll, he asked me, "Do you think you actually go through with seducing that girl?"

I hadn't thought about that question before, but I answered.

"No," I finally said.

"Interesting," he said. "Why?"

"Well," I said, "as a Sicilian, I'd lead her to the point where she would want me to and then leave her stranded, but I wouldn't actually do it."

"Good idea," he said, "play it that way."

Kazan's approach didn't always work for everyone. Late one evening, I was supposed to shoot a scene with Carroll Baker where she was supposed to cry. Kazan ordered her to stand behind a nearby barn and prepare. She went behind the barn and then fifteen minutes went by. It was getting dark outside and the crew had already moved the camera in position to catch the last bit of the setting sun.

Kazan looked at me. "What will I do?" he asked.

"Get her out," I said. "Just get her out."

Kazan ran behind the barn. There sat Carroll looking bewildered.

"What's the matter?" he asked.

"I don't know how to prepare," she said.

But as soon as Kazan dragged her into position in front of the camera, she began to cry—not because of the wonderful scene Williams had written, but because she was upset that she hadn't been able to carry out Kazan's order. Once the camera began to roll, however, she played the scene beautifully.

After a few weeks of filming, Karl Malden took me aside and tried to give me some pointers on acting on film. He was an old pro and had already acted in more than a dozen films, including *A Streetcar Named Desire* and *On the Waterfront*.

"Eli," he said, "I'm an old hand at movies; this is your first film. Do you realize that on-screen your head is about thirty feet high? So be careful, don't open your mouth too wide. If you do, the audience will be able to see your tonsils and gold inlays."

The next day the scene called for me to appear at the top of a flight of stairs. Carroll looked up at me and shouted, "Hiyo, Silva!" I looked down at her and, remembering Karl's advice, clenched my teeth and said, "Hiyo!"

"Cut!" Kazan yelled. "What's the matter? Why didn't you say 'Hiyo'?"

"I did say it," I said.

"No, no," he said, "Open your mouth and say the line. I don't want the Japanese version." Then, he paused and smiled.

"Oh, Malden has been at you, has he?" he asked, and laughed.

The shoot wasn't over yet, but Christmas was approaching and I was looking forward to a chance to get home to Peter, Roberta, and Annie. I called Anne and told her that I'd be coming home. Shortly thereafter, Kazan called me into his office.

"Sorry, you can't go home," he said.

"But the whole crew is going," I said. "Why not me?"

"Because the crew is not on film," he said. "You are, and if the plane crashes, I'll have to shoot all of your scenes over again."

I was furious and didn't talk to him all week. I even refused to have Christmas dinner with the rest of the cast: I just moped around on the set with the post-Christmas blues.

When we started shooting again, I had to play what would become one of the film's most controversial scenes, where I would put my seductive prowess into effect. Carroll and I were sitting on a double wooden swing in the front yard. Mississippi could be damn cold in winter, so Carroll had wrapped an electric blanket around her legs. I wore long johns and warmed my hands down around my legs on a tiny electric stove. Before the scene, we'd suck on ice cubes so that our breath wouldn't be visible in the cold. As soon as Kazan called "Action," we'd spit out the cubes.

When the film was released, the critics had a field day with that scene. "Where was his hand?" they asked, not knowing that I was actually warming it against the electric stove just out of frame. "What was he doing to her in that big, hot sexy scene?" they asked. Hot? Hell, we were freezing.

After finishing location shooting on *Baby Doll,* I stopped in Philadelphia, where Anne was still appearing in *Middle of the Night.* In the dressing room, I found our new daughter, Roberta Wallach, sleeping peacefully. Anne had refused to tour with the play unless she could take the baby with her.

Once *Baby Doll* was released, the critical assault began, with *Time* magazine leading the charge. "This is just possibly the dirtiest American movie ever legally exhibited with 'priapean' detail that might well have embarrassed Boccaccio," the *Time* reviewer wrote. When I read that, I immediately ran to the dictionary to look up the words *priapean* and *priapus* and this is what I found. *Priapus:* the Greco-Roman God of procreation, guardian of gardens and vineyards, and personification of the erect phallus. An image of the god Priapus is often used as a scarecrow in ancient gardens. *Priapism:* persistent, usually painful erection of the penis, especially as a consequence of disease.

"Well," I thought, "it was even painful just to think of the definition. I didn't know that was happening to me while I was making the film."

From his pulpit in St. Patrick's Cathedral, Cardinal Spellman forbade Catholics from seeing *Baby Doll.*

"Any Catholic who sees this movie is in danger of being excommunicated," he said.

Strangely, though, when asked if he had seen the movie, he said no. "If the water supply is poisoned, I don't drink it," he replied.

The December 18, 1956, edition of the *New York Post* printed a further declaration from Cardinal Spellman, who said that it was "the moral and patriotic duty of every loyal citizen to defend America, not only from dangers which threaten our beloved country from beyond our borders, but also the dangers which confront us at home."

After all of those reviews came out and I was back in New York, I sulked around the city, eyes downcast, shoulders slumped. I was sure that people were glaring at me. "Ah! Here comes that sinner, that pornographic pedophile priapean!" they were thinking. Suddenly, I found myself in front of the Capitol Theater on

Broadway. There was a long line of people snaking around the block waiting to get tickets to see the "dirtiest American movie" ever made. Above the entrance to the theater was a fifty-foot sign for *Baby Doll* with Carroll Baker lying in a baby's crib, sucking her thumb.

"Well," I thought, "give the people what they want and they'll come get it."

As for my wife's review of the film, Anne sat next to me at the premiere. The moment I played my first scene with Karl Malden, she observed, "Never have two noses filled the screen so completely."

12

An Actor's Dilemma

BACK IN NEW YORK, I shaved off my *Baby Doll* mustache and set
out to honor my agreement to return to the cast of *Teahouse,* touring with the show to Boston, Philadelphia, and Washington, D.C.
We closed at the National Theatre in Washington; with a heavy
heart, I stepped in front of the bamboo curtain and uttered my
last lines for the final time: "Little story now concluded, history
of world unfinished. Lovely ladies, kind gentlemen, go home to
ponder. What was true at beginning remains true. Pain make man
think, thought make man wise, wisdom make life endurable. Our
play has ended. May August moon bring gentle sleep."

Following the end of the run of *Teahouse,* I returned to the usual
actor's plight: What next? And now there was a new question too:
Theater or film? I often compare the two media to lovemaking.

In theater, onstage one goes through the entire experience: curtain up, foreplay, excitement, then finally an orgasmic release, curtain down. In film, there's action, foreplay, excitement, and just before you reach the glorious moment of release, the director yells, "Cut! Let's do this scene again." I didn't find that very satisfying. But still, I found it difficult to escape the lure of fame that film offered.

As a boy, I used to practice writing my signature in preparation for the day when I'd be asked for my autograph. My first taste of fame came when I saw my name in lights on the marquee of the Martin Beck Theatre. I walked past the sign ever so slowly. Fame also meant that I'd appear on talk shows in the earliest days of TV and that my name would appear in newspapers. At one point, Peter Witt strongly urged Anne and me to get a press agent, so I hired one for quite a sum—about $125 a week. The first item he planted in Ed Sullivan's *Daily News* column was "The Wallachs lost their yacht in a storm at sea." Many friends called us the next day. "Are you all right?" they asked. And then, "Why were we never invited on your yacht?" I fired the press agent. That kind of fame I didn't need. But deep down, there was a large kernel of envy. Whenever other actors were lavishly praised, I used to ask, "Why not me?"

I remember riding the bus in New York. One day there were two people sitting behind me. One kept saying, "It's him; it is." The other said, "No, no, it's not." I kept nodding my head thinking, "Yes, it's me, it's me."

Once while I was wheeling my cart down the aisle of a supermarket, a woman kept following me, then stood in line behind me at a checkout counter. She smiled, pointed at me, and said, "I know you; you're George C. Scott."

"No," I said.

"Oh," she said, "I mean E. G. Marshall."

"No," I repeated.

"Aha! Martin Balsam."

My third negative reply seemed to dampen her spirits.

"Well, who are you, then?" she asked.

"Eli Wallach," I said modestly.

"Oh," she said, "my favorite!"

I used to feel sorry for the great stage stars; their fame seemed to fade. Films seemed to pay greater dividends: more money, recognition.

Once I got a package of old theater programs for Christmas, and it was one of the most depressing gifts I'd ever received. I turned page after page and couldn't find one name that I recognized. And yet, all of these actors had egos, each one had a drive to succeed, all of them had dreams of making it, and no one remembers them. Yet even now, if I say "Katharine Cornell" to people who saw her perform, their eyes light up, for she lives in their memory.

Cornell did appear in one film during World War II, in which she doled out food for hungry soldiers at the *Stage Door Canteen*. In the film, a scene was shot based on a real experience that Cornell had had while dishing out food for soldiers. She was standing behind a table when a soldier stopped, read her name tag, and said, "My drama teacher told me about you. You were in *Romeo and Juliet*. My teacher cast me as Romeo."

"What was your favorite scene?" she asks.

The soldier puts his tray aside and launches into a soliloquy: "See, how she leans her cheek upon her hand! O, that I were a glove upon that hand, that I might touch that cheek!"

Cornell magically turns into Juliet; the screen lights up as she begins to play the balcony scene with the young soldier. Someone at the back of the crowd shouts, "What the hell's holding up the line?" Miss Cornell kisses the young soldier's cheek, he moves on, and she continues doling out the food.

Irving Thalberg, Hollywood's youngest and most successful producer, tried to lure Miss Cornell into making a film, but she adamantly refused.

"You're frightened," he told her.

"Yes, I am," she said.

"I tell you what I'll do," he said. "Pick any script you like, we'll make the movie, and if you don't like it, I'll burn it."

"Thank you, but no," she said, and never made another film.

Alfred Lunt and Lynn Fontanne only made one film—*The Guardsman,* based on Molnár's play. Fontanne came home after seeing a rough cut of the movie, but Lunt was too frightened to go.

"Tell me, please, how was it?" he asked her.

"Well, I'll tell you," she said. "You were tall and handsome. You looked so wonderful in your Russian uniform, but your lips were a little thin. However, you played all of your scenes beautifully." She continued to praise his performance for ten minutes, and when she was through, all he could say was, "My lips were thin?"

ⓠ ⓠ ⓠ

In 1956 Charles Laughton was going to direct a production of Shaw's *Major Barbara.* As his film career had wound down,

Laughton, who had played such roles as the hunchback of Notre Dame and Captain Bligh in *Mutiny on the Bounty*, had performed readings from Shakespeare and the Bible for hospitalized soldiers. He then moved on to direct such plays as *The Caine Mutiny Court-Martial* and *Don Juan in Hell*. We first met in his small flat in Greenwich Village.

"Come in," he said. "Make yourself comfortable. Tea?"

"Yes, I'd like that," I said. He looked as though he had slept in his clothes, he was unshaven, had heavily lidded eyes, but he still spoke with that magical, musical voice. I asked if he wanted me to read for him.

"Never mind reading," Laughton said. "Bob Joseph, our producer, has told me all about your work and that you're a member of the Actors Studio. I'm casting you as Bill Walker, one of the greatest comedy creations since Falstaff." He paused briefly and then added, "Furthermore, I want no Stanislavsky shit from you."

I assured him that he'd get none, but that I was very concerned about using a Cockney accent.

"Not to worry," he said.

Not trusting the actor to master the accent, Shaw had written Walker's dialogue phonetically: *Gaow* for *go, alown* for *alone, loy* for *lie, mauth* for mouth.

"I want you to play the situation, that's what I want," Laughton said. "Walker's a street urchin and he's not afraid to terrorize anyone he meets. Think you can do it?"

"I'll try," I said. "I'll give it a *gaow*." Laughton didn't smile at my lame joke.

For *Major Barbara*, Laughton assembled a cast of veteran actors, including Burgess Meredith, Glynis Johns, Cornelia Otis

Skinner, Colin Keith-Johnston, and Laughton himself. At the first rehearsal, he stood before us and asked, "Do you know the clown Grock?" He didn't wait for an answer but continued talking.

"Grock would appear onstage with a yellow wig, feathered hat, red nose, big shoes, carrying a tiny concertina," he continued. "He'd growl at the three spotlights he didn't like, and they would go out. Kneeling down, he'd blow out the footlights, and in the pitch-black darkness he'd whimper loudly. A pink spot would blink on, he'd sigh contentedly, and then begin to play his concertina. That's the way I shall stage the opening of *Major Barbara.*"

I wondered briefly if he had lost his mind, but he stayed true to his word and staged the opening much as he said he would: Cornelia Skinner enters and looks around as if something were missing. Just then, some drapes descend. She's still not satisfied, so several butlers and maids bring on some furniture and potted plants. Then they bring in her writing desk. She sits down and picks up a pen, then slowly turns upstage and watches as a huge portrait of Charles Laughton as the character of Andrew Undershaft is lowered into place. A deep sigh from the lady, the lights shift, and the play begins.

We were booked into the Martin Beck Theatre. I'd had a happy history playing in that lovely theater. While appearing with Miss Cornell in *Antony and Cleopatra,* I'd gotten married. Our son, Peter, was born when I was appearing there in *The Rose Tattoo.* And Roberta was born during *The Teahouse of the August Moon.* When I told Annie that *Major Barbara* had been booked into the Martin Beck, her eyes narrowed. "Well, don't come near me!" she said.

Shortly thereafter, the booking was changed to the Morosco Theatre.

On the fifth day of rehearsal, I received a notice for jury duty. "Not to worry," our producer Bob Joseph said to me. "My father is the comptroller of New York. He'll take care of it."

Not long afterward, my doorbell rang just before I was going off to rehearsal. Standing before me was a hefty uniformed man. A big star glistened above his coat pocket.

"Are you Eli Wallach?" he asked.

"Yes," I stammered. "What's wrong?"

"I'm the sheriff," he said, "and you're to see the judge down at Centre Street tomorrow morning, no excuses, is that understood?"

"What have I done?" I asked. I felt like a character out of Kafka.

The sheriff stared at me. "Jury duty," he said. He handed me a subpoena, turned on his heel, and was gone.

Next morning, I was ushered into Chief Justice Steur's office. Steur was a little man who looked as though he were sitting on three telephone books. His mouth was drawn tight. Staring over his horn-rimmed glasses, he sneered.

"Are you going to do jury duty?" he asked.

"Sir," I said, "I'm in rehearsal with Charles Laughton. It's important that I get to the theater."

"Quiet! No excuses!" he said. "Are you going to do jury duty?"

"Well, you don't understand," I began. " As the actor . . ."

"I don't want to understand," he said. "Answer my question: Are you going to do jury duty?"

"O Hamlet," I thought, "Give me your sword and I'll dispatch this little king."

Weakly, I answered, "Yes sir, I'll do jury duty."

His growl changed to a big smile. "Not to worry," he said. He climbed down from his telephone books. "Now, let's see how we can make it easy for you to serve and to rehearse at the same time."

Justice Steur solved the problem judiciously. Early each morning I'd come to the courthouse, and names would be drawn out of a large bowl. If my name was drawn, it would be quickly thrown back into the bowl, at which point I could leave just in time to get to the theater and rehearse. I erased all the hateful thoughts I had about this judge. I never saw him again, but I was tempted to leave two tickets for him at the box office.

In those days, the curtain would rise at 8:30. In the case of *Major Barbara*, this meant that men who had left home early in the morning and had many business conferences during the day followed by a two-martini lunch before meeting their wives for dinner were now obliged to listen to lengthy discussions of economics, religion, war, and the struggle of the Salvation Army against the corporate world. The gentle sound of snoring often filled the theater.

In one scene Laughton played in a trombone-drum duet. Meredith would bang his drum, Laughton would blow heavily into his trombone, and all the men in the audience would awake with a start.

During rehearsals, whenever Laughton's character was onstage, he would ask Burgess Meredith to sit out front and help to direct. Whenever he was onstage with Burgess, I was asked to take on that role. At one point, over dinner with Meredith and myself, Laughton said, "I'm sorry. I feel I dominate Wallach's scene in the second act." I turned to Burgess and asked for his comment.

"Of course you do, Charles," Burgess said. "You relegated him to a dark corner stage left, and there you stand stage center blinking your eyes, your jowls shaking like a bowl of jelly. Of course that's why you dominate the scene."

"How could you say that? I do no such thing," Laughton said. But for the run of the play, Laughton, like a scolded child, would go sit in the darkened corner, allowing me to shine at stage center.

Laughton had many differences with Glynis Johns about her performance in the title role, so she left the company. He asked Anne to replace her. Burgess was very helpful in easing Anne into the play, while I was too selfishly busy with pretending to be a tough Cockney to give Anne much assistance.

Laughton often talked about how impressed he was by the work of a theater innovator down in Texas named Paul Baker. Baker had staged a daring production of *Hamlet* starring Burgess. Laughton was interested in producing a national tour of *Major Barbara* in repertory with Baker's *Hamlet*, so he closed *Major Barbara* for a long weekend so that Anne, Burgess, Cornelia Skinner, Bob Whitehead, and myself could fly down to Waco to see a revival of Baker's production that he was directing with his students at Baylor University. Baker had so many students that he cast three Hamlets, three Ophelias, three queens, and three kings to represent each of their ids, egos, and superegos.

"This is crazy," I thought. "It's like a whole damned deck of cards." But the production surprised me. When the three Hamlets delivered their soliloquies, I had no idea whether Hamlet's id, ego, or superego would win out, but somehow Baker's staging made it all work.

Frank Lloyd Wright had designed the Dallas Theatre Center to Paul Baker's specifications. His design fit the *Hamlet* production very well. There was a severely raked stage, with two levels on either side of the audience, and in the orchestra, there were several hundred swivel chairs. As actors walked directly down the raked stage, the audience would lean back in their swivel chairs. As the action went from left to right all up and down the auditorium, all the chairs would swivel simultaneously. After three hours, we all had quite an experience riding our swivel chairs, but I wondered whether the theater would be well suited to other productions.

Major Barbara had a successful and critically acclaimed run. Unfortunately, Laughton couldn't raise the money for the national repertory tour he had in mind. And so, *Barbara* and Baker's *Hamlet* were put on the shelf.

Years later Burgess Meredith told me a startling story about Charles Laughton. Laughton was hospitalized and in a coma. Each evening Burgess would sit beside his bed. One evening Laughton emerged from his coma, sat bolt upright, and grabbed hold of Burgess's hand and said, "Burgess, do you think this director knows what he's doing?"

Startled, Burgess said, "Uh, I don't know; I don't think so."

"Neither do I," Laughton said, then went right back into his coma. Early the next morning, Laughton was gone, off to the great theater in the sky.

After *Major Barbara*, Anne was more than ready to put away her Salvation Army uniform and put on her maternity dress. Apparently, switching from the Martin Beck to the Morosco Theatre had no effect on our ever-growing family. Anatole Litvak had offered Anne a role in a film called *The Journey* that was going to be shot in Vienna, featuring Jason Robards, Robert Morley, Deborah Kerr, and Yul Brynner. The entire film was to take place over a long weekend in an airport.

"I'd love to do it," Anne said, "but I'm pregnant."

"Exactly what we want for the character," Litvak told her. "You'll play E. G. Marshall's pregnant wife."

Now the tables were turned. I was to be the stay-at-home husband and Anne would be the movie-star wife. For some reason, this seemed to work out. We took turns when jobs came in. Two months into the shooting, I brought Peter and Roberta and our nanny Nellie to join Anne in Vienna. The fact that Nellie was black was something of an oddity in Vienna; people stared at her constantly. So Anne looked up the appropriate German response for Nellie to use: *Starren sie nicht, bitte* (Do not stare, please). It seemed to work.

During the filming, Anne wore an inflatable belt so that her tummy would remain the same size during the filming. One day Litvak looked through his camera lens and said, "Cut! Cut! Hold it! Her stomach looks too large." Annie smiled and said proudly, "That's me. I'm not wearing the damn thing."

After filming was finished, we all returned to the States and Anne gave birth to a beautiful blond bambina on July 13, 1958. We named her Katherine Beatrice after Anne's two sisters. Ten days later Litvak was on the phone. "I must have one more take of you, Annie. You must come back to Vienna." Annie did so, but reluctantly. At least she didn't have to wear the inflatable tummy belt anymore; all Litvak needed was a close-up.

☉ ☉ ☉

Recalling that Katharine Cornell and the Lunts only lived in the memory of their contemporaries because their work was confined to the stage, and because I had a growing family, I decided enough "art" for a while; I was going to try to get rich and famous. This meant facing the cameras again. My second film would be with Don Siegel, who was adapting the hit TV series *The Lineup* for the screen. It was to be shot in San Francisco.

I first met Siegel at the plush Columbia Pictures office in New York, where he told me he wanted me to play the role of Dancer, a sadistic professional killer.

"Dancer?" I asked. "Why Dancer? Do I have to dance in this movie?"

"No," he said. "Just read the script. You'll see why."

The next day we met for lunch.

"The guy has to kill five people in one day," I said. "That's not for me; I'm not that sadistic."

"Oh, it's only a movie," he said. "Besides, you'll enjoy San Francisco."

"All right," I said, then added as a joke, "But I want ten grand a killing."

"No problem," said Siegel. "Welcome aboard."

In the film, Dancer would stand on the dock and wait for a

luxury liner to nestle up against the pier. He would follow passengers who were inadvertently carrying drugs hidden in souvenirs they had purchased in Hong Kong. If the innocent carriers

...fused to hand over their drug-laden articles, Dancer would

ld make an ominous click-

iatic pistol, he'd attach a si-

shoot the carrier.

slick action films. During

sensed it. I felt I'd made a

ie money seemed more im-

n a worthwhile project.

in Los Angeles, me in black

wn. Our eyes smarted from

ed us.

vies!" I thought, but during

ced each time I shot some-

hter whom she had taken to

inal victims in the film. The

ill.

e child began to cry. I opened

I reached in to get the gun,

woman, I'll never talk to you

ng movies mean that I would

an, a hired killer?

characters?" I wondered.

ind confesses. Even as a non-

ie for my behavior.

13

My Brief Atonement

TO ATONE FOR *The Lineup*, I flew to London, where I appeared in a live BBC television play adapted from Elmer Rice's *Counsellor-at-Law*—at least I was on the right side of the law now. Afterward Anne joined me and we flew to Rome, where we lectured about the Method at the Teatro Quirino and performed scenes from Clifford Odets's *The Country Girl* and Sean O'Casey's *Bedtime Story*. Anna Magnani was our host, and she gave us an enthusiastic introduction. I'd memorized one Italian sentence, which I proudly delivered: "E un gran piacere per me dividere il palcoscenico con Anna Magnani." (I'm very pleased to share the proscenium with Anna Magnani.) She gave me a wide-eyed smile and kissed me.

After the scenes, the Italian audience asked questions about the Method. "We do the same thing," said one Italian actor. "Why do you call it 'the Method'? We have our method."

I tried to explain, rather lamely, that we didn't have all the answers but that we used the idea of "effective memory" in order to create a character. Another Italian actor jumped to his feet. "Yes, yes, I do the same thing," he said. "Tell us something different."

I did not intend to make any remarks about their style of acting. It had always seemed to me that calling it *the* Method was incorrect; each country, each society, each theater, and each actor devises his own method. Thus, rather than go into all the technical details, we described what life in the Actors Studio was like.

"It's sort of a gymnasium," I said. "An actor could come in and work out and exercise. We did improvisations. We pretended to be animals." We could hear tittering from parts of the auditorium. But soon the questions got sharper. "Well, we will try," one actor said. "We could do the same thing, maybe—who knows?"

Upon my return to New York, I appeared with Joan Plowright in Eugène Ionesco's *The Chairs*, directed by Tony Richardson. Joan was now seeing Sir Laurence Olivier, whom she would later marry. Once while in London, I had spent a day with Olivier and watched him prepare to play Othello at the Old Vic. I remember accompanying him as he took his voice lesson, then to the gym. I watched him put on his makeup before the show; it took him about an hour and a half. It took another hour for him to take it off. Every hour of his day was dedicated to playing that role of Othello. Now he was in New York starring in John Osborne's *The Entertainer*. Anne and I would often join Joan and Sir Laurence for late supper. At one point, I asked if he'd like to sit in and observe a class at the Actors Studio.

We sat in the rear of the classroom and watched two young actors performing a scene—there was a lot of stage business before either actor spoke. The young girl then removed her blouse and started for the bed at center stage. Lee Strasberg leaned forward, as did most everyone else in attendance. Olivier tapped me on the shoulder and whispered, "Eli, dear boy, let's you and me start a school for fucking; I'll name the school after you."

I couldn't believe what I'd heard—here we were in the sacred temple of the Method, and Olivier was naming a fucking school after me.

Anne and I attended the opening of *The Entertainer.* At Sardi's after the show, we talked about the play and Olivier's performance; he had been impressively sharp as a down-at-the-heels actor.

"I see you were using a lot of our method," I told him. "You really moved me when you slowly slid down the wall at stage right."

"Ah," he said, "we do take from each other, don't we?"

The Chairs was to be my last act of contrition for all the killings in *The Lineup.* The play concerned an old couple who decide to invite all their old friends to a gala party. As each guest arrives, the old man (aged ninety-five) orders his wife to bring in additional chairs. By play's end, the stage is covered with chairs.

The old couple have to be in great physical shape because they spend much of their time rushing offstage, coming back with a chair and setting it in position. Later on they stand at open windows, say, "Farewell, my dear friends," and jump to their death. An orator is hired to deliver their eulogy. He appears with a scroll, unrolls it, mumbles and mutters, and we find he is a mute. Irony, O irony—Ionesco; curtain.

◎ ◎ ◎

By now, I had had a good taste of theater and movies and loved them. But I soon became intrigued by a new medium—television. I doubt there were more than five thousand TV sets in the whole United States in the early 1950s. At that time, the major film studios did not permit their stars and contract players to appear in a free medium. That left the way clear for New York stage actors, such as myself, who were not under contract to a film studio and who could do live TV including long scenes.

David Susskind, a young, volatile, and bushy-haired entrepreneur, had dreamt up a show called *Play of the Week.* Actors would rehearse for ten days, and on the last few days, we would walk around the set and allow the cameraman to study all of our moves. It was a tedious operation, but as opposed to film, whole scenes could be played without interruption, which gave stage actors great satisfaction. The first performance was taped on a Monday in front of a small audience. Then that tape was played for the rest of the week.

Anne and I were cast in a light comedy called *Lullaby.* I played a shy truck driver who elopes with a nightclub cigarette girl. The play drew great ratings, far better than the usual fare of heavy dramas. Several weeks later Susskind asked us up to his office and began a smooth, seductive pitch.

"Listen," he said, "I think *Lullaby* can be developed into a series." Anne and I had never even heard of a series.

"I'll own a third, you'll own a third, and the network will own a third. And if it's successful, your children will never have to work again," Susskind said.

In the taxi on the way home, Anne turned to me, wrinkled her brow, and said, "Why shouldn't the children work?" We decided not to do the series.

Later I was cast as a boxer in a live TV drama on NBC. Growing up, I was an avid follower of prizefighting. Glued to the radio, I would listen to the blow-by-blow. At the end of the fight, a microphone would be stuck right in the boxer's face and he'd always breathlessly say, "Hello, Ma, hello, Pa, I won!"

In the TV drama, I boxed three rounds. At the end of the show, I rushed to the phone and called my father. "Well, Pop, what did you think?" I asked.

No answer.

"Pop, did you hear me?" I asked.

Again no answer. And then he spoke up. "You couldn't say hello?" Pop asked sadly.

TV was a strange hybrid. It used the machinery of filmmaking, but at the same time had to satisfy the demands of networks and advertisers, who had the power to censor scripts. For example, the gas company would never allow a program that dealt with the gassing of Nazi victims during the Holocaust. Swear words were bleeped. I recall that a supermarket owner in Syracuse, New York, terrified the networks by threatening to expose actors sympathetic to Communism in a publication called *Red Channels*. One time I was sitting around a table in a TV studio rehearsing a script. We broke for lunch, and on our return there were two empty chairs; the actors had been fired. It gave us goose bumps. It was like finding your photo on a WANTED poster in the post office:—only this one would read: NOT WANTED ON TV.

During the time of red-baiting and the House Un-American Activities Committee, *Red Channels* and *Aware* were publications that listed names of suspected Communists, liberals, and petition-signers. These were distributed to radio and TV stations and advertising agencies. HUAC was cleaning house, stating that the people called to testify before its committee were secretly inserting liberal ideas into films. To its credit, Actors' Equity was the only entertainment union that did not participate in black-listing, while AFTRA (American Federation of Television and Radio Artists) and SAG (Screen Actors Guild) were feeding the frenzy to root out "un-American" actors. Years later both organizations apologized to their members who had suffered from these tactics and promised never to repeat such a "cleansing" again.

At CBS suspected actors were required to sign a loyalty oath. One prominent actress said she would sign under one condition—that the head of the network sign the oath as well. "If my loyalty is suspect," she said, "unless he signs, I must presume that he is disloyal." She was kept on, and her political leanings were never questioned again.

☞ ☞ ☞

TV offered me a wide variety of roles. I played the Dauphin opposite Julie Harris in *Saint Joan;* I played a gypsy in *For Whom the Bell Tolls;* much later I would appear in *The Executioner's Song,* an adaptation of Norman Mailer's Pulitzer Prize–winning book about convicted killer Gary Gilmore. Gilmore told TV writer and producer Larry Schiller that he would give him the rights to dramatize his story on the condition that he be able to choose the star.

"Well, who might that be?" asked Schiller.

"Gary Cooper," Gilmore said. "He's a good actor and we have the same first name."

"He's been dead for many years," Schiller said.

Gilmore soon revealed that he was joking, then offered the rights to the story if Schiller would attend his execution. (Utah gave convicted killers the choice of hanging or a firing squad, and Gilmore had chosen the latter.) Schiller agreed.

I was cast as Gilmore's uncle, Vern Damico, a shoemaker who was also the archery champion of Utah. To research the role, I met Vern, who was a gentle giant of a man. When we shook hands, my little hand was lost in his big, strong gnarled hands.

"I don't want to know about your nephew's personal life," I told him when I met him. "I just want you to teach me how to fix shoes."

Schiller kept the promise he had made to Gilmore and attended the execution. He staged the scene exactly as he had witnessed it: The firing squad, the priest who had given Gilmore last rites, and the warden all played themselves. We actors were issued ear plugs.

My heart began racing as I watched Tommy Lee Jones, the actor playing Gilmore, being led to a tall chair and strapped in. Behind the chair, there were large sandbags to slow the bullets after they had broken through the chair. A tiny yellow patch was placed over his heart. The four-man firing squad was secreted behind a large black curtain with holes to accommodate the rifles, only one of which contained a live bullet—the other three were blanks.

"Do you have any final words?" asked the warden.

"Let's do it!" Gilmore said.

The rifles were pushed into the tiny openings, and at a signal from the warden, they fired. I was grateful that they had issued earplugs because the shots echoed throughout the building. Even though I knew it was only a movie, my heart throbbed and I found myself shaking.

◎ ◎ ◎

Despite my detours into TV, I soon found the route right back to the movies. In 1960 I made *Seven Thieves,* a caper film starring Rod Steiger, Edward G. Robinson, and Joan Collins. I was to take a mammoth leap by playing a homosexual American saxophone player. In one scene I danced with Joan Collins, who played a stripper. She and I performed a very suggestive dance with me blowing away on the saxophone while she climbed all over me.

The director, Henry Hathaway, hired the stripper Candy Barr as a technical adviser to choreograph the dance. Candy's specialty was her ability to run naked up a wall and do a back flip. She was also out on bail for marijuana possession; noted gangster Mickey Cohen had posted bond for her. But when he found out that she had had an affair, he made sure that her bail was revoked. Once she was done choreographing our dance, she was sent back to jail in Houston for a four-year stretch, during which she played the drums in the prison band.

For me, the most memorable moment of the shoot happened during a crucial scene in which we seven thieves sat around a table planning a daring casino robbery in Monte Carlo. After a brief rehearsal, Hathaway had walked over to check on the lighting. While waiting for him to return, Steiger kept repeating his line, "If we go in the front door, I think we can make it." Again and again, he repeated this line, putting a stress on different words.

"If *we* go in the front door, I think we can make it."

"If we go in the *front* door, I think we can make it."

"If we go in the front door, *I* think we can make it."

"Action!" shouted Hathaway.

Steiger said his line: "If we go in the front door, I think we can make it."

Edward G. Robinson's eyes narrowed, and in his famous growl he said, "And I can't remember my goddamn line!"

Hathaway always referred to me as "that New York actor," and I enjoyed the title. I was very impressed by his directorial ability to make the scenes come to life. Robinson, Steiger, and I pulled off a great robbery, but the film sputtered and failed, and soon disappeared.

ⓔ ⓔ ⓔ

During my film career, I would become known for Westerns. My first experience in that genre came right after *Seven Thieves*: *The Magnificent Seven*, a remake of the classic Akira Kurosawa film *The Seven Samurai*, to be directed by John Sturges. I had seen the Kurosawa film and was especially taken with Toshiro Mifune's wildly funny samurai, but when I met with Sturges in Los Angeles, he told me that he wanted me to play Calvera, the lead bandit.

"Can't I do the Mifune samurai?" I asked. "To me, he's the most colorful and interesting one."

"No, no," said Sturges, "that part will be the love interest in the film and it's already cast. We've got a young German actor named Horst Buchholz to play it. "

"But the head bandit only appears for a few minutes in the beginning of the film," I complained, "and you don't see him again until much later when he returns with his gang. Mostly you only see horses' hooves. And the head bandit has an eye patch."

"You'll do fine as the bandit chief," Sturges said. He nodded. Interview over.

After rereading the script, I realized that even though I only appeared in the first few minutes of the film, the natives spoke about my return for the next forty-five minutes—"Calvera's coming." "When is he coming back?"—so, I decided to do the part.

The movie moved the action of Kurosawa's film to a small Mexican town being victimized by a greedy bandit named Calvera. In order to save their village, the peasants travel north to recruit a bunch of gunslingers to protect them. The Mexican censor had asked Sturges, "Why do you have to send up to the border to bring 'Yankees' down here? Why can't our own people do it?"

Sturges said, "Well, Hollywood is paying the bill."

A few years earlier, Mexican audiences were so upset by the depiction of the local peasants in the film *Vera Cruz,* starring

Gary Cooper and Burt Lancaster, that they ripped up their chairs and threw them at the screen. From then on, Mexican authorities appointed a censor to read scripts and to make sure that Mexicans were portrayed as real people, not caricatures. Sturges made sure that the peasants in *The Magnificent Seven* would all wear clean white clothing.

During the shoot, a Mexican assistant director was assigned to Sturges. He was supposed to sit on the set and help out where needed but would not receive any film credit. The assistant, Emilio Fernandez, was a fascinating character nicknamed "El Indio." He was mustachioed, black-eyed, and stocky; his once-pearly teeth were now turning brown. He always carried a small silver pistol and had a reputation as a short-tempered, wild-eyed demon. In 1947 he had directed the film *The Pearl* adapted from John Steinbeck's story. One critic turned in an acid review of the film and Fernandez's direction, so El Indio shot him in the balls. He was blacklisted by the Mexican Film Society, but they allowed him to work as an assistant director on *The Magnificent Seven.*

"You must have an authentic Mexican hat," El Indio told me when I got on set. "One of my jobs is to get you one. So tomorrow we go to Mexico City."

After the store clerk in the Mexico City hat shop took my head measurement, El Indio said, "*Muy bien!* Now, we celebrate. We go on the town." And on the town we went. I awoke the next morning remembering nothing of what had taken place. I think it had something to do with the tequila.

The next day, off we went to get my specially made Mexican sombrero. The clerk proudly handed me the hat: deep black with a leather band. I stared in disbelief. The circumference of the hat was almost that of a cocktail table.

"Listen, Emilio," I said. "If I'm wearing this big hat and my horse goes into a gallop, I'll sail right off his back."

"No, no, no, it's perfect," he said, and grinned.

On the way back to Cuernavaca, I changed my mind. "Oh, sure. I'll wear the damned thing," I thought. "All I have to do is push the hat to the back of my head; the screen will all go black except for my smiling face."

John Sturges greeted us at the hotel. "Let's see the hat," he said. He took one look at the four-foot brim and shouted, "Props! Bring out the scissors." They cut the hat down to a normal size, and that was what I wore for the rest of the film.

This was my first Western, but I'd learned to ride horses in Texas, while at the university. In all the cowboy pictures I saw as a boy, the bandits held up trains, robbed banks, stole cattle, but no one ever knew what they did with the money. That was the key I needed to create my character; I would be a dandy spend-thrift. I asked Sturges, and he smilingly agreed, if I could have a beautiful horse, a silver-studded saddle, red silk shirts, silver rings on all my fingers, and two gold caps for my teeth.

"There's a dentist in Cuernavaca," said Sturges. "Get him to help you with your teeth."

The local Mexican dentist that Sturges recommended tried to dissuade me from using the gold caps.

"Señor," he said, "I will drill two little holes in your front teeth, insert a diamond in each, and you will light up the screen; same price as caps."

"No thank you, I'd prefer gold," I said. "And make the caps so they will just snap onto my own teeth."

I enjoyed working with Sturges; he often offered easy solutions to what seemed to me like difficult problems.

One time as I was walking back to my horse, after my character had slapped one of the local peasants, I lifted my leg to reach the stirrup. My pants were so tight that I couldn't do it. I suggested to Sturges that I get looser-fitting pants.

"No," he said, "I'll show you how we'll fix the problem. Just start to lift your leg. I'll film that. And then I'll cut to one of your gunmen; he'll look up, and then I cut back to you and you'll already be sitting on the horse."

I did as he suggested. It was, after all, my first Western, and I was most grateful for an expert director to show me that trick about how to get on a horse.

⊚ ⊚ ⊚

Throughout the filming, I had asked Anne to come visit me, and she finally consented to my urgent plea. I picked her up at the airport in Mexico City, and sent a mariachi band out to greet her as she got off the plane. On the hour ride back to our hotel, I kept smiling broadly, showing off my gold caps. She stared at me but never said a word.

I thought, "Gosh, she doesn't like the costume. I don't understand it."

Later she explained that she thought my horse had kicked me in the mouth and that the local dentist had filled my mouth with gold.

While Anne was visiting, we stayed in a small cottage near the swimming pool of a luxury hotel called La Posada Jacarandas on the outskirts of Cuernavaca. Showering off after a day's worth of grime and dust, I noticed that my tissue-wrapped spare pair of gold caps—which I kept neatly stored over the john—was missing.

"Anne!" I called out. "Anne, did you see that little package I kept near that toilet?"

"Oh yes," she said. "I decided to clean house like a good wife, so I tossed the little package down the john."

"What?" I asked. "Those were my spare teeth; that's $300 worth of gold gone."

After a long pause, she looked at me.

"I'll bet you're happy I came down to stay with you," she said.

◎ ◎ ◎

While I was in Cuernavaca, Sturges introduced me to the head horse wrangler.

"I'd like the most beautiful horse in that corral," I told him, "but he must be gentle, amiable, and know exactly how to act in films."

"This is Frederico; he's seven years old," the wrangler said. "He fits all of your requirements."

As soon as I mounted up, I swear the horse turned around and looked at me and snorted; his thoughts were clearly stated: "Oh god, I'm going to have to spend the next seven weeks with this New York actor."

I met the members of my bandit gang—thirty-five Mexican men. For most of them, this was their very first film; they had all been hired because they were excellent horsemen. As we left the corral, the wrangler shouted, "You must take your gang for a long riding workout every morning."

I felt great riding along at the head of my gang: silk-shirted, gold-toothed, with a black sombrero (cut down to size). We rode up and down hills. One time we passed a small cemetery with monuments that caught my eye. I raised my hand to halt the gang. One of the horsemen approached me and told me that this cemetery was made for the local people; instead of a traditional tombstone, they could select their favorite building (school, church, house, bar) and have it reproduced in wood in miniature, colorfully painted. There were flowers at the front door of each building; it made for a colorful little village.

On we rode until we reached the village of Tepoztlán. It had been settled by Indians and was about an hour's ride from Cuernavaca. We were dirty, sweaty, dusty, but eager to get to work.

The one regret I had in making *The Magnificent Seven* was that I never heard Elmer Bernstein's musical score while making the film. That music was later used as the Marlboro cigarette theme song. If I had heard that score, I think I would have ridden my horse differently. In the days of silent movies, mood music was played on the set to enrich the actors' feeling for a scene. That would have helped me. During the shooting, Sturges always teased me about my horsemanship. "Why do you type while galloping?" he asked.

"Type?" I asked. "I don't know what you mean."

"Your right hand is holding the reins with authority," he said. "Your left bounces up and down as you gallop. It looks like you're typing. Cut it out!"

Sometime later I said to Bernstein, "I wish I'd heard your music. If I had, I would have sat upright in my saddle, ridden with authority, and felt like the head of my gang."

The cast of *The Magnificent Seven* was extraordinary. The seven were Yul Brynner, Steve McQueen, James Coburn, Charles Bronson, Robert Vaughn, Horst Buchholz, and Brad Dexter. Whenever they ask a contestant on a quiz show to name the seven, the most difficult one to remember is Brad Dexter. But he and I had a close relationship while we were making the movie; he was the only one of the seven with whom I really socialized.

One time John Sturges asked me to stand beside the camera and watch a scene being shot in which the seven gunmen ride across a river. Brynner was the head man, and sometimes he would resent the tricky pieces of business that McQueen used to draw attention to himself. Brynner led the seven across the river, riding high in the saddle with a determined look on his face. McQueen took his hat off and dipped it in the water. In another scene, as they were riding on a hearse to the cemetery, Brynner was fixing his holster and lighting a cigar by striking a match on his boot while McQueen pretended to test the shotgun cartridge by shaking it next to his ear before loading it into his gun. Yul's eyes darted toward McQueen with a look of "What are you doing there?" It was a wonderful competitive moment. Sturges loved the competition and never chastised his actors for it.

McQueen and I had trained together at the Neighborhood Playhouse and the Actors Studio. Even then, McQueen had the raw skill. His greatest talent lay in being observant. He could always find what in an earlier scene had led logically to what he was doing just then. In *The Magnificent Seven,* McQueen once asked Sturges to cut some of his dialogue. "Please," he said, "movie acting is reacting. Silence is golden on the screen." Nobody quite grasped the poetry in the flow of film like he did. What McQueen had learned to do was what separates the true artist from the ham—to watch and, above all, to listen. McQueen was the best reactor of his generation.

The final scene was a long shoot-out between my men and the seven. Yul Brynner finally traps and shoots me. Sturges said, "Okay, Eli, now I'd like the light to go out of your eyes as you die."

"How the hell do I do that?" I wondered, and asked him to give me a minute.

I racked my brain. I'd seen many movie death scenes. Often actors enjoyed themselves and it took them an eternity to die. "Make it simple," I thought. "Just let go, relax." And then it hit me: "Don't focus, just stare, and let your heavy head roll to one side." And that's what I did. Sturges seemed to like my choice.

A year later my son Peter came to a screening of the film. He had only one comment about that last scene: "Gee, Dad, couldn't you outdraw Yul Brynner?"

"Ah, Peter," I said, "one must follow the script. And if it says I get shot, I get shot."

14

The Misfits

LATE IN 1959, my agent Peter Witt called to tell me that United Artists had offered me a leading role in *The Misfits,* a film that had been written by Arthur Miller. At the time, I had never met Miller and had only seen him from a distance when he testified in front of the House Un-American Activities Committee in Washington, D.C., where, during the run of *Teahouse,* I attended hearings in which people would be grilled about their leftist leanings. *The Misfits* was to be directed by John Huston and shot in Reno, Nevada. Miller had written the film as a valentine to the film's star—his new wife, Marilyn Monroe.

"Marilyn's name will appear above the title," Witt told me. "And you'll get first billing under the title."

A week later Witt called with the latest bulletin.

"Ow, Eli," he said—Witt was German, and whenever he was excited, he would began his statements with *ow*. Witt told me that Clark Gable had signed on to do the film. "So," Witt said, "the billing will be Gable, Monroe, and you'll be in first position under the title."

The following day another *ow* came from Witt informing me that Montgomery Clift was on board now too. "So the billing will be Gable, Monroe, Clift, and you'll still have first position under the title," he said.

The day before I was to leave for Reno, Witt called up with his final bulletin. "You lost out," he said as my heart sank.

"Lost out?" I repeated. "What does that mean?"

After a long pause, Witt continued, "Ow, Eli, Thelma Ritter has joined the cast, and she'll get first position under the title."

I laughed and let out a sigh of relief. I thought that Witt was calling to tell me that I was being replaced.

I was looking forward to appearing in the film, which was Arthur Miller's first screenplay—he had based it on a short story he had written for *Esquire*. Clark Gable was to play Gay, an aging cowboy; Montgomery Clift would be Perce, a footloose rodeo rider; I would be Guido, a hypocritical widowed tow truck driver. The three of us would vie for the heart of Roslyn, a divorcée played by Marilyn Monroe. Her best friend, Isabelle, was to be played by Thelma Ritter. I wasn't exactly sure how I'd gotten the role in the film, but I had a suspicion that Marilyn had had something to do with it.

I had first met Marilyn Monroe when she came backstage after seeing me perform the role of Sakini in *Teahouse* on Broadway. She was in the midst of a contractual dispute with 20th Century Fox, and while the air was full of suits and countersuits, she decided to spend some time in New York. After that night's performance, a press agent had ushered her into my dressing room—I remember that she looked nothing like the movie star I'd seen on-screen; she wore a simple dress and had short blond hair. She was pale, shy, and wore no lipstick.

The first thing she said to me was, "How do you do a whole play?" Though she was by now perhaps the world's most famous movie star, she had never appeared in a play, and she seemed both awed and curious about it. I had the impression that she might not have ever seen a stage production. After we'd talked for a while, she asked if she could come see the show again and watch from backstage. I told her I was afraid that management wouldn't allow it, so she said she'd watch from the balcony, which she did many times after our first meeting.

While she was in New York, Marilyn and I would have lunch and we would discuss books and plays. Once I brought her a copy of James Joyce's *Ulysses* and suggested that she read the last chapter of it. At lunch a week later, she told me that she couldn't believe her eyes. "How could the publishers ever put that in a book?" she asked.

"Oh," I said. "The Supreme Court finally allowed it."

Sometimes Marilyn and I would go out dancing. One tabloid columnist wrote about how Marilyn was often seen about town with me and that I was the "beard" who would mislead the press before turning her over to Arthur Miller at a secret hideaway. One time while Marilyn and I were cavorting on the dance floor,

I looked up to the balcony, where I noticed Milton Berle, Frank Sinatra, and Marilyn's husband of the time, Joe DiMaggio, watching us. I gulped and said that I didn't feel like dancing anymore. She looked up at them and smiled. "The hell with them," she said. "Let's keep going!"

Often when we talked, we would discuss the work that I did in the Actors Studio, and Marilyn soon began attending biweekly acting classes as an observer. She'd sit quietly in a back row, mesmerized by the scenes being presented.

"The Studio is a place where an actor can afford to make mistakes and sharpen his talents; that's what it's for," I told her. "You should try it."

"Someday I hope I'll be courageous enough," she told me.

Two months later she and Maureen Stapleton performed a scene from Eugene O'Neill's *Anna Christie*. The other members of the Studio sat quietly as Marilyn played the scene simply and with self-assurance. Everyone was moved by her performance.

One Friday morning on the way to the Studio, we passed a sign advertising the film *The Seven Year Itch*. The sign showed her standing over a subway grating. As the subway roared underground it shot a big gust of air up through the grating which raised her skirt above her hips.

"You see that?" She sighed. "That's all they want me to do in films. I told 20th Century Fox and the press that I want to play Grushenka in Dostoevsky's *Brothers Karamazov*. They all laughed, but none of them have read the book; I call them 19th Century Fox."

Marilyn began taking private lessons with Actors Studio head

Lee Strasberg, and my wife and Marilyn soon became very friendly. She would come to visit us at home and play with Peter and Roberta. She even occasionally babysat for us while Anne and I went off to the theater. I was impressed with her adjustment to the world of theater and her determination to remake her image, also with her professionalism. She once even helped me rewrite a contract to make sure that I got the best possible deal. I remember her putting on her little Ben Franklin spectacles to read the contract. "All right," she told me, "take out clauses three and four. And make sure they clarify your billing."

After shows at night, a lot of actors would gather at Downey's on Eighth Avenue to eat, drink, and talk shop, and Marilyn often joined us.

"I enjoy the people here," she said of the actors she met from the Studio. "They love their work, they listen, and they look you in the eye."

But by the time we began work on *The Misfits* in 1960, she seemed to have become a different Marilyn than the one I had known in New York, and the action that happened off-screen during the making of the film sometimes seemed to rival what was happening on-screen. Although she had only recently married Miller, when she arrived there were already rumors that the marriage was in trouble.

When I first came to Reno, Marilyn wasn't there yet. I was told that she was still in L.A. finishing the film *Let's Make Love*, co-starring Yves Montand, with whom, it was rumored, she had had an affair. My first evening at the Mapes Hotel, there was a party attended by the mayor of Reno and all the cast and crew with the exception of Marilyn and Montgomery Clift, who was joining the shoot later. Mr. and Mrs. Clark Gable were there. So was the producer Frank Taylor and his wife. At one point, John Huston proposed a toast.

"We've got a wonderful cast and crew," he said, "so let's all work together to bring Arthur's screenplay to life." We all raised our glasses in a solemn salute.

The first day of shooting, I was scheduled to play a scene opposite Gable. I was a bit intimidated—Gable was, after all, the king of the movies, and this was only my fifth role. We had never rehearsed together. I remember the first night at the Mapes Hotel, I had ordered room service and almost immediately afterward there came a knock on the door.

"That's the quickest room service in the West," I said to myself. But when I opened the door, instead of a waiter I found Gable's stand-in and bodyguard standing there.

"My name is 'Bama Davis," he said, and handed me the call sheet, which listed the scenes that we were to shoot the following day.

"Mr. Gable asked that you read a scene or two," he said.

"Well," I said, "does he want me to read in his room or here?"

"No," Davis said, "he wants you to read the scene with me."

This seemed to me to be a strange request. I figured that this must be the way Gable works all the time or that maybe he was a little uneasy about working with a Method actor. So we read and then 'Bama Davis left. I turned my alarm clock back from midnight New York time and switched to 9:00 P.M. Reno time. I closed my eyes, and when the alarm went off, it was 6:00 A.M.

The first time I saw Gable on the set, I was sitting in the driver's seat of my tow truck. He was tanned and fit and he wore a red shirt and a Stetson hat. As he leaned in, I felt nervous—I could almost see his credits rolling before my eyes: *It Happened One Night, Gone with the Wind.* I stared at him and he stared back. Neither one of us wanted to plunge in first. John Huston, who was wearing a well-tailored beige safari jacket with huge pockets and epaulets, took charge. He tapped on the window with his riding crop.

"All right," he said. "Let's start acting."

He then handed us each a shot glass filled with Jack Daniel's.

"Drink it down," he ordered, and we did. The spell was broken. After the brief scene, Gable smiled and shook my hand—his hands were huge. I smiled, too, and for the rest of the film, Gable was Gay and I was Guido, his pal.

The next scene was to be with Marilyn Monroe. I was supposed to stand in front of her wood frame house and call up to her. But since she had not arrived yet, I had to play the scene to an empty window. Near the door to the house, a brand-new Cadillac was parked—Huston appeared and ordered the crew men to put some dents in the car. In the film, it was explained that local high rollers would often bump into Monroe's Cadillac, jump out, and then apologize and try to date her.

Across the street, the police kept many spectators behind waist-high ropes. Everyone wanted to get a glimpse of Marilyn. But they did not know that she hadn't arrived yet. Thelma Ritter and I joined the spectators as each blow of the sledgehammer smashed into the car. The people watching must have thought that moviemaking was some sort of insanity—beat up a new Cadillac and talk to an empty window.

In the early days, the shoot went well. Sometimes I would be teased for the Method exercises or the push-ups I would perform before my scenes, but I viewed the teasing as a sort of professional compliment. Once, Huston and the crew played a practical joke on me—in one scene in the studio I was supposed to sit in an airplane where the motor had sprung a leak. I climbed up into the cockpit, put on my helmet with my goggles, and waited as the crew set up the lighting. I looked over the cockpit and there, on a ladder, stood the prop man. He was supposed to spray me with some of the oil from the leaky motor. "Action!" Huston said, and the prop man opened up what I thought was a fireman's hose and sprayed me completely with black oil. Someone in the crew yelled out, "Get him to sing 'Mammy.'" I took the goggles off slowly, staring down a crew member with one of the Mexican bandit looks I had perfected in *The Magnificent Seven*, and the laughter stopped. I was not teased anymore.

When Marilyn Monroe finally appeared in Reno at the Mapes Hotel, she came with an entourage—Whitey Snider, her makeup man; Ralph Roberts, her physical trainer and masseur; and her acting coach Paula Strasberg, wife to Lee Strasberg. In addition to being expert in their respective fields, they served to help her work through her tensions and fears. Worn out from a schedule of back-to-back movies and aware of the Hollywood rumormongers' columns filled with the details of an affair with Yves Montand, Marilyn would need all the help her backup team could provide.

Producer Frank Taylor gave a small party to welcome Marilyn the night before she was to shoot her first scene. She greeted me warmly. "Arthur has written a wonderful scene for us," she said, smiling, "and we dance too. I'm so happy we'll be working together."

The next day of filming, Marilyn looked out of her second-floor window perch, and we did the scene where I was doing an appraisal of her damaged Cadillac. It went very well. At the end of the scene, I swear she winked at me.

But gradually, her mood waned and she began to lose her self-confidence. One day, out of curiosity, I stood near Huston and watched as he directed her in a scene in which she was to cross a busy street on her way to the courthouse, where her character's divorce hearing was to be held. Huston quietly said, "Action," and Marilyn started to cross the street. But then she stopped midway, turned, and dashed back to her starting point. She did this two more times. Finally, Huston asked if something was wrong.

"No," Marilyn assured him, "I just forgot my motivation."

Huston glanced back at her coach, Paula Strasberg, and decided he'd handle this himself.

"All right," he said, "your motivation comes from your need to cross the street without getting hit by any of the cars." On the next take, she crossed the street without a hitch.

Marilyn's mood brightened considerably when Monty Clift joined the film. He was a superb actor, but he also shared many problems with Marilyn—self-doubt, neurotic fears, and a need for painkillers, sleeping pills, and stimulants. Monty and Marilyn were two sides of the same coin; they seemed to bond.

I knew Clift back in the mid-1950s when we were both members of the Actors Studio. A handsome leading man, he was highly regarded by the theater elite and had starred in a number of plays on Broadway. While out in California, he was involved in a terrible automobile accident and it took months of plastic surgery to repair his face. When he returned to New York, we met at a party. I had arrived in a brand-new Burberry trench coat with military epaulets. Clift walked over to me, reached up, and tore off one of my epaulets.

"That's for failing to recognize a fellow actor," he said.

At the time, I felt like punching him in the nose, but then I remembered all the news coverage about his surgery and resisted the temptation to deck him.

"Have your tailor sew it back on; I'll pay for it," he said.

I didn't see him again until his first day on the set of *The Misfits*; he was friendly, and I doubt that he remembered the epaulet incident. In Clift's first scene in the film, Gable, Monroe, Ritter, and I sat in a car and watched him as he entered a phone booth and spoke for about three minutes, which is an eternity on-screen. He stepped out of the booth and said, "That was my mom. She sends her best wishes."

"Cut! Print it! Let's move on!" said Huston. Clift pleaded with him to let him take the shot again. "I'm sure I can improve it," he said.

"No, no," Huston assured him. "You'll never do it better." All of us in the car applauded. Our response was a gesture of welcome; Clift was now one of the Misfits. For the most part, during the shoot Clift was amiable, and I looked forward to each day we worked together, although one time during a bar scene, he shoved me aside so that the camera would focus on him instead of me. "Jesus," I thought, "here's a big star and he has to make sure that he gets his screen time."

In one rodeo scene, Marilyn and I sat up in the stands while Clift tried to ride a bull. He rode, holding on for dear life, but just ten seconds later, he was on his back, looking like he'd just been hit by a truck. In the scene Marilyn runs down the steps and stands over him shaking, but to me it looked like she was not concerned about the film at all, but terrified that her new best friend was seriously injured.

"He's the only person I know who's in worse shape than me," Marilyn once told me.

As the film progressed, I began to notice a tension growing between Arthur Miller and Marilyn. And then other symptoms began to arise in Marilyn: lateness, having to repeat scenes over and over, forgetting her lines, having difficulty separating reality from the film she was making.

Each male character in the movie spoke of how beautiful and how wonderful she was. And each one was going to be the one to save her. Whenever these sorts of lines were spoken in the film, they seemed to make Marilyn even more unhappy. In one scene Gable's character says to her, "You're the saddest girl I ever met. What makes you so sad?" Marilyn was so shaken by the question that she burst into tears. Her backup crew stepped in to try to help her, but they couldn't. "No! No!" she cried. "I don't want makeup or hair! I don't want any of that!" Marilyn tearfully begged Huston to stop the scene and let her go for the day. He agreed to do so. The episode seemed to set a pattern for what was to come over the next weeks. Marilyn seemed to feel that the camera could detect her innermost thoughts.

Huston was the one person on the set who seemed to know how best to handle Marilyn. His style of direction was one of indirection. "I tell an actor as little as possible," he once said to me. "When I have to step in, I feel defeated."

I recall that one day I had to do a drunk scene with Gable. We sat at a table covered with empty shot glasses, watching Clift and Monroe dancing. In the first take, I displayed all of my drunken rage at the dancing couple. While I was waiting to do the scene again, Huston approached me.

"Do you know the drunkest I ever was in my life?" he asked.

"No," I said. "When?"

"Yesterday," he said.

"Wait a minute," I said. "I was with you all day yesterday. I saw you riding a camel. I never saw you drunk."

"That's the drunkest I ever was," he said, and walked away.

For a minute I was confused, but then I said to myself, "My god, he was drunk and I didn't even notice." And when I did the scene again, I played the drunken bit simply, knowing that drunks always try to pretend that they're sober. After I finished that take, Huston grinned at me.

"Cut. Print that," he said.

In another scene I had to play opposite Marilyn in my tow truck. Huston had set the camera up on my side of the truck, shooting over my shoulder for a close-up on her. Feeling secure in my knowledge of making movies, I directed all of my lines to Marilyn. After we finished the scene, Huston said "cut," then told the crew to set up the next shot.

I couldn't believe it. "Aren't you going to shoot the scene over Marilyn's shoulder now for my close-up?" I asked. "I directed all of my lines to her."

Huston stared at me. "Never," he said slowly, "*never* tell a director where to set up the camera."

I was embarrassed and ashamed, and thought he'd never trust me again.

"I'm sorry, but I thought...," I began.

"Don't think," he said. "Let's move on."

Three days later the call sheet indicated that we would be reshooting the truck scene. I climbed into my position behind the steering wheel. While the crew set up the shot for my close-up, Huston stuck his head above Marilyn's shoulder. "And I don't want to hear a goddamn word out of you," he told me. I just smiled, happy to be back on his good side.

Occasionally, Huston would have difficulties with Miller, but he always seemed able to solve them. In one scene shot in the desert near Reno, Gable, Clift, and myself were roping wild horses that would then be sold to dealers, slaughtered, and made into dog food. Huston directed Marilyn to stand about fifty yards away from us and scream, "Murderers! Murderers!" at us. Miller felt that Huston had erred in having Marilyn standing so far away from us and that no one would see or hear her. Huston said no, he wanted her at that distance, as if she were a voice lost in the wilderness. But Miller was adamant, and Huston finally agreed to shoot the scene both ways and see which was better. After seeing the rushes of the film, Miller agreed that Huston was right.

If Huston did have anxieties sometimes, he also had a ready outlet for them in Reno; he gambled. Craps seemed to fascinate him; though he never seemed to give a damn about winning or losing, he'd roll the dice all night long. One morning at seven while Huston was still shooting craps after not having slept the whole night, his first assistant director, Tom Shaw, tapped him on the shoulder and told him they had to go in order to be on location on time.

"All right, get me some coffee; let's go," Huston said, and he worked all day without showing any sign of fatigue.

I owed Huston a great debt—he took me over many hurdles as an actor. Once just before I was to play an emotional scene, he uttered one name to me—"Edwin Booth"—and at that moment I knew that I should emote as much as I needed to, as if I were playing Hamlet, Macbeth, Richard III, or even Lear. Years later Huston would direct me in a short film called *Independence* made for the American Bicentennial, in which I played Benjamin Franklin and my wife played Abigail Adams. Huston had just finished making *The Man Who Would Be King* for $5 million and shot *Independence* for about $5,000.

During *The Misfits*, Huston was the calm captain of the ship, skillfully maneuvering past problems with the script, the crew, and, above all, the tensions in the Monroe-Miller marriage. He was always amenable to suggestions. He never said, "Do this!" or "Do that!" If he liked what you did in a scene, he'd say, "That's nice, kid."

Huston always praised and charmed Marilyn. The first time they worked together was when she was given a bit part in *The Asphalt Jungle*, a role that had brought her to the attention of the major studios. Knowing that Monroe was most dependent on her coach Paula, Huston always repeated a take when Marilyn or Paula requested it. What Paula and Marilyn seemed not to know was that Huston had final say in the editing. Huston stopped all the malicious gossip about "Black Bart," the nickname that some of the cast and crew had given to Paula since she always dressed in black—a black silk dress, a black sunshade hat—and carried a black parasol. Huston freely said that he would have been unable to finish the film without Paula.

With his great knowledge of actors' psychology, it was not surprising that he would tackle the life of Sigmund Freud for his next film. On one day when Marilyn was unable to shoot because she was indisposed for one reason or another, I asked the makeup and costume crew to make me up to look exactly like Sigmund Freud, hoping that this would put an idea in Huston's mind when he cast his next film. The photographer Inge Morath (who would later marry Arthur Miller) took pictures of me in the Freud get-up to appear on the cover of a photo album that was to be given to Huston as a present for his fifty-fourth birthday. As he accepted the album at the party, Huston looked over at me and shook his head. "Oh, Eli," he said with a smile of pity and amusement. Montgomery Clift wound up getting the role.

As we got deeper into production on *The Misfits,* tensions kept growing. Some of the crew members were getting upset with Marilyn's lateness. Stories were leaked out about difficulties on the set. Journalists filled their columns with gossip on the Monroe-Miller marriage. One hot item said that they had arrived on the location in different vehicles. I didn't know which side I was on: Miller and producer Frank Taylor, on the one hand, or Marilyn with her backup team, on the other.

In the one scene in which I was supposed to dance with Marilyn, she arrived late. In the scene her character (Roslyn) suggests that we turn on the car radio since there were no radios in the shack. As Guido, I rush out to turn on the radio and step back in the house to find her dancing with Gable while Thelma Ritter keeps time by beating a pan in the kitchen. My character cuts in, saying, "It's my turn," and Marilyn and I begin to dance. In the scene I talk about my character's late wife.

"Didn't your wife dance?" Roslyn asks.

"No," I say. "She had no gracefulness."

"Why didn't you teach her to be graceful?" she asks.

"Well," I say, "you can't learn that."

"How do you know?" she asks. And here, Roslyn's eyes tear up. "If you loved her, you would have taught her anything."

Throughout the scene Marilyn seemed upset and unhappy. Every time we went through another take, she would squeeze my shoulder very hard. It wasn't until later when I was taking a shower that I noticed my shoulder was black-and-blue.

I remember one morning when Marilyn was a few hours late. She ran up and threw her arms around Gable and said, "Oh, forgive me. I'm so sorry I'm late." Gable smiled and said, "No hurry, honey." By this point, Gable was getting overtime of $50,000 a week.

"Why is it that sexy women are never on time?" Gable once quipped.

And still, the problems did not stop: a forest fire west of Reno, an electrical outage, a publicized item about Marilyn being released for a week to visit her doctor in Los Angeles due to exhaustion. One day my wife, our three children, and our nanny arrived on set, and I had some free time to spend with my long-lost family. The whole Wallach family trooped down to a local clothing store and emerged an hour later in complete Western outfits: boots, hats, colorful shirts, and tight jeans. My son was eager to see Marilyn, whom he hadn't seen since she had babysat him, and show her his costume. But the moment we got to her trailer, she looked out and when she saw us, she shut the door.

I found myself spending most of my time on the set with Clark Gable. To me, he was no longer a big movie star—he was an inordinately shy man who enjoyed the camaraderie of his fellow actors. He was a true professional, always on time and line perfect. He had one iron-bound clause in his contract—at 5:00 P.M., no matter where he was in a scene, he'd leave the set, waving a polite good-bye as he drove away. He had a great laugh and enjoyed teasing me when I'd prepare for a scene using exercises I'd learned at the Actors Studio. "Oh, you're at it again," he would say with a laugh. "Maybe I'll try those exercises in our next scene."

When Gable's wife, Kay Spreckles Gable, came down to Reno to visit Clark, she met my family and invited us all to have a swim at the Gable pool. Gable said, "Let's go sit in the shade and talk while the kids swim." He made a sharp martini, so sharp that I could barely speak, and he told stories. He never talked about movies; he talked about growing up in Ohio, doing summer stock, acting Shakespeare. He told us about his first screen test, which Lionel Barrymore had helped him to arrange. He described the test, where he was made up to look like a Hawaiian native with a flower over his ear. He said that when he was first offered a movie contract, he was already contracted to do a Broadway show with the producer Al Woods.

"How much are they going to pay you?" Woods asked him.

"Seven hundred dollars a week," Gable said.

"Forget the contract," Woods said. "Stay out there."

"And I did," Gable told us. "And I never did a play again."

Several times while waiting for Marilyn to appear, Gable would invite me over to his trailer and we'd share a beer and talk about theater and film. He was curious about the Actors Studio and this mysterious Method.

I was impressed with Gable's devotion to his craft. He told me how insecure he had been about accepting the role of Gay in *The Misfits* and how Miller's script and Huston's love for the story had convinced him to do it. Gable was always generous with other actors. Of Clift, he said, "He surprises me with his understanding of his character; he's a master."

There was one scene that Miller had written in which Guido runs into Gay carrying bags of groceries, approaching the back of the house where Roslyn was staying. Guido turns and walks away, knowing that he's been defeated in his attempt to win Roslyn's heart. Gable read the scene and vetoed it—contractually he had that power. I was devastated, feeling that I had lost out on a key scene. Gable immediately sensed my disappointment and took me aside and explained why he felt the scene was too sentimental and not what his character would do. "I'd never take a woman away from a friend," he said.

I finally got up the courage to ask him about Marilyn's difficulties and why he never expressed anger or irritation with her.

"I'm just unhappy about her problems," he said. "Her fears, her personal life, but if I were to chastise or criticize her, it would only deepen her despair."

All the scenes he acted with Marilyn were beautifully played. Whenever she would finally arrive on set, Gable would hug her and compliment her on the work she had done in earlier scenes with him. Marilyn told me that she was happiest working with him.

For a time during the last third of shooting when we were filming with wild horses, Marilyn seemed rejuvenated and ready to work. But then the lateness started up again, and after my family left to go back to New York, I began to get tense, too. Each day's delay in completing the film came into direct conflict with a contractual deal I had: I was signed on to appear in the Broadway production of Eugène Ionesco's *Rhinoceros* costarring my wife and Zero Mostel. The New York producer Leo Kerz was angry with me.

"You'll never get here," Kerz said. "I have a theater booked, tickets sold, and no Wallach. Tell Gable and Monroe that you have to return." He signed another actor to replace me. But my agent got Actors' Equity to stand by me. I was assured that I'd appear in the play. My heart stopped pounding and I felt relieved.

Ultimately, though, matters did not improve on the set. The tensions between Monroe and Arthur Miller became so palpable that all of us in the cast and crew felt uneasy. Sometimes on my hallway in the hotel, it was impossible to avoid hearing the arguments they were having in their room. Marilyn remained at a distance from everyone, spending most of her time with Paula

Strasberg—Huston once remarked that he saw Miller standing alone on the main road to Reno; apparently, Marilyn had left and driven off without him. I began feeling sorry for Miller—he looked hollow-eyed and lost; give him a beard and he could have passed for Abraham Lincoln.

A good many parties were held during the months when we were filming. At one particular party, all of us were gathered to celebrate a crew member's birthday. There was a big cake and some people were singing songs; there was much drunkenness and dancing. Suddenly, Marilyn, who had been having a heated discussion with Miller at the table, jumped up, erupting like a blazing volcano.

"You don't understand women!" she screamed. "I am a film actress and I know what I'm doing. Stop interfering. Why don't you let John direct?"

Miller lowered his head and stared at his plate as the entire room went silent.

Later that evening I ran into Marilyn in a hallway of the hotel, and she lashed out at me. "Oh, you Jewish men," she said, walked down the hall, and slammed the door to her room.

It was the last thing I recall her saying to me. I only saw her once more on set—the last time was during a scene with Gable in the cab of my flatbed truck. Magnum, the photographers' co-operative, had an exclusive contract for *The Misfits*. They were to shoot all the stills on the set. But one of my hobbies was photography, and though I respected the Magnum deal and took no pictures during the filming, I couldn't resist shooting this last scene with Gable and Monroe.

After the shoot was over, I caught a night flight back to New York. Not long after I got back and was getting ready to exercise my stage-acting muscles by appearing in *Rhinoceros*, two pieces of news came to me. On November 11, 1960, Armistice Day, Marilyn Monroe announced to the press that her marriage to Arthur Miller was over.

I never saw her again after the filming of *The Misfits*. I was acting in a play on Broadway the night the film had its premiere. About a year after she died in 1962, I was working in London in a play and John Huston was filming *The List of Adrian Messenger* with Burt Lancaster, Frank Sinatra, and Kirk Douglas. I met Huston under Big Ben; he was doing a cameo in the film where he was buying a newspaper, and he asked me to walk with him while he did the scene. While we were walking, he asked me what I thought of all the rumors about Marilyn and how she had died. I told him that I didn't believe most of what had been said and thought her death had been accidental, that she had mixed up her prescriptions.

"Yeah," Huston said. "That's what I think too."

Five days after I heard of Marilyn and Arthur's divorce, on November 16, I learned that Clark Gable had died of a massive coronary. As I watched the news on television, I thought of the months I had spent with this wonderful and unique man. His death was a complete shock to all of us because of his vitality on the set. Reports in the press suggested that Gable had suffered from all the stressful scenes he had to shoot in the film struggling with wild horses. But everyone who appeared in the film had had to pass a physical. Gable had passed his test with flying colors. Nobody knew he had a heart condition; even he didn't know.

Forty years later Anne and I were attending a ceremony at the Beverly Hilton Hotel for the Golden Boot Awards, honoring myself and several stars of Western films. It was an elegant affair with many old Western stars in attendance. Anne and I had rented cowboy outfits especially for the occasion. After dinner and dancing, Anne went off to rest—jet lag. I wandered into the bar and a young man stopped me. "Can I ask you a favor?" he asked.

"Yeah, sure," I said.

I looked at him carefully. "Have we ever met before?" I asked. "You look familiar."

"No," he said. "My name is John Clark Gable. You made the last film with my dad. Could you tell me a little about him?"

We settled down in a dark corner of the bar, and we had three or four beers. I asked him what he did for a living. He told me that he was a race car driver.

"Well, that must be an inherited trait," I told him. "Your dad was car crazy. He often visited the Harrah Collection at the National Automobile Museum in Reno. He was so proud of the Chrysler station wagon that he bought for your mother. I remember him saying, 'All the doors have fake wood panels!' One day he tapped me on the shoulder at the end of filming and he said, 'Why don't we go for a drive?'"

"'Sure,' I said. 'I'll be happy to go.'

"He said, 'I want your eyes closed when we get to the dry lake.'

"I closed my eyes as we walked, and then he tapped me on the shoulder and said, 'Open up.' And there sat an odd-looking vehicle. It was a gull-wing Mercedes with two doors that rose above the roof like the wings of a gull when they were opened.

"'Hop in,' he said. 'We'll go for a spin, and I'll show this little baby who the boss is.' As we drove, we seemed to float above the dry lake bed. My shoulders were pinned back against the seat. I didn't dare look at the speedometer, but he handled the car like a true race car driver."

I told John Clark Gable about how his mother had come to visit Clark on the set and how I had danced with her at a party. Later on, when I heard that she was pregnant, I asked Gable, "Why did you let me jump around dancing like a madman with Kay if you knew she was pregnant?"

"'Well,' he said, 'at her last pregnancy, the doctor ordered bed rest for several months, but she miscarried. I didn't expect this youngster; this is a dividend. I guess there's some life in the old man yet! I figured let her dance and have fun and see what happens.'

"So here you are," I told Gable's son. "You are what happened! And welcome."

"Thank you," he said quietly, and walked away.

John Clark Gable had never met his father—Clark Gable had died four months before his son was born.

15

Rhinoceros

IT TOOK WEEKS to shake the memory of working on *The Misfits*, and I was grateful to plunge into *Rhinoceros* by Ionesco. In the play, Ionesco states that everyone who conforms, obeys, doesn't make waves or question the authority of the state slowly and inevitably becomes a rhinoceros. I was to play the role of Berrenger, a gentle, hard-drinking simple man who does question authority and, in the final scene, decides to fight against becoming a rhinoceros. In the 1960 London production, the play starred Laurence Olivier and was directed by Orson Welles—it was the last theatrical production that Welles would ever direct. Years later Olivier told me that he found the play "boring, my boy, boring." I did not agree.

In New York *Rhinoceros* starred Zero Mostel, myself, Anne Jackson, Morris Carnovsky, Michael Strong, and Phil Coolidge. The director was Joseph Anthony, who had had a big hit with the off-Broadway play *Bullfight,* and I thought the fact that he was moving from bulls to rhinos was a good sign.

During rehearsals I sometimes had to struggle to compete with Zero Mostel, and in my efforts to keep pace with his bullhorn voice, I lost my own. The show's stage manager recommended that I see a Dr. Max Jacobson to help restore my voice. Dr. Jacobson had an elegant office on Park Avenue, and some of his patients included Tennessee Williams, Cecil B. DeMille, and John F. Kennedy. A nurse ushered me into his office—Jacobson was wearing a blue work shirt with the sleeves rolled up to reveal big muscular arms.

"So what's your problem?" he asked in a German accent.

In a crackling voice, I said, "I've lost my voice. I'm in a play and we'll be opening next week." He stared at me, sighed, and said, "Ah, a genuine hysteric; pull up your sleeve for a shot." He poured several different colored medicines into a large hypodermic—the kind that could have been used on a horse after a long race—and gave me a shot.

"You feel better?" Jacobson asked.

"No, no," I croaked.

"Undo your belt and lower your pants," he said. Each time he gave me an order, his accent got stronger. In went the needle: "You feel warm in your throat now?" he asked.

"Yes, yes," I said, my voice strong and clear. As I started to compliment him on the miraculous restoration of my voice, he put his finger to his lips and whispered, "Go home, drink some warm tea, and tomorrow go back to rehearsal; you'll be fine."

A few days later, still struggling to keep up with Mostel, my voice cracked again. Dr. Jacobson called and Anne answered the phone. "I want to talk to Wallach," he said.

"This is his wife," Anne said, and as she started to explain that I had lost my voice again, he snapped, "I don't talk to wives," and hung up. This set off alarm bells for Anne, who called our own doctor and told him about Dr. Jacobson and how he was treating me. The doctor said, "Get Eli away from that man. He's dangerous. Eli is full of amphetamines and other drugs." I did not return to Dr. Jacobson, and two years later he was tossed out of the medical profession. At rehearsal I finally learned to stop competing, and my voice slowly returned.

I had a stormy relationship with our producer, Leo Kerz. He had been worried that I wouldn't be able to do the show because *The Misfits* had gone overtime. But I did finally get to rehearsals, and because of Kerz's lawsuits and harassments, I had a clause added to my contract: Kerz was not to come into my dressing room during the run of the play nor was he allowed to speak to me. Kerz agreed to the clauses and obeyed them throughout the play's nine-month run until the final night when we met backstage and shook hands. Peace was then restored.

Opening night was a triumph. The critics were unanimous in their praise. "No need to go to the zoo," one said. "Drop in at the Longacre Theatre and watch Zero Mostel turn into a rhino." On our second night, after many curtain calls, Kerz asked us to remain onstage, then told us he would not be using quotes from critics in his advertising despite the fact that the reviews were uniformly positive. The cast gasped—"Why in hell shouldn't we use the quotes?" Zero asked. "We're a hit!"

But Kerz said he wouldn't do it. "A critic can write, 'This show is the greatest piece of junk of the season,' and if I wanted to, I could delete the last half of the sentence and make the comment read, 'This show is the greatest!'" Kerz explained. "A review," he continued, "is an important comment only in its entirety, and it is insulting to the critic and the public alike to reduce such a comment to the level of a consumer report." He said that he would print up all of the reviews—good or bad—and distribute them in the lobby of the Longacre Theatre, where theatergoers would be able to read them and make their own decisions. In the packet of reviews that Kerz assembled, he wrote, "I especially want to thank all of you for lining up at the box office two weeks before the reviews were written." Kerz's innovative and daring approach to theater advertising seemed to work very well.

Anne played the role of Daisy—once during rehearsal while hugging Berrenger (me), she raised her leg, as girls sometimes do while being kissed. "Are you going to do that?" I asked her.

"Yes," she said. "My director approved of it—it's appropriate and inventive, and I'm definitely going to do it."

In many of the reviews, the critics praised her leg-lifting bit. That taught me to never doubt her choices. In short, I promised never to criticize her again.

Onstage Zero Mostel truly was a force of nature. Although heavyset, six feet tall, with ten wisps of hair that couldn't quite cover his bald spot and a voice that could shatter glass, he could still move like a gazelle. Despite the fact that he had been black-listed during the McCarthy era, he had not lost his spirit of fun. One of the crazy stunts he liked to pull was to carry around a large pair of scissors; if he met someone who wore an ugly neck-tie, he'd pull out the scissors and cut the tie in half.

Offstage he spent most of his time painting in a tiny studio on Twenty-seventh Street. Anne and I showed him two paintings by our ten-year-old son, Peter. One was of a dragon with reddish hair and green eyes, spouting flames. "That's you," Zero said to Anne. And then we showed him a portrait that Peter had made of a huge, green-faced Frankenstein monster wearing a suit. "That's you, Eli," Zero said.

"What, me?" I asked. "You mean I look like Frankenstein?"

"Look at the hands," he said. "See how sweet the hands are; that's you." After such praise, those portraits were prominently displayed in our dressing rooms.

I had acted once before with Zero in an off-Broadway production of *Ulysses* directed by Burgess Meredith. To boost the box-office take, renowned actors were invited to appear onstage and narrate. At one point, I read the line "Leopold Bloom kisses the oozing, pussy bedsores of a palsied veteran." Zero, playing Bloom, stared at me for a moment and asked me to read that line again. This was not part of the script, but I repeated the line about kissing the veteran's bedsores. Zero paused, then in pantomime pretended to taste an oozing sore on his arm, savoring the flavor, then smiled and said, *"Mmmmmm."* I could have killed him, but this got the biggest laugh of the entire reading.

In the craziest scene in Ionesco's play, Zero became a rhinoceros. In the French and English productions, the actors playing

John (Zero's character) would go offstage from time to time and a makeup man would paint their faces green and paste a small horn on their foreheads. But director Anthony and Zero decided to forego that method—instead, Zero stayed onstage all through the scenes and through his stance, his growls, and his movements slowly transmogrified into a rhinoceros: I swear he did it. I was onstage with him all through the scene.

When I first entered, he was sitting up in bed, dressed in a green bathrobe, reading *Playboy*. A pencil stuck out of his mouth, serving as a thermometer. "Let me see if you have a temperature," I said. Remembering how difficult it is to read the mercury in a thermometer, I rolled the pencil around and around. Zero glanced at me, grabbed the pencil out of my hand, and did a three-minute sketch of a man trying to read a thermometer—this was not rehearsed.

"You have a fever," I cried. "I'll get a doctor."

"No, you won't," he shouted. "I'll kill him. I detest doctors."

"I'm going," I said, and as I started for the door, he grabbed my hand and growled and tossed me back into the room again. He growled, seeming to get angrier and angrier, and started chasing me around the room. I opened the center stage door, and he ran through to the bathroom. I locked the door and started breathing hard. One loud scream from Zero and he drove his head right through the center panel of the door, which was made of balsa wood. The audience would always scream with surprise.

I will always remember the night in 1961 when we performed *Rhinoceros* when a blackout had struck the city. The cast was busy onstage at the Longacre when the lights went out and then the air conditioner gurgled three times and went silent. The theater had a special backup system that went into action; up went the lights and on went the air conditioners. At the time, Anne and I were playing our final scene, one in which she stops speaking her lines and starts roaring like a rhino as she leaves the stage.

At our curtain call that night, Anne whispered to me, "I've lost my voice." We immediately went to the emergency room at Roosevelt Hospital. After Anne had been examined, I asked the ear, nose, and throat specialist what had happened. I was told that Anne had had a hemorrhage on her vocal cords, apparently caused by the sudden off and on of the air conditioners.

"Ten days of rest and she'll be able to go back to *Rhinoceros*," the doctor told me. "Oh, by the way, I saw the show and loved it!"

Anne made the recovery as predicted, and I was thankful that we hadn't gone back to Dr. Jacobson, who had treated my voice and almost transformed me into a drug addict.

One evening as Zero and I stood behind the curtain getting ready for the second act, the stage manager ordered, "Curtain up!" At this point, we heard a strange sound—the heavy red velvet curtain began to tear. As the audience watched in amazement, Zero stepped through the gaping hole and assured the audience that everything was okay. He then proceeded to do a five-minute comedy routine while the stagehands ripped down and removed the torn curtain. When they were done, Zero held up his hand and said, "And now, with your kind permission, we will continue with the play." The audience gave him a big hand, relaxed, and we went on with the show.

Ionesco, as it turned out, didn't like our version much. He sat in the audience and watched our first run-through and claimed that Joseph Anthony had completely misinterpreted his play. He kept shaking his head and saying, *"Mon dieu, mon dieu,"* as he walked out of the theater.

My struggle with playing the character of Berrenger intensified as more and more reviewers kept suggesting that people should see the play in order to watch Zero become a rhinoceros. At the end of the play, as the rhinos in the wings kept trumpeting, I spoke these final lines: "Oh how I wish I was like them. I haven't got any horns. My skin is slack. I can't stand my white, hairy body.

"I can't stand the sight of me. I'm so ugly," I continued. The script then indicated that I should suddenly snap out of it and say, "Oh well, too bad. I'll take on the entire horde. I'll put up a fight against the lot of them. I'm the last man left. I'm staying that way till the end. I'm not capitulating. I will not capitulate. Do you hear? I will never surrender."

I always hated that stage direction—"suddenly, he snaps out of it." I had spent the whole play as a weakling, a spineless character. I could never understand this sudden transformation into a principled, brave, strong-willed hero. I never forgave Ionesco for that last speech. Nor could I excuse his leaving the theater after our run-through with a weak *"Mon dieu."*

16

The Good, the Bad, and Me

IN THE MID-1960s, while I was in Los Angeles making a TV movie, my West Coast agent, Paul Kohner, called me to set up an appointment with the Italian film director Sergio Leone. "I'm sending you a script by messenger," he said. "It's called *The Good, the Bad and the Ugly.*"

"What kind of movie is it?" I asked.

"A spaghetti Western," Kohner said. I had never heard of a spaghetti Western, but Leone was offering good money, so I agreed to meet with him.

The following morning at Paramount Studios, I met Leone. I was expecting to meet a dark-haired Italian sporting an embroidered Western shirt with a bolo tie and a Stetson hat. Instead, I met a tall, fair-haired man wearing tortoiseshell glasses. He was dressed in a silk summer suit, which almost disguised his paunch—he must have weighed three hundred pounds. His interpreter explained to me that before we discussed the movie, Leone wanted me to see the opening credit sequence for his previous Western, *For a Few Dollars More*. In the darkened Paramount screening room, I watched as Leone's name popped up on the screen. Suddenly, a gun appeared in the left corner and proceeded to shoot down each letter of his name to the sound of music. I was hooked.

"Where and when does he need me?" I asked.

As the interpreter explained my acceptance, Leone beamed and shook my hand. "*A Roma*," he said.

"*Sì*," I said. "I'll see you in Roma."

Back in my room in the Chateau Marmont hotel in Hollywood, I sat down and read Leone's screenplay for *The Good, the Bad and the Ugly*. At the time, I thought it was an awful title; later it would become a catchphrase in a lot of American political campaigns. I began to question myself. Why did I agree to do the movie so quickly? Was it the money? The challenge? I wondered why Leone was so keen on me playing the role of Tuco. I thought it was because he had seen me playing a Mexican bandit in *The Magnificent Seven*. Years later I would learn in an interview with Leone in a book about Italian Westerns by Sir Christopher Frayling that he chose me because of a small scene in *How the West Was Won*, in which I used my index fingers to pretend to shoot the children of a local sheriff, played by George Peppard. Leone once said that he had been warned to stay away from me because of my Actors Studio training, but that scene had convinced him that I had the right comic talent for the role.

When I got back to my hotel, I called director Henry Hathaway, with whom I had made *How the West Was Won*. I told him that I had met with Leone and that I had made a quick and rash decision and now I felt trapped.

"They want me to play a Mexican bandit in a spaghetti Western," I said.

"Well, you made your bed; now lie in it," Hathaway said.

"What does Leone know about Westerns?" I asked. "An Italian Western sounds like Hawaiian pizza."

Still, Hathaway made a gracious gesture: He offered to take me to a Western costume shop to help me pick out an outfit for the film. He found a pair of unusual Mexican chaps (worn by horsemen to protect them from prickly bushes) that went from the knees down and a wonderful straw hat with a painted eagle above the brim.

Back in New York, I had to face up to the problem of leaving Anne and our three children. Separations in a marriage are always difficult—over the course of my career, I would make several movies that would take me away from home for long periods of time: two months in Angkor Wat in Cambodia (*Lord Jim*), two months on the island of Crete (*The Moon-Spinners*), five weeks in Paris (*How to Steal a Million*). And every time I'd come home, I'd bring guilt gifts for the children. I once said to our middle child, Roberta, "I'm sorry I've been away for so long."

"Well," she said, "we always had the feeling you wanted to come back."

Anne had a career too—she had Nell, our nanny, to look after the children, but I'm sure she felt trapped. "Oh, you're off moviemaking again," she'd always say. "You hardly get home, then one of your bicoastal agents comes up with another film, and you go off to another part of the world. Whenever you boast about how long we've been married, make sure you divide the years by two."

I always rationalized career decisions. "But I have to work," I'd say. "We have big expenses," then my stomach would churn and I'd say, "All right, I'll give up the damn movies. I'll stay home; is that what you want?" Her eyes would roll and fill with tears. She'd sigh and shake her head and make an exit, and the conflict would remain unresolved. She knew that the movies were like a magical magnet for me, and that I'd soon be off to Italy and Spain to film the movie with Leone.

The following month, I was met at the airport in Rome and driven to Leone's office. He greeted me warmly. "You'll grow a little beard," he said. As I showed him the outfit that Hathaway selected for me, I noticed that he was wearing a pair of suspenders and a belt. "That's an interesting way to hold up one's pants," I thought. The first thing that popped out of my mouth was, "Do you mind if I wear suspenders and a belt?" Leone smiled as his assistant explained my request to him. He snapped his suspenders and grinned.

"*Oui, certo*, of course," Leone said. The last two words surprised me.

"I learn a little English every day," he said, and over the course of filming, I would learn that he knew a lot more English than he let on at first.

One of the first things that Leone explained to me was that for the part of Tuco, the Mexican bandit, he didn't want me to wear a holster.

"So where do I put my gun?" I asked.

"You have rope around your neck with gun on end of it," he told me.

"So the gun dangles between my legs?" I asked.

"*Oui*," Leone said. "You twist your shoulders hard, I cut to your hand, and there's the gun."

I asked him to show me how to do it. He grabbed a gun on a rope from his desk and placed it over his head. He twisted his shoulders quickly. The gun jerked up, but it missed his hand and hit him in the groin. He groaned and caught his breath. "Just keep it in your pocket," he said.

I was glad to be able to skip the holster bit. Clint Eastwood, Steve McQueen, and most of the leading Western stars took lessons and became very skillful at spinning their guns and popping them into their holsters without looking. But I hadn't taken lessons, and whenever I had appeared in Westerns, I always had to look down to find the damn holster.

The next day Leone gave a small party where I was first introduced to my costars, Clint Eastwood and Lee Van Cleef; both were veterans of Leone's previous Westerns. This would be Clint's third film working with him. Also in attendance were the members of Leone's technical crew. The wine and the Italian food all served to relax me. Leone talked about the film, the shooting schedule, and the locations and, at one point, he pulled me aside.

"Rest today," Leone said. "And the day after tomorrow, we will start with scenes six and seven."

Upon reading the call sheet for the first day of shooting, I couldn't believe my eyes. We were to leave the hotel at 6:30 A.M., drive for one hour to a Western set outside Rome, get into makeup, and be on set ready to shoot by 8:00. This was a far more grueling schedule than anything I had ever experienced in Hollywood.

In the first scene we were to shoot, my character, Tuco, is taken to a public square to be hanged. "E-*li*," Leone said to me as I stood on the set—he always used my first name with a strong stress on the last two letters—"You will be on the back of the horse screaming. Clint will turn you over to the sheriff and collect his reward for your capture."

"Fine, fine," I said.

"We will not shoot in sequence," he said. "You will be hanged after we move to location in Spain. Clint will shoot the rope and you will ride off on horseback."

Two days later Clint and I flew to Madrid, where we were to spend the night before we would fly to Almería on the southern coast of the Mediterranean. North Africa was visible in the far distance. In Madrid all the hotels were booked with conventions and trade shows. Clint told me that he had a friend who had an apartment and who would gladly put us up for the night.

Pancho Kohner, whose father was my agent in Los Angeles, was most happy to see us, and he showed us to his spare bedroom, which had one small bed. "Do you want the left side or the right?" Clint asked.

"I don't know," I said. "I guess I'll take the left side." This made sense—politically I was always to the left. I wondered if Clint would snore, but soon I was asleep. Later in the shoot when Anne was visiting me with the children, I told her the story. She laughed and said, "Now you can brag that you're the only man to have slept with Clint Eastwood."

Clint and I were to leave Kohner's apartment at nine the following morning, but when we woke up, Clint told me that he hated to fly "in those rickety crates the Spaniards call planes." He said he would rent a car and driver and asked if I would ride down to Almería with him.

"Sure, I'd be happy to," I told him.

On the long ride down to Almería, Clint filled me in about Italian westerns, how there were no unions, how the hours went from sunrise to sunset, and shooting took place six days a week, how the food on location would come in little white boxes. It was usually pasta or half a chicken or a pork chop stuck between two pieces of bread, some fruit, and a bottle of red wine.

"Don't eat too much or you'll fall asleep by midafternoon," Clint told me. "And don't volunteer to do any dangerous scenes. Let the stuntmen do the tricks."

"Oh, I've made Westerns before," I told him. "I know how to take care of myself."

"No," Clint said, and gave me a hard stare. "You've never made a Western like this. Don't show off."

We arrived in Almería that evening, a tiny town with one main street and no hotels. We were to spend the next two months here in a boardinghouse where each of us had a small room. Max Sloan, an Englishman, was the proprietor. "You'll get a good breakfast," he told me, "and we'll all have a drink after you return from the shoot."

After a day of shooting, that drink always felt like a fresh glass of ice water after the desert.

The second day of shooting in Almería, we picked up the scene where Tuco was being turned over to the sheriff to be hanged. Remembering Clint's warning about not showing off or doing dangerous stunts, I asked Leone if we could discuss this hanging scene.

"It is my understanding," I said to Leone, "that the special effects man has a put a small charge of dynamite in the top of the noose around my neck. Am I correct?"

"Yes. Correct," Leone said.

"And then Clint, hidden in the barn at the edge of the square where I'm to be hanged, takes aim and shoots the noose around my neck. Correct?"

"*Sì, sì,*" Leone said.

"I urge you to put some cotton in the horse's ears," I said.

"Why?" Leone asked. "I've never heard of that."

"In Hollywood they always put cotton in the horse's ears—to calm them," I lied. "Otherwise, when they heard the shot, they would take off."

Leone didn't buy it. "Don't worry," he said, then added in Italian. "*Non c'e pericoloso.*" (There's nothing dangerous.) His use of Italian at this point indicated to me that he didn't give a damn whether it was dangerous or not. "Get on the horse," he ordered. "It's getting late."

I sat on the jittery horse, my hands tied behind my back, the noose tight around my neck. The heat was intense; the horse kept twitching the mosquitoes off his flanks. Most of the extras who were standing around to watch the hanging were English. They had all migrated to sunny southern Spain, where living costs were low and they could escape from rainy, foggy England.

The scene began with the sheriff unrolling a long document and intoning in a loud voice, "Wanted in fourteen counties of this state, the condemned is found guilty of the crimes of murder, armed robbery ... inciting prostitution, kidnapping, extortion ... rape."

As the sheriff got to the final crimes on the list, I looked down at this poor little old English lady and growled at her. Leone called cut, ran up to me, and said, "Do that again."

"Do what?" I asked, literally at the end of my rope. "What in hell do you want me to do again?"

"Look at the lady and growl," he said, and demonstrated, "*Grrr!*"

I did as he asked; I scowled and snorted as the poor lady winced, and Leone stood beside the camera and applauded.

"Therefore," the sheriff continued, "according to the powers vested in us we sentence the accused here before us, Tuco Benedicto Pacífico Juan María Ramírez and any other aliases he has, to hang by the neck till dead. May God have mercy on his soul. Proceed!"

The sheriff raised his whip. Just then Eastwood shouldered his rifle, aimed carefully, and fired. At that moment, to give the illusion that Clint's aim was flawless, the special effects man pressed a button, the rope exploded and snapped, and the horse took off like a bat out of a hell while my hands were tied behind me. I kept yelling at the horse to stop, using my knees to try to control him, but it was no use. It took about a mile before the horse stopped.

That night I reread the rest of the film script—there were three more hanging scenes left. "Goddamn it," I thought. "Leone better order a box of cotton. Not only for the horse's ears, but mine as well."

I did little to no wandering around Almería. Worn out after a week of shooting, I'd have my usual cocktail-hour drink with our English landlord, have a fish dinner, memorize some of the scenes we would film the following week, then drift off into a deep sleep. After filming one Saturday night, Leone asked if I would like to join him, his wife Carla, and his young daughters for a Sunday at the beach. I happily agreed and spent the day playing games with his young children, eating tapas and sardine-and-egg sandwiches, and drinking good Spanish wine. Being with the Leone family, though, brought on a fierce longing for my own wife and children. My letters to Anne were filled with pleas to come join me in Spain and bring the children and fervent vows never to go off to these crazy locations again.

About ten days later, my hands shook as I opened a special air-mail letter from Anne. "You go off to all of these exotic locations; now the whole family will come join you," she wrote, and asked me to pick them up when they arrived in Almería. The letter was signed, "Love, from your lonely wife and abandoned children."

"What had I done?" I wondered. I remembered Clint saying that he didn't trust Spanish airplanes, but thank god my family arrived safely. I rented a suite for us at a newly opened hotel near the beach. It was a joyous reunion with Anne, Peter, Roberta, and

Katherine. Leone invited them all to the set. They would watch me do a scene, then have lunch, where they would open their little white boxes and be surprised by the size of the chicken sitting between two slices of bread; but they were pleased by the red wine. In the evening we'd all take a swim in the hotel pool. Leone even gave me a day off so that the Wallach family could wander around and do some shopping in Almería.

After a week of filming, the cast learned that we would be flying north to do some location shooting near Burgos—the land up there looked like the Virginias and would serve perfectly for the Civil War battle scenes. Leone had spent a year doing research on that war, studying Mathew Brady's book of photographs. Generalissimo Franco had agreed to lend a thousand of his regular army soldiers for the battle scenes. He also allowed Leone to borrow American Civil War cannons and guns from the Madrid army museum. Leone's costumers were able to reproduce the blue and gray uniforms for the soldiers so that they'd look authentic.

Anne, the children, and I flew up to Madrid and from there were driven to a little town called Covarrubias. Our hotel looked out over the town square. After we settled in, I stepped out onto the tiny balcony and about a million mosquitoes flew in. We slammed the French windows shut. Roberta said that the town looked like the shtetl in *Fiddler on the Roof.* Katherine suffered from stomach cramps. Anne took her to the drugstore only to find that all the bottled medicines were covered in dust. After three days, Anne decided that she and the children would return to Madrid. "I'll never call your locations exotic again," she said.

As for me, I was not allowed to leave the new location because we had many Civil War scenes to film, the most important being the main battleground where the armies of the North and South were separated by a bridge. Leone's technical crew with labor supplied by the Spanish army had spent a month building that bridge, and a dam was constructed to deepen the little stream that ran underneath. Clint and I were to place dynamite at the base of the bridge, then blow it up so that the two armies would then cease fighting one another and move on, leaving us to wade across the river to where we were sure a large sum of money was buried beneath a soldier's grave bearing the name "Arch Stanton." The morning after Clint and I set the dynamite, we gathered around three or four cameras. Clint asked Leone, "Where do you want Eli and me to be when you blow up the bridge?"

Leone pointed to a small ditch about ten yards from the dam. "Over there," he said.

"And where will you be?" Clint asked.

"Well," Leone said, "I have one camera using long lenses up on top of the hill two hundred yards away. That's where I'll be."

After a long pause, Clint said, "I think Eli and I will be standing right at the top of the hill with you. We want to see the bridge blow up too."

"But, but," Leone stammered, "I want to pan down the hill past you and Eli lying in the ditch and then up to the bridge and then we blow it up."

Clint's reply was short and crisp. "No, Sergio," he said. "We will stand right up here by you. That's it."

The man who had planted the explosives for the scene was a

captain in the Spanish army. The Italian special effects man was effusive with thanks for the captain's help—not only for the dynamite planning, but for building the bridge as well. "The honor for pressing the button to blow it up should be yours," the special effects man said.

"No, no," the captain said. "I don't want the honor. If we were at war, I would happily blow it up, but this is a movie."

"It's simple," said the Italian. "When I say *vaya* [go], you press the button. Please, please do it." The captain reluctantly agreed.

At the top of the hill, Leone stood, holding a blackened piece of glass, staring up to the cloudy sky. "Don't turn on the camera until that cloud moves away from the sun," he ordered. Clint was holding a golf putter and playing with it as I kept an eye on the bridge, waiting.

Down below, one of the crew members asked if he should turn the slow-motion camera on. "*Sì, sì,*" the special effects man said. "*Vaya.*"

The captain heard the word *vaya* and pressed the button. Clint and I stared at the bridge. Leone stood still, his eyes still glued to the blackened piece of glass as the sound of the explosive charge echoed down the valley. He let out a slow moan and then began screaming—"No cameras are shooting! No cameras! Half my bridge is gone! I'll kill that son of a bitch!" The special effects man jumped into his jeep and headed straight for the airport. Leone grabbed his megaphone and cursed in Italian—"May your seed dry up! May you drop dead! You're fired, you bastard! I'll kill you if I ever find you."

The Spanish captain walked over to Leone—his voice was low but firm. "It was my fault," he said. "I pressed the button at the wrong time. My soldiers and I will rebuild the broken part of the bridge in three days on one condition: You bring that man who drove away back here. You do not fire him, you understand?" Leone reluctantly agreed.

Three days later, as promised, the bridge was rebuilt and stood shining in the morning sun. Clint still fiddled with his golf putter. Leone was standing beside the camera. He stared at the special effects man and nodded. The Italian expert pressed the button and the bridge went up in flames.

During the weeks that followed, Clint continued guiding me through the emotional explosions that were yet to take place. When I was a little boy, my mother used to tell me, "You only have so many words programmed into you. Don't use up your quota; don't waste them." So I didn't talk much as a child. I wondered if Clint's mother had told him the same thing. I often thought that Clint didn't do much acting. He seemed to underplay every speech he made. But when I saw the rushes, I realized that he showed more through his silence than most actors do with a page of dialogue. The week before we finished filming, we sat and had dinner together. "This will be my last spaghetti Western," he told me. "I'm going back to California and I'll form my own company and I'll act and direct my own movies."

"Oh sure," I thought. "That'll be the day." Little did I know.

He certainly succeeded in making his dream come true. Years later in the film *Unforgiven,* in which he starred and won an Academy Award for direction, a card flashed on the screen. The film was dedicated to Don Siegel, who directed Clint in *Dirty Harry* and me in *The Lineup,* and to Sergio Leone. I thought that was a lovely gesture by a classy man.

One of the underestimated aspects of *The Good, the Bad and the Ugly* was Lee Van Cleef. Lee was an experienced professional. As "the bad," he gave the film its needed vitality, danger, and force. He was tall, dark-haired, with sparkling black eyes and a mustache. Part of his right index finger was missing. Leone always liked to use non-actors with disabilities—legless war veterans, for example—and he focused the camera on Van Cleef's finger during the final cemetery shootout.

Leone was a fine director—intelligent, innovative. He had assembled a great group of technicians—his cameraman, scenic artist, and composer had all worked together on his two previous Westerns. From time to time, he and I engaged in a sort of game. I'd try to outwit him with odd behaviors—for example, turning my back away from the camera. He'd retaliate by changing the lines I was supposed to deliver at the last minute to throw me off balance. In one scene he directed me to walk into a gun shop. He told me to take apart some of the guns, then put them back together using different pieces.

I hate guns, have never had any use for them. But I pretended to be an expert as I squinted through the barrel of a Colt pistol and stared down the owner of the gun shop. I then spun the bullet chamber of a Winchester and put it to my ear, finally putting the parts of the different guns together until I created a monstrous weapon. I loved the fact that Leone kept the camera running, figuring that I'd eventually run out of creative impulses. But I trumped his king by playing my ace: As I began walking out of the shop with my new gun, I spied an OPEN sign hanging on the door. I reversed the sign to read CLOSED and then ordered

252

the bewildered gun shop owner to open his mouth wide and shoved the CLOSED sign into it. "Cut, cut!" Leone cried as he burst out laughing.

I used to joke with Leone about his directing methods and his nervous habits. He'd often open and close his fists or tear pieces of paper. I stopped once while filming and said, "Sergio, all I see are your hands; I can't concentrate on acting." He responded by stage managing some surprises to distract me. In the finale of the film, my character, Tuco, discovers the grave where some gold is supposedly hidden. Leone directed me to enter with reverence and gravity, and to walk on with hope and tension in perfect silence. And just as the camera began rolling, without warning me, he released a trained dog to start running toward my legs. Later on he told me that he wanted to break the dramatic tension and film my natural response of surprise. "This was *my* method," he said. "So our little game is even now."

There were two incidents that brought an end to our game playing. In one scene I board a train en route to a Union army prison camp. I was handcuffed to a giant of a soldier who kept pulling at me. In the scene I ask him if I can take a piss. The guard slides open the train door to let me pee. "I can't while you're watching me," I say. As he turns his head, I jerk on the handcuffs, jump, and pull him off the train with me, then bludgeon him to death.

Handcuffed, I'm unable to get away, but in the distance, I hear a train whistle. I pull and push the dead guard (actually it was a dummy) between the tracks and lay my handcuff on the rail. Our great special effects team had created soft handcuffs that could easily be cut as the train ran over them. I watched Leone twitch his hands with excitement. "As the train approaches, I want you to turn around so your face is to the camera," he said. "I want to know that it's you and not a stunt man or a double."

I began to follow Leone's direction, but noticed as the train went past that each car had a small iron step leading to the door of the train car. And if I had raised my head from the ditch where I was lying just a few inches higher, I would have been decapitated. After the train passed, Leone sat beside me and told me he needed to redo the scene.

"Not with me," I said. "I'm not doing it again."

"I need this shot; it's important," Leone said.

"All right," I said, but insisted that the ditch in which I was lying be dug deeper. The train went into reverse, I settled back into my hole, laid the handcuffs on the tracks, and waited for the scene to start over. As directed, I turned my head to face the camera as the train passed. When the scene was over Leone approached me with Tonino Delli Colli—the expert cameraman who shot all of Leone's films. They huddled together, gesturing and arguing. Finally, Leone said that the cameraman couldn't see my face because I was too far down in the hole.

"Did you see that goddamn step on the train?" I asked. "Do you want me to finish the movie without a head?" Leone stopped and stared as the train disappeared into the distance.

"All right," he said. "We'll use the first take."

The second incident took place in a cemetery, where I was supposed to use a shovel to break open a leather sack of gold. It was rather tough leather, so the prop man had put some acid on the sack to make it easier for me to crack it open. I remember that it was hot as hell in the cemetery, and in the heat, I usually drank lemon soda that came in special bottles with a little porcelain cap and wires to hold it in place. Taking a break from the scene, I saw a little bottle, flipped back the lid, and started to drink. I got a mouthful of acid. As soon as it hit my mouth, I spat it out and the whole crew stopped chattering. Leone handed me a bottle of milk—"Drink, drink," he said, "it will help you." "Goddamn it," I thought. If I had swallowed some of the acid, it would have destroyed my vocal cords. Leone was shaken but philosophical about it. "We didn't know," he said apologetically. "It's terrible. He never should have left it there, but accidents happen."

One of the stranger aspects of how *The Good, the Bad and the Ugly* was made was the Italian style of recording the actors' voices using a cue track. As the recording went on, it didn't matter if planes flew overhead, if the wind was howling, or if someone on the crew was cursing somebody out—all of these problems were taken care of in the editing room after the film was finished. Actors could speak their native language—Greek, Spanish, French, German—and they would be dubbed into Italian or English, depending on the country in which it was to be shown. For the Italian release, the man who dubbed my voice had the deep, rich, melodic baritone of an opera star, and whenever I did interviews in Italy, journalists were always surprised by my scratchy voice. In one scene Leone used an Italian non-actor, a man who had lost an arm in World War II. He was hired to play a one-armed soldier in the Civil War sequence. The man, who was dressed in his Civil War uniform, heard me speaking to Leone in English, shook his head, and said in Italian that he didn't like Americans because he had lost his arm in the war. Calling on my poor command of Italian, I said, "*Non fatto questo.*" (I didn't do it.)

Since the dialogue would be dubbed in later, Leone saw how angry the man was and told him to count to ten instead of delivering his actual lines. "*Uno, due, tre,*" the man counted angrily. "*Quattro, cinque, sei, sette, otto, nove, dieci.*" I guess as he counted, the man must have been thinking about the loss of his arm and my lame remark that it hadn't been my fault. He spat out the numbers and got angrier as he reached the number ten (*dieci*). When I saw the completed English version of the film at the New York premiere, his performance was brilliant—Leone had dubbed a barrage of curse words over the man's counting, and it worked perfectly. "Damn it," I thought. I'd spent my life learning my craft, going to acting school, joining the Actors Studio, working on Broadway, using the Method, and here was this man who stole a scene from me by counting from one to ten. "Well," I sighed, "that's moviemaking, Italian style." I grew to admire Leone's innovations—he was the man who controlled the rhythm and the pace of the film. As a young man, he had been an apprentice to Federico Fellini, from whom he learned firsthand all the tricks of the directing trade.

◎ ◎ ◎

I actually met Fellini later on a trip to London at the Carlton Hotel, where he was casting a new movie and wanted to discuss the possibility of my starring in it. He was a great storyteller, and

I was mesmerized by the film he described. The story was about a cellist who is supposed to appear at a concert in Venice. The cellist explains that he has business in Rome but would fly up to Venice rather than take the train. The orchestra conductor agrees. But the cellist's plane crashes in a strange white city—everything in the city is white: the automobiles, the streetcars, the hotels. The cellist survives the crash and asks a policeman dressed in a white uniform how to get to Venice so that he can appear at his concert.

The policeman takes out a book and reads from it: "All your life has been recorded on film," the policeman says, "and applicants for leaving this city must appear at a screening room where you will watch as your life unrolls on the screen. If an unselfish moment appears, the film will be stopped. The unselfish moment will be clipped out of the roll, then attached to your passport, and you will be released."

The cellist watches his film in amazement. At one point during the film, he sees himself stopped at a traffic light. To his right, there is a beautiful woman in a white car with a handsome white puppy. The puppy sticks his tongue out at the cellist, and the cellist, for no particular reason, sticks his tongue out at the dog. The film is stopped; the tongue-wagging frame is cut out of the film and attached to the cellist's passport, and the last scene of the film shows the cellist sliding into his seat at the Venice concert hall as the conductor raises his baton.

I thought the idea of Fellini's film script was wonderfully fanciful. I asked him why he was talking to me instead of Marcello Mastroianni. "I love him," Fellini said, "but I feel it is time to use another actor with whom I can fall in love." We parted, and I never heard from him—I later learned that Fellini had also been interviewing such British film stars as Paul Scofield, Alan Bates, and Albert Finney, but the film was never made. As it turned out, Dino De Laurentis, the prolific Italian film producer, became so excited when he heard Fellini's story of the cellist, the dog, and the unselfish moment that he spent three-quarters of a million dollars building the set of the white city where the cellist's plane crashes. But Fellini, who was quite superstitious, told De Laurentis that he had a dream that if he made the film, he would die. De Laurentis didn't pause: "Federico," he said. "I didn't have a dream, but if you *don't* make this film, you will die." The dispute continued in court, and Fellini did not make another movie until Alberto Grimaldi, who also produced *The Good, the Bad and the Ugly*, heard of Fellini's plight, went to De Laurentis, and wrote him a check for $750,000. The lawsuit was dropped, and Fellini made his next three films with Grimaldi. He never made the film about the cellist, though, and I never got the chance to appear in a Fellini film.

◎ ◎ ◎

After all of the months spent in Spain, it was good to get back to Rome. Leone threw a lavish dinner party for us at the Eden Hotel and reminded us that he would be in New York for two months, where Van Cleef, Eastwood, and I would be required to dub the dialogue that was on the rough cue track. Months later I met Leone at a voice recording studio in Manhattan. At the studio, I was happily surprised to find that my old friend Mickey Knox was on hand to work on the dubbing as well. Knox, affectionately known as the Mayor of Rome, had settled in that city after being blacklisted in Hollywood. Mick was a tough bird—willing to lock horns with anyone who irritated him. He was a master of adapting screenplays from Italian to English; his credits were enormous—he'd worked with Leone, Orson Welles, Fellini, Mastroianni, Vittorio De Sica, and Anna Magnani.

The big problem with *The Good, the Bad and the Ugly* was its cue track—like a master detective, Mickey labored over all the lines spoken by Eastwood, Van Cleef, and me. Leone owed Mickey a medal for his work. Mickey taught me how to lip-synch, how to capture the emotion of a scene in a studio. In one scene I was sitting on my horse, yelling my lines—horses hate the hot sand and this one was not cooperative. This was not an easy scene to recapture while sitting on a stool in a recording studio in New York. "Just yell the goddamn line," Mickey reassured me. "We'll take care to match your yelling with what's on the screen."

Some time later, Henry Fonda called me in New York and told me that there was an Italian film director who wanted him to appear in a Western in Spain. "Is it Leone?" I asked. "If so, by all means take the job; you'll enjoy working with him."

"But he wants me to play the villain," Fonda said. "I even have to shoot a young boy."

I told him it would be a change of pace for him. "It's called *Once upon a Time in the West*—what the hell does he know about the West?" Fonda asked.

"You'd be surprised; take the challenge," I said. He did and the film turned out to be a success; Fonda even called to thank me.

A year later Leone came to America, this time to scout locations for a film that he would make only many years later—*Once upon a Time in America.* I took him to Brooklyn and showed him around Red Hook and Little Italy. We walked around my old neighborhood for hours, stopping in front of the store my mother and father once owned on Union Street, my old school, and the boys' club where I first knew I wanted to become an actor.

Leone stayed in touch. "We will make more movies together," he said. "I keep my promises."

One time he called me and said he wanted to make another Western in Spain called *Duck, You Sucker* (*Giù la testa*). He told me that there was a wonderful comedic part in it for me. I explained to Leone that I had a conflict with the dates of the production—I was supposed to do a film in France with Jean-Paul Belmondo—but Leone pleaded with me. "Please agree to do my movie, please," he said. I foolishly turned down the film I was offered and agreed to star in Leone's.

Leone went to Hollywood to try to raise money for "our picture"—I thought it was a grand gesture that he referred to it as "ours." In California the studio he was going to work with asked him about the cast. He told them that he had Eli Wallach in the lead role. "No, no," he was told. "We have an actor, Rod Steiger, who owes us one more picture on his studio contract. You'll have to use him; otherwise, we can't put up the financing."

Leone agreed. "Sorry, E-*li*," he told me over the phone. "But I have to use Steiger." I told him that I had had to turn down the other film and had now lost out on two jobs. I asked if he could at least give me a token payment.

"I'm sorry," Leone said. "But I have to do what the California producers want."

"I'll sue you," I told him angrily.

"Get in line," he said, and slammed down the phone.

The breaking of that connection also broke our relationship. We never spoke again.

Leone may have ultimately won our battle anyway. Since *The Good, the Bad and the Ugly* was an Italian film, I was not entitled to any residuals (in America an actor receives payments when the film is replayed on TV). I'd be a multimillionaire if I had stuck that clause in my Italian contract. As the French would say, "*C'est la* goddamn *guerre,*" or, to quote my first theatrical agent, "That's life in the Balkans."

◎ ◎ ◎

I didn't see much of my friend Clint Eastwood during the intervening years. But whenever he came to New York to receive an award for directing or acting, I would be asked to give a brief speech about him. I once told him that if and whenever I do get an award, I would expect him to reciprocate.

A few years ago, Clint was directing a film called *Mystic River* in Boston, and his agent called me with an offer to appear in it.

"How many weeks?" I asked.

"One day," the agent said, "but Clint thinks it will be a wonderful reunion."

My agent, Clifford Stevens, wisely told me to accept the offer with one caveat—since I would only be doing one day of shooting, I would not be listed in the cast credits or used in any of the advertising. Clint consented.

I flew up to Boston on a Wednesday knowing nothing of the

story or the script. I found that I was to play a liquor store owner. I memorized the three pages of dialogue that were given to me and prepared to act in the scene the following day. On Thursday morning I walked out to the set. Clint greeted me warmly. "I'm happy you agreed to do the cameo," he said, and told me that I'd be playing opposite two wonderful actors—Kevin Bacon and Laurence Fishburne.

Clint waited patiently while the scene was lit, then walked over to me and whispered, "Any time you're ready, Eli." Not one word of direction was given. I felt relaxed and happy to be before the camera again. Bacon and Fishburne assured me that my scene would not be deleted in the final cut.

"You give us an important clue to the solution of the crime we're investigating," Kevin Bacon said.

Many months later I sat next to a woman in the rear of a movie house on Broadway to watch the film; it had gotten great reviews. As I watched, I kept wondering when my little scene would appear. About an hour and a half into the film, my patience was almost at an end. Then finally, there I was behind the counter in my liquor store. The woman seated next to me stared at the scene, puzzled. Then, she turned to look at me, then looked back at the screen.

"Is that you?" she asked.

"Yes, yes, it's me," I said. "Please let me watch the scene."

I walked out of the film, unknown and unrecognized, save for my lady friend in the seat next to mine.

17

@@@@@@@@@

Schisgal, Gielgud,
Sharif, and Me

OVER THE COURSE of our careers, Anne and I have had the good
fortune to work closely with a number of great American playwrights, among them Tennessee Williams, with whom we worked
on *This Property Is Condemned* and *The Glass Menagerie*. Anne was
also in *Summer and Smoke*, while I performed in *The Rose Tattoo*,
Camino Real, and the film *Baby Doll*. How lucky we were. And how
lucky we were in the 1960s to join up with a young playwright
and gifted social satirist named Murray Schisgal, with whom we
did *The Typists, and The Tiger*; *Luv*; and *Twice Around the Park*.

Jean Guest, whom I had met while I was performing in *The
Teahouse of the August Moon* in London, was now our neighbor in
Greenwich Village. Jean held an important position in ANTA

(American National Theatre and Academy). One evening at her home, she handed us a script to read: two one-act plays. "I think you'll be perfect for them," she said, and told us she had contacted Claire Nichtern, who was a young producer interested in putting these plays on.

Lying in bed one night, I had the chance to read the first one-act play, *The Typists*, about a young man and a young woman typing away in a small office; every time after the boss summons one or the other to his office, they return to their typewriters and ten years have passed. The play begins at 9:00 A.M., and by 5:00 P.M., after four visits with their boss, the typists have aged and are now in their late sixties (the actors had a few moments to put on their age makeup while in the boss's office). I thought the writing was superb and the aging trick was quite creative.

While I had been reading *The Typists*, Anne was reading *The Tiger*, and every time she'd turn the page, she'd roar with laughter. "How the hell can I concentrate with you laughing all the time?" I asked. "You'll see," she told me, and again yelped with joy. When she was done, she handed me the script; it dealt with an angry postman who, hating his job and society as a whole, decides to kidnap a girl (anyone would do), take her to his basement flat, and rape her. I had recently seen the film *The Collector*, which had a similar plot, and had hated it.

"I don't think I want to do this play," I said. "I don't see anything funny about kidnapping and raping someone. It's tasteless and violent."

"All right," Anne said. "Then we'll get another actor to play the postman."

"No," I said, almost shouting. "I'll read the damn play again." And when I was done, I had to concede that it had some funny moments.

"All right, I'll do it," I told Anne. "And I don't want any triumphant roars from you."

For years after that production, I'd have Anne read scripts that had been offered to me, and if the room shook with her laughter, I'd happily agree to sign the contract.

At the first reading of the play, we met the author, Murray Schisgal. He was a fairly tall, bald, and bearded man. His most distinguished features were his eyes—they were so sad. He looked like a basset hound. How could he have written such amusing plays, I wondered. I soon became aware that apart from his basset hound eyes, Murray was also gifted with a wicked sense of humor. He was a cross between a brilliant social satirist and a psychoanalyst. He had passed his bar exams and was a licensed attorney, but hated the profession, left it without ever practicing, and chose to enter that minefield called playwriting. I immediately understood his decision—after all, I had happily abandoned the teaching profession and entered the equally dangerous minefield of acting.

The Typists, and The Tiger, directed by Arthur Storch, opened at the Orpheum Theater on the Lower East Side. Established Broadway actors rarely ventured off-Broadway at the time, but Anne and I never regretted taking that chance. The reviews for the plays were glowing. Schisgal was hailed as a great new author, and we were given kudos as a newly discovered acting couple, even though we still did argue every once in a while. I remember one afternoon, while on our way to the theater, we ran into Joseph Heller, author of *Catch-22*, in front of Zabar's on the Upper West Side. I was, and still am, a nut about time, but Anne never cared particularly about that four-letter word. As Anne stopped to chat with Heller, I let out another four-letter word: "What the hell are you doing?" I asked Anne. "We have a matinee and you're still standing around talking. I'll take the subway down and you can drive." And I did.

At the Orpheum, Anne and I shared a dressing room, and we had a wardrobe girl who helped us with our quick costume changes. That day I sat in front of a mirror doing my makeup as Anne sat alongside me. "Tell him," she growled to the wardrobe girl, "that I never wish to speak with him again. He abandoned me and made me drive to the theater, and I didn't even have my glasses."

"Tell her," I said quietly, "I had a matinee to do and she better learn how to get to work on time." Our young lady assistant went from chair to chair, trying to mediate, as if she were a frightened referee in a championship fight.

The Tiger opened in a blackout. Suddenly, a rear door was kicked open, and I entered as the postman carrying a kicking figure wrapped in a raincoat over my shoulder. As the lights came up, I would tie Anne in a chair as she would whimper, "I have a husband in Long Island."

"Shut up," I would order. "You do not have my permission to speak." During this particular matinee performance, I delivered that "shut up" line with a special emphasis.

During one evening performance, I noticed a young man sitting in the front row who seemed to be asleep while I made my entrance in *The Typists*. Now, actors do have a tendency to talk to themselves onstage from time to time, and my internal conversation went a little like this when I saw that young man sleeping.

FIRST SELF: I've just come on and he's already fast asleep?
SECOND SELF: Well, he's bought his ticket. He has a right to sleep.
FIRST SELF: Why the hell doesn't he rent a room somewhere?

This conversation went on for some time, and that sleeping figure never once looked up. After the show, the stage manager came up to tell me that there was a man who wanted to see me. "If it's that sleeper, I'll kill him," I thought. A young man was ushered into my dressing room; it was him. He was carrying a cane.

"My name is Ved Mehta," he said. "I'm a writer for the *New Yorker*." He put his cane into his left hand and reached out to shake my hand with his right; he was blind. I'm glad he never could read my thoughts.

At another matinee, a tall Englishman came to see the play. "Sorry," he was told. "We're all sold out." He started to walk away, but when our producer Claire Nichtern caught sight of him, she ran out of the lobby to catch him; it was Sir John Gielgud. "Come back, come back," she cried. "We'll put out an extra chair for you."

Gielgud later recommended our plays to Binky Beaumont, the managing director of H.M. Tennant, the most prestigious theatrical producers in London, and they agreed to stage the plays in the West End on the condition that Gielgud direct. So, after closing in New York, we went on a cross-country tour with stops in Chicago, Los Angeles, and San Francisco. But before we would go off to London to do the Schisgal plays there, I would have to embark upon another exotic adventure, this time to Angkor Wat in Cambodia, where Richard Brooks was filming his adaptation of Joseph Conrad's book *Lord Jim*, which was to star Peter O'Toole. Brooks wanted me to play a half-breed warlord.

Peter Witt was instrumental in getting me this role, and usually he would try to finagle a trip out of any job he got me outside of the United States. Not this time. "There are too many snakes," he said. Anne refused to join me as well. She had done research and discovered that Angkor Wat was known as the home of the deadly krait snake. Getting there took twenty hours with stops in Hawaii and Tokyo, after which we finally landed in Siem Reap, where the airport consisted of one small room with a large framed photo of Cambodian ruler Prince Sianouk. He had offered the ruins of Angkor as the main location of the film on one condition: that the crew build an extension to his motel. Columbia Pictures agreed to the arrangement.

The ruins had been discovered by the French in early 1865, and all the buildings were overrun by banyan trees, whose roots ran along the ground and slowly grew up the sides of the sandstone structures, crushing them. Cambodia was once part of the French empire, and the French had cleared away all the trees to restore the temples of Angkor.

Brooks was an ex-marine who became a top director, famous for his work on *In Cold Blood* and *Elmer Gantry*. He was a hot-tempered loner who would purchase famous novels and adapt them for the screen. Originally, Brooks had to do some work to convince me to play a half-breed warlord, but after a while I figured that I had already played an Okinawan, a Mexican bandit, a Greek jewel thief, and a Latin American dictator, so I might as well give it a try. He also wanted me to be bald, but I was not willing to give that a try.

"No," I said, "I can't do that because when I finish with this film, my wife and I are appearing in *The Typists, and The Tiger* in London."

"We'll get you a wig," Brooks said.

"I can't wear a wig every night in the play," I said. "I have too many quick changes to make."

Upon my arrival in Cambodia, the makeup man proposed to shave my head about two inches above my ears. "You'll look so strange that the movie audience will think you are a Cambodian warlord," he said. Brooks stared at me on my first day on set and said, "You look like a warlord."

Peter O'Toole, who was to play Lord Jim, was already famous for his role in *Lawrence of Arabia*. I had met him in London when he'd been studying at the Royal Academy of Dramatic Art and had helped backstage on *The Teahouse of the August Moon* at Her Majesty's Theatre. In O'Toole's autobiography, *Loitering with Intent*, he tells of how he brought his girlfriend backstage to meet me. "That impressed her mightily," O'Toole wrote. "She was astonished that I knew the star."

During one scene in Brooks's film, I was to torture O'Toole's character—as a boy I used to watch movies where villains would heat a sword, then press it to the flesh of the hero in order to get him to confess. And here I was in the jungles of Cambodia doing the same thing to O'Toole.

Peter was a skillful, well-trained actor. He had played Hamlet for the opening of the National Theatre in London, directed by Sir Laurence Olivier. And he and I became good friends on location; we were to work together on another film, *How to Steal a Million.*

I had ten days off during the latter part of the filming and spent it with Paul Lukas, a well-known stage and screen star who was traveling with his wife to Thailand, Penang, Malaysia, and Singapore. I was delighted to go; anything to get out of the jungle. But our last stop was Saigon; at night in our hotel there, we could hear cannon fire. It scared the hell out of me, and I was glad to get back to Angkor Wat to complete the film.

On the final day of filming, Brooks told me that I had one more scene to do—a final shoot-out with O'Toole—and it would be shot at Shepperton Studios outside of London. "The makeup man has created an exact clay duplicate of your head, and as you try to escape, you'll be blown up," Brooks said, "then you can go back to your one-act plays and say good-bye to *Lord Jim.*"

On the way home, I stopped in Hong Kong to meet with a film technician who had worked on *Lord Jim* with me. He said that he had a daughter who wanted to go to London and could I please take her with me to work as an au pair to look after our children while Anne and I were acting in the Schisgal plays. I agreed, we shook hands, and set a date for her arrival.

At home Anne and I busied ourselves with arrangements for our London trip. We sailed out of New York and arrived in

Southampton five days later and were met by a representative of H.M. Tennant. We were driven to an elegant home on Astell Street in Chelsea. We had quite a staff: a cook named Minnie, a cleaning woman named Mrs. Mumford, and while we waited for our Hong Kong girl to arrive, our agent friend Roz Chatto recommended a blond, blue-eyed beauty named Juliet Harmer to look after the children while Anne and I went off to rehearsals at the Globe Theatre on Shaftesbury Avenue. Peter, age thirteen, immediately fell in love with Juliet. We also got him a tutor who helped him with his math, history, and science, while Roberta and Katherine were enrolled in a girls' school in Chelsea. They were compelled to wear uniforms and would depart for class early each morning.

Our young au pair, age sixteen, finally arrived. Her name was Helen Fok. Our cook and cleaning woman immediately took a dislike to her; after all, she was a foreigner in their midst. Helen became homesick and our daughters took care to soothe and comfort her. She became like our third daughter. Peter also got along very well with his tutor and even began to enjoy his math and science sessions. On off-days the family would go to flea markets, museums, and the zoo, while Juliet would make sure that we got to see parts of London not seen by the usual tourists.

At rehearsals Gielgud seemed most happy with us and Schisgal's plays. Just hearing him make a comment from the rear of the theater was energizing, but the plays opened to mixed reviews. After opening night Vivien Leigh told us that audiences would love *The Tiger* because "English audiences are always impressed with threatened rape and sexy scenes." But, she said, the

British would give a critical thumbs-down to *The Typists* because "they see nothing wrong with spending one's life in an office as you do in the play."

Leigh turned out to be exactly right. Our signed contracts were for six months, and we had no idea that we'd be able to last that long. Our financial obligations were huge: house rental, cook, cleaning woman, school fees, tutor. I had even rented a used car—a Wosley—but Binky Beaumont assured us that we'd make it through. Toward the end of the fourth month, the ax fell; we were to close. It was a most painful situation to face, but our agent Roz Chatto managed to get me a job to take care of some of the remaining expenses. I was to play the role of the emperor of China in *Genghis Khan*, which was being filmed in Yugoslavia.

"How many weeks do I do?" I asked.

"About six," the producer told me. "You have many scenes."

"I've only got one free week," I said. "My whole family's sailing back to New York."

"All right," I was told. "Read the part of the shah of Khwarezm."

I looked but couldn't find any lines for the shah. "Oh," the producer said, "I forgot. You're in scene 38 and that one was omitted from the script. When you get to Belgrade, you can write the scene."

When I arrived in Belgrade, it looked abandoned. All the stores had empty shelves; the film studio had dirt floors. In the run-down hotel, I wrote scene 38, in which I, as the shah, was hiring a warlord to capture and kill Genghis Khan. I specified that the set have an elegantly painted throne and I would have my two daughters by my side. "If you agree to this offer," I say to the warlord, "I will give you one of my daughters." He shows his refusal with a mere shake of his head. "All right," I say. "How about two?"

The producers were thrilled by the scene I had written. Genghis Khan was to be played by Omar Sharif, who had already made a name for himself with Peter O'Toole in *Lawrence of Arabia*. I told him of my recent work with O'Toole on *Lord Jim,* and we became friendly. But when he made his first appearance on set, where we were to film his capture, I could barely recognize him. He was wearing what looked like a wooden doughnut over his head; he was handcuffed and his hands were attached to the doughnut.

"How many weeks are you going to be on this job?" Sharif asked me.

"I'll only be here for one week," I said.

"Goddamn it; I've already been here for two months," Sharif said. "What are they paying you?"

"Twenty-five thousand dollars for the week," I said.

The wooden doughnut shook angrily as Sharif shouted, "That's my salary for the whole goddamn picture."

I couldn't resist—"Well," I said, and gave him the smile of a shah, "if the Egyptians enslaved the Jews, they are now getting their revenge!"

Sharif glared at me. "I'm not an Egyptian," he said. "I'm Lebanese."

I remember one day I watched the director, Henry Levin, instructing the horse wrangler. "In this scene I want all the horses to appear on the ridge of the hill," he said. "It will be a great cinematic sequence." He explained that in a lot of American Westerns, all the Indians would suddenly appear on the horizon. "I want the shah's men to appear just like the Indians," he said.

On the call of action, thirty men appeared on horseback as directed. Levin screamed at his horse wrangler. "Spread the goddamn horses out," he said. "This is for widescreen Cinerama."

The wrangler rode up to the indignant director. "I can't spread them out," he told Levin. "They're plow horses; they stand two by two and they won't separate."

"Okay," Levin said. He was stumped. "We'll have to film the scene in sections."

At the end of the week, I turned in my shah's yellow and gold costume, said a fond good-bye to my new friend Omar Sharif, and flew back to London. Our last days there were sad as we said good-bye to our household staff—Helen, Mrs. Mumford, Minnie. Gielgud and Beaumont sent Anne a bouquet of roses and wished us bon voyage. I returned the old Wosley car and took the family to Southampton, where we boarded the ship back to New York.

Once we were back, we got a lovely surprise. Claire Nichtern told us that she had optioned Murray Schisgal's new three-character comedy, *Luv,* and had signed Mike Nichols to direct it. Nichols had most recently had a great hit with Neil Simon's *Barefoot in the Park.* He was lined up to direct four more plays on Broadway, but *Luv* was the one he wanted to direct first. Anne and I were to play a husband and wife, and we were asked to see whether Alan Arkin would be right for the third character, who was named Harry Berlin. We saw him in Joe Stein's wonderful play *Enter Laughing,* and before the first act was over, we knew that Arkin was exactly right—he had the gifts of Groucho Marx, Buster Keaton, and Jack Benny all rolled into one.

We did the first reading of the play with Nichols at our apartment. Nichols stressed that Schisgal had written a deadly serious play, a Chekhovian comedy for the 1960s. He also told us that we were the best cast he could imagine for the play. At one point during the reading, Schisgal was asked why he had chosen to call the play *Luv*. He volunteered that love had been so commercialized, so distorted, and so inauthentic that people could no longer even spell it correctly.

We all loved *Luv*, no matter how it was spelled. The day after the first reading, I talked to my brother, Sam, who had become a devoted fan of my theater successes. "Tell me," he said, "why can't you read a play and tell if it will become a success?"

"I'd become a millionaire if I could do that," I said, then handed him a copy of *Luv*. "Here's a play Anne and I are going to do next," I said. "We believe in it so strongly that we're buying shares in it for each of our children. Read it and tell me if you could predict its chances."

After he'd read it, he called back and asked, "Are you sure you're going to do this? Save your money. If it's successful, it'll be a miracle."

Rehearsals went smoothly for the most part. But at one point, we were confused about the rhythm of a scene, so Nichols gave us a rather unusual direction: "Anne," he said, "I want you to play your part with a heavy Tallulah Bankhead southern accent; Alan, you are to imitate Tennessee Williams's southern drawl; and Eli, I want you to use the heaviest Jewish accent possible. But do not change one word of the script; let me hear you play the scenes that way."

One of Nichols's most recognizable traits is his laugh; it sounds like an elongated whistle. And as we played the scenes for him, accents and all, he laughed and whistled all the way through. At the end, he rushed to the front of the stage, tears in his eyes. "It's miraculous," he said. "Maybe we should keep the accents." Actually, his miraculous direction helped us to get rid of all our tensions. We were free now to dispense with the accents and just have fun with Schisgal's witty lines.

As the rehearsal process went on, Nichols revealed that he was a stickler for details. As the set was being put up for the show, Nichols took the producer, Claire Nichtern, aside. "Claire," he said, "we can't bring the curtain up on this set. The floor is lemon yellow; it's bilious. Whoever painted that bridge floor must have been color-blind. Have the set designer redo it."

"It would cost over $750 to redo it," Claire said, "and our expenses are already too high."

"Redo it," Nichols said as he stormed out of the theater.

Claire, aside from being a Broadway producer, was also an experienced housewife. She went home, brought back a box of Clorox, got down on her hands and knees, and sponged the entire floor with bleach. The next morning, Mike came back for rehearsal. He looked at the floor. "Perfect," he said. "That's exactly the color I want."

"Thank you," Claire said. "I knew you'd like it."

The set of the play was a bridge, a bench, a lamppost, a sandbox, and a garbage can. Behind us, there was a backdrop of the New York skyline. "When the curtain goes up," Nichols said, "I think the audience will feel disoriented. 'Where's the furniture?' they'll ask. 'Where's the telephone, the liquor bar?'"

Maybe the audience got too disoriented. After the second preview performance at the Booth Theatre on West Forty-fifth Street, we sat onstage as Mike gave us our notes. The Booth is a tiny theater and the box office is a mere fifty feet from the stage. During the performance, we could hear loud, angry voices yelling at the box-office man. "This is the worst play I've ever seen! I want my money back!" someone said. "My wife almost threw up," said another.

"I don't understand," I said to Nichols. "We love the play."

"Well," Nichols said, "they probably just hate you. But don't get upset; we'll solve it."

Opening night, Nichols gathered the three of us onstage. "Remember the fun we had during the 'accent rehearsal'? So, relax and enjoy!

"Oh," he added, "I have one more idea. We've hired a specialist to use a smoke machine. As the curtain goes up I want the bridge to appear to be drowned in a heavy fog."

On opening nights, the audience usually applauded when they saw the set. Not this night at first, however. After the stage manager had whispered, "Houselights out" and the curtain rose, some mysterious breeze from the back of the theater sucked the stage fog off the set, and it drifted out into the audience. They couldn't see their hands in front of their faces. What a novel way to open a play, they must have thought. Still, Nichols was noted for his dramatic effects, and so they figured that it must have been intentional. At first bewildered and then amused by this effect, they roared with laughter and burst into applause.

Unlike our experience with producer Leo Kerz, who refused

to quote critics in advertising, Claire Nichtern ran full-page ads in all the papers. "Glowing," one said. "The funniest play on any stage this season. We were lost in a fog of fun." The next day there was a long line in front of the theater that went all the way up to Eighth Avenue. I called my brother. "Well?" I gloated. "What do you think? Did you read the reviews?"

"Well," Sam said, "it was a miracle."

Anne and I had corresponded often with Sir John Gielgud after our engagement in London with *The Typists, and The Tiger.* He was now appearing in Edward Albee's *Tiny Alice* on Broadway. Anne arranged for us to have an early dinner with Gielgud at Sardi's after our matinee performances.

That afternoon, while Alan and Anne were playing a scene, some man in the audience laughed so hard that he fell out of his seat. Alan, who was sitting on Anne's lap, turned his face upstage, his shoulders heaving with laughter. Anne joined him, thus committing what I always considered to be an acting sin. She spoke directly to the audience. "Please forgive us," she said as she tried to control her laughter. "We couldn't help ourselves; I hope that man didn't hurt himself." The audience applauded, a sign of understanding and forgiveness. But as I stood offstage, waiting for my cue, I was shocked. Earlier in the scene, I had fallen off the bridge. Now, soaking wet, I dashed onstage, glared at Anne, and whispered, "Amateur! You're both amateurs!" After the curtain call, Alan, frightened, ran to his dressing room. "I'll report you to Actors' Equity," I said. "You oughta be fired for your amateurish behavior."

Anne dressed quickly and dashed up Shubert Alley and into Sardi's across the street. Gielgud was already at the table. "Where's the old boy?" he asked.

Anne said, "I don't know if he'll join us. He intends to report me to Equity for breaking up on the stage. Did you ever do that?"

"Good god, no—I'd be too frightened," Gielgud said, "but Larry Olivier is a great giggler."

I joined them at the table, scowling at Anne. "Oh, do forgive her," Gielgud said. "She's terribly upset and she's crying." Anne's tears always seemed to erase my crazy anger.

"All right; I'll forgive her," I said.

During our meal, Anne told Gielgud that we had both seen him in *Tiny Alice* and were puzzled by its final scene. "You remember that long speech you gave in the last scene?" Anne asked him. "Do you understand what it means?"

"Good god, no. I haven't the faintest idea," he said. The rest of the meal went peacefully, and back we went to our respective theaters, Gielgud probably trying to figure out what his last speech meant.

ⓠ ⓠ ⓠ

After playing to sold-out houses in *Luv* for about five months, my agent Witt called with another "Ow!" He said that his friend William Wyler had an emergency. He was directing a film called *How to Steal a Million* in Paris with Audrey Hepburn and Peter O'Toole. One of the other actors had taken ill and had to be replaced.

"Can you get out of *Luv* for three weeks?" Witt asked.

"I doubt it," I said. "There are only three of us in the cast and we're a team, but I'll ask."

Claire Nichtern listened to my request and then surprised me by using the same strategy that Maurice Evans had used when I asked for a leave of absence from *Teahouse*. She asked how many weeks I would be gone and added two weeks' work in *Luv* for each week I would be in Paris. "But first," she said, "you'd better make peace with Anne." How I worked that out, I'll never know, but Anne finally said okay, and for three weeks I was replaced by my understudy, Gene Wilder, and I flew off to begin filming with Hepburn and O'Toole.

In the film I was to play a millionaire art collector who wanted to purchase the Cellini *Venus* for his Los Angeles museum. Once I arrived, I was greeted by William Wyler and the cast as though I were the lifesaver who had pulled them out of a sinking ship. Audrey Hepburn was as beautiful as the Venus coming out of her half-shell. In one scene I had to kiss her. She was a little taller than me. Before the scene she whispered, "I'll take off my shoes if that will help you."

"Help me?" I thought. "She's an angel."

"Oh, that would be lovely, thank you," I said.

I had a long weekend off from the shooting and flew down to Nice on the Côte d'Azur to revisit the hospital where I had served in World War II. At the hotel, I ran into an old friend, the actor E. G. Marshall, who was in Nice doing a film for UNICEF starring Trevor Howard, Rita Hayworth, and Yul Brynner. The film, based on a story by Ian Fleming, was called *The Poppy Is Also a Flower*, and it dealt with the drug world. The director, Terence Young, asked if I could do a cameo as a Mafia drug dealer.

"I'd be happy to do it, but I have to be back in Paris on Tuesday," I said.

"You have my guarantee," Young assured me, adding that there was no salary and my payment would be six Lanvin shirts.

To play the Mafia drug dealer, I called upon my memory of Albert Anastasia in Murder Incorporated and some of the other gangsters I'd played on TV. I finished the job and flew back to Paris to complete *How to Steal a Million* before returning to New York and the cast of *Luv*. I was just in time to celebrate *Luv's* first anniversary. While I'd been in Paris, Anne had taken a fall on the bridge set and had hurt her hand, but being a trooper, she had continued to perform. Claire Nichtern had found a mink piece that she could use to cover the splint on her hand. When I found out about Anne's injury, my guilt thermometer shot up to a new level. "What is it in my makeup that makes me grab any offer and fly around the world," I wondered. "Will I ever be satisfied? Can't I ever just rest?"

Luv closed after a triumphant year-and-a-half run. Shortly thereafter, my friend Paul Bogart, who would later direct the TV series *All in the Family*, was nominated for an Emmy. At the awards ceremony at the Waldorf Hotel, he reserved a table and asked Anne and myself to join him. We showed up in full evening clothes and sat with Paul and his lovely wife, Jane. It was a gala affair. A huge screen showed clips of all the nominated TV shows. At one point, the spotlight picked up the emcee as he announced the award for Best Director in a TV series—Paul Bogart. Paul followed the spotlight to the stage, made a brief heartfelt speech, and rejoined our table.

Again, the spotlight returned to the emcee and he made another announcement: "And now, the Emmy for the Best Supporting Performance in a TV film: Eli Wallach." I looked at Paul. "What kind of joke is this?" I asked him. "Did you know about it? What am I getting an award for?"

"*The Poppy Is Also a Flower*," he said, and added that he had had no idea that I had even been nominated.

I have always hated long acceptance speeches, the ones where actors pull out a long list and mention their agents, their managers, their teachers, the landlady of their building, and even God. I stood in front of the mike and said, "I'll be brief. I want to thank UNICEF. I want to thank Lanvin for giving me six shirts as my salary, and Paul Bogart, who lured me here on false pretenses." And with that, I walked back to my table with my gold-plated Emmy.

18

Reflections on
a Golden Career

THE STAND-UP COMEDIAN Henny Youngman became famous for
a four-word joke: "Take my wife," he'd say. Then he'd pause and
say, "Please."

Well, I have taken my wife and I have always been pleased.
Anne cries aloud in theaters, loses ten pairs of glasses annually,
mentally tears down ugly office buildings, dreams of directing
traffic and issuing parking tickets, never went to college but has
an honorary doctor's degree, can't carry a tune but has always
been musical; her timing is as perfect as a Movado watch.

Anne has a wicked sense of humor too—from time to time,
we'd appear as guests on TV talk shows. One time a host talked
on and on about our lengthy marriage, asking questions such as
"How do you make your relationship work?"

Anne surprised me and the host by responding with a new twist to that familiar question: "I'm so sorry," she said in a voice heavy with guilt. "We have a terrible announcement to make." She stopped for a moment and the host gasped. "Our relationship has worked," Anne said, "simply because I am a saint."

But I believe we found an answer to the question of why our marriage lasted. We often chose plays that had tremendous fights in them—like *The Waltz of the Toreadors, The Typists,* and *The Tiger.* Onstage we could, with the help of brilliant writing, air our personal grievances and thus avoid expensive psychiatric sessions. I also believed that it was important to respect Anne's fighting spirit and her need to grow as an actress. She juggled several careers—wife, mother, and actress—and did them brilliantly.

During one radio interview, Anne was publicizing the Tennessee Williams play *Summer and Smoke.* The hostess asked Anne what it was like to be kissed onstage by a romantic leading man from Hollywood.

"Well," she said, "the leading man in my life is an actor from Brooklyn, and as we speak, he's at home ironing my blouse, and I find *that* very romantic."

When I heard that broadcast, I immediately pulled the plug on the iron, left the ironing board standing, and went out to see a movie that she wanted to see.

There are, of course, many battles in any long relationship, but one was particularly memorable. We were at home and the argument volume meter kept rising. At one point, I ran into our bedroom and slammed the door hard so that Anne started getting the message—this battle was meant to grow into a war. After ten minutes of cooling down, I decided to return to the fight. I tried to open the door, but it was stuck. I began banging on it, and Anne was starting to become terrified by all my yelling and screaming.

"Goddamn it, goddamn it, get me out of here!" I yelled.

"I'll call the super," Anne said.

The super, a giant with the physique of a professional wrestler, approached the door. "Is there anyone in there?" he asked.

"My husband," Anne said.

The super stepped back, took a deep breath, and began a run to knock down the door.

"No, no," Anne cried, "stop. That door always sticks; just bang on it."

He did and the door finally popped open.

When Anne is nervous or frightened, she often laughs. But there was no laughter this time. I glared at her as I walked out. Dinner was a long, silent affair. The thing that puzzled me most, though, was the fact that to this day, I still can't remember what the goddamn fight was about.

My children are adults now—Peter Wallach has become a superb film animator (I had once bought him a Beaulieu 16-millimeter camera and this led in part to his development as a photographer); Roberta and Katherine knew they wanted to become actresses—when journalists would ask us if we would encourage our children to go into the world of the theater, it was asked with this intent: Do you think it's worth pushing your daughters off a cliff?—but actresses they became.

I remember one time when Anne and I were going on the road with the play *The Waltz of the Toreadors*. We asked our two daughters to appear with us in the play. Katherine was fifteen at the time and having second thoughts about being a performer. "I don't want to be an actress," she said. "They're all phony."

"You're coming on the road," Anne said.

"The only reason you're taking me is because you don't want me to be alone in New York," said Katherine.

"You're damn right," I said.

"Okay," she said. "How long are we going for?"

"Well," I said, "Mommy and I are going for sixteen weeks all across America. But when we get to Chicago, you and your sister will go back to school in New York and Mommy and I can go on to play Los Angeles."

"Not play Los Angeles?" Katherine suddenly asked. "But that's the whole point of touring!"

When our kids were younger, they would always plead with me to get parts on the television shows they liked—"Dad, please do *Captain Kangaroo!*" "Dad, please do *Batman!*" I'd call my agent to see if he could get me on any of those shows.

The most fan mail I ever got for anything I've ever done was for an appearance as Mr. Freeze on the TV series *Batman.* I was the villain of the episode, and I spoke with a heavy German accent—"I *vill* freeze *zee* whole *vorld!* I *vill* conquer every country!" I felt like a haughty Hitler. It was a half-hour program and my pay was $350.

In 1997 Arnold Schwarzenegger, now the governor of California, played Mr. Freeze in the film version of *Batman.* His salary—$20 million. I could hardly eat dinner the night I read that in the newspaper. I spend my whole life onstage and in films and I got a measly $350, and Arnold walks away with $20 million? I continued to complain to Anne, my anger growing into a mighty roar.

Anne held up a hand to silence me.

"Lift weights," she said.

☙ ☙ ☙

The theater has often been called "the Fabulous Invalid," but having survived the onslaught from radio, film, and television, it is still here and it remains my first love. Now that I am in my eighties and continue to act, I, too, feel at times like a fabulous invalid. Aging actors remember the old joke—I always open the paper to the obituary page and if I'm not listed, I feel better for the whole day. Still, one now feels abandoned, lost, and sad as one's fellow actors leave. I was recently startled to find that six of the "Magnificent Seven," my enemies onscreen, had died.

In June 2004 I called Marlon Brando in California. "I haven't heard from you in twenty years," he said. "Why are you calling me now?"

"You want me to hang up?" I asked.

"No," he said, "let's talk. How are things in New York?"

We began to flip through the pages of our memories. Brando, who always loved to tease me, asked me at one point, "Can you afford this call?" Two weeks later he left us, and we lost a great theater and film talent.

When my old Neighborhood Playhouse pal Tony Randall was in the hospital, I visited him. We spoke of our days at the Playhouse, and I praised him for his great efforts to bring plays to

Broadway with his National Actors Theatre. My heart was racing as I watched my friend lying before me.

"I hear you were here last week," he said.

"Yes," I said, "but you weren't. You were in a state of disrepair."

"Next time you drop by," he said, "don't come back empty-handed."

He smiled and waved good-bye as I left. Two weeks later Tony was gone. I spoke at the memorial service for him. At the end of my talk, I said, "Dear Tony, I didn't come back empty-handed; I've come back brokenhearted."

Film actors can remain alive now through TV and DVDs; the stage actor lives on only in the memory of the audience. I owe a great debt to the stars of stage and screen whom I've known and who've left us—Henry Fonda, Charles Boyer, Charles Laughton, Clark Gable, Montgomery Clift, Yul Brynner, Steve McQueen, Jessica Tandy, Hume Cronyn, Jason Robards, Edward G. Robinson, Rod Steiger—and to my directors: Sergio Leone, Elia Kazan, John Sturges, Richard Brooks, John Huston, William Wyler, and Stanley Donen. All of them contributed to my growth as an actor.

◎ ◎ ◎

Some years ago, while doing dishes in my home in East Hampton, my right eye went dark, like a lightbulb that flickered and went out. Anne drove me to Southampton Hospital, and all during the ride, I didn't say a word, but my mind was racing. Did this mean that I could never be behind the wheel of a car again? I recalled what Tennessee Williams said about eyes in his play *Camino Real*—that they were the windows of the soul. Would this affect how I could work before the cameras?

The ophthalmologist worked quickly. With drops in my eye, I rested my chin on a bar and looked into a lens; again, the actor in me came to the fore—I imagined that I was a German U-boat commander getting ready to deliver the order to fire a torpedo.

"Please don't hold back anything," I said. "Just give me your prognosis."

He shook his head. "You've had what we call a stroke in the eye," he said. "A bit of plaque broke off somewhere in your arterial system, went up your carotid artery, and instead of going to your brain, lodged in your right eye. There is nothing we can do for you."

On the ride home, I thought about other actors who had not let accidents and vision problems interfere with their careers: Peter Falk, who has a glass eye; Hume Cronyn, who lost an eye to cancer—while he and I were working on the play *Promenade, All!* he used to make me shudder when he'd use the ring on his finger to tap on his glass eye. "Well," I thought, "if they could work with their handicaps, so can I."

A few years later while working with Whoopi Goldberg on the film *The Associate,* I began to have terrible hip pain. The director, Donald Petrie, told me that I would have to run up a flight of stairs. "Sorry, I can't," I said. "You can cut to another actor looking up the flight of stairs and staring and then cut to me at the top." And that's what he did. I hated being handicapped by the pain, but I worked my way through the film despite it.

I was puzzled as to why my hips were troubling me so. I could blame it on all the horse riding I'd done in films, or I could blame it on the fact that eight times a week during Tennessee Williams's *Camino Real* I had to jump from a box seat in the theater onto the stage.

The noted orthopedic surgeon Dr. Ranawatt of Lenox Hill Hospital ushered me into his office. He was tall, Indian, handsome. "I've studied your x-rays carefully," he said. "You have an arthritic hip and will need a hip replacement—the sooner the better."

Before the operation, Anne insisted that we take a week's vacation in Florida. We swam in the ocean, lay on the beach, and relaxed. At 6:00 A.M. on the morning after our return to New York, I was wheeled into the operating room, and there were six white-gowned men, all wearing clear glass bubble helmets. They looked like they were aliens from outer space. Dr. Ranawatt nodded to one of the bubble heads, who approached me with a shiny hypodermic and ordered me to sit up.

"It's just a simple spinal injection," he said. "No pain."

I lay back and went into bye-bye land.

After the operation, I was wheeled back to my room. Anne turned to our daughter Roberta and said, "He looks so healthy and tanned and relaxed. If this were a film, they'd send him back to makeup to remove all the tanning lotion."

The next morning, Anne and Roberta came to visit. A young woman walked into the room—"Hello," she said, "I'm Cynthia, your physiotherapist." She placed a wheeled metal walker alongside my bed. "Up you go," she said. "Sit up, wait a few seconds, and then get out of bed. Use this walker and head for the wall."

"What do you mean walk?" I asked. "I still have about fifty stitches in my left leg."

"You'll do it," she said with the authority of a prison matron. "Walk!"

I got up ever so slowly and, using the walker, I headed for the wall. I stood there facing it for a moment.

"Turn around and come back," she said. I didn't move. "Turn around," she said again.

Anne whispered to her—"Tell him you're a camera," she said.

Cynthia seemed puzzled, but she repeated what Anne had said: "I am a camera."

Instantly, I turned around and headed for my bed. "That'll teach her," I thought—give me a camera and I'm ready to go.

After six months of physiotherapy and exercise, I could walk with no pain. Dr. Ranawatt asked me if I would talk to the doctors and nurses at Lenox Hill about my operation and recovery. At the hospital auditorium, several hundred people came to hear me talk. I walked out onstage using crutches. "I'll be brief," I said. "Some people go to Lourdes for a miracle cure, but I came to Lenox Hill." I threw my crutches to the floor and walked out; the audience gave me a standing ovation.

Two years later I returned to Dr. Ranawatt's office. "Now my right hip is driving me crazy," I told him.

"I didn't want to tell you before, but you'll have to go through the same hip-replacement routine again," he said.

"Why didn't you do both hips at the same time?" I asked. "Two hips for the price of one."

"You weren't ready," he said. "I'll operate on you in two weeks."

Recovery from the second hip operation was smooth, and I returned to work on stage and screen. Several years later I began to get pains in my left hip again. I went back to Dr. Ranawatt, who slid my x-ray on the lighted wall in his office.

"When I do an operation, it is perfect," he said. "Look at these beautiful hips; they're like brand-new shock absorbers in an old car. Your problem is not your hips; it's referred pain from your spine."

"So what do I do?" I asked.

"Painkillers and physiotherapy," he said.

Recently, during plays in which I've performed, I've experienced a sort of miracle. Standing in the wings, just before I would have to go out onstage, I'd take a deep breath and, upon the moment of my entrance, I would feel no pain at all. Acting before an audience has been my best painkiller.

Although I limp in life as a result of my two hip operations, whenever I go onstage with Anne, the lights give my body a lift and I prance onto the stage and dance off. I feel I can play a sixteen-year-old if the author calls for that. Which is why I prefer live acting to film—I come alive with the lights. Although the money is better and the exposure is greater with film, movies are not as much fun.

◎ ◎ ◎

Now it's time for me to reflect on my life and upon my choice of profession. From the time I left the army in 1945 until 1955, I concentrated on theater. After that, I made films but would continue to rush back to New York to find a play. Film work paid dividends in name value and money, but theater presented an opportunity to sharpen my skills. Facing a live audience always gave me great satisfaction.

The navy had its motto—"Join the navy and see the world." For me, it became "Join the movies and see the world." Movies have taken me to Canada, Crete, Cambodia, Mexico, France, Italy, Spain, Yugoslavia, Great Britain. I hope one day to work in India, New Zealand, and Australia. Working in far-off places sometimes put a strain on my marriage, but whenever Anne and the children would visit and spend time with me, that eased the problem somewhat.

I often accept requests to speak at colleges and acting schools—there, students bombard me with questions, mostly dealing with theater, film, and the mystery of the Method. They want to get information about what to do with their lives. I always tell them choose what you want to do and don't let anyone ever dissuade you.

Recently at home, I spotted a big envelope from the Screen Actors Guild on my desk. I knew it contained a residual—a check from the union for a rerun of a film on TV. "Good," I thought. I may not be making as many films as I once did, but residuals are always a welcome addition to my income.

I quickly tore open the envelope; the residual was for the movie *Mistress,* which I had made with Robert De Niro. It was for *two cents.* I'm sure my first agent, Bill Liebling, would have said, "Well, that's life in the Balkans," but for me it meant that I was still in the race, that even two cents was a residual.

As for me, I intend to keep working and to stay true to the words spoken by Lord Byron in Tennessee Williams's *Camino Real:* "Make voyages, attempt them, there's nothing else."

Film Credits

King of the Corner (2004)—Sol Spivak

The Root (2003)

Mystic River (2003) (uncredited)—Mr. Loonie, the liquor store owner

Advice and Dissent (2002)—the Rebbe

Monday Night Mayhem (2002) (TV)—Leonard Goldenson

The Bookfair Murders (2000) (TV)—Erich

Keeping the Faith (2000)—Rabbi Ben Lewis

Uninvited (1999)—Strasser

Naked City: Justice with a Bullet (1998) (TV)—Deluca

The Associate (1996)—Fallon

Two Much (1996)—Sheldon

Honey Sweet Love (1994)

Vendetta II: The New Mafia (1993) (TV)—Frank Latella

The Godfather Trilogy: 1901–1980 (1992)—Don Altobello

Nonesense and Lullabyes: Poems (1992)

Night and the City (1992)—Peck

Teamster Boss: The Jackie Presser Story (1992) (TV)—Bill Presser

Mistress (1992)—George Lieberhof

Legacy of Lies (1992) (TV)—Moses Resnick

Article 99 (1992)—Sam Abrams

Nonesense and Lullabyes: Nursery Rhymes (1992)

Vendetta: Secrets of a Mafia Bride (1991) (TV)—Frank Latella

The Godfather: Part III (1990)—Don Altobello

The Two Jakes (1990)—Cotton Weinberger

A Matter of Conscience (1989) (TV)—Ira Abrams

The Impossible Spy (1987) (TV)—Yacov

Nuts (1987)—Dr. Herbert A. Morrison

Something in Common (1986) (TV)—Norman Voss

Tough Guys (1986)—Leon B. Little

Rocket to the Moon (1986) (TV)—Mr. Prince

Murder: By Reason of Insanity (1985) (TV)—Dr. Huffman

Our Family Honor (1985) (TV)—Vincent Danzig

Christopher Columbus (1985) (TV)—Father Hernando DeTalavera

Embassy (1985) (TV)—Joe Verga

Sam's Son (1984)—Sam Orowitz

Anatomy of an Illness (1984) (TV)—Dr. William Hitzig

The Executioner's Song (1982) (TV)—Uncle Vern Damico

The Wall (1982) (TV)—Mauritzi Apt

The Salamander (1981)—Lieutenant General Leporello

Skokie (1981) (TV)—Bert Silverman

The Pride of Jesse Hallam (1981) (TV)—Sal Galucci

Fugitive Family (1980) (TV)—Olan Vacio

The Hunter (1980)—Ritchie Blumenthal

Winter Kills (1979)—Joe Diamond

Firepower (1979)—Sal Hyman

Little Italy (1978)—Gerolamo Giarra

Circle of Iron (1978)—Man in oil

Movie Movie (1978)—Vince Marlow/Pop

The Pirate (1978) (TV)—Ben Ezra

Girlfriends (1978)—Rabbi Gold

Nasty Habits (1977)—Monsignor

The Domino Principle (1977)—General Reser

The Deep (1977)—Adam Coffin

Seventh Avenue (1977) (TV)—Gus Farber

The Sentinel (1977)—Detective Gatz

Eye of the Cat (1976)—Cesare

Plot of Fear (1976)—Pietro Riccio

Independence (1976)—Benjamin Franklin

Shoot First . . . Ask Questions Later (1975)—Sheriff Edward Gideon, aka Blackjack

Stateline Motel (1975)—Joe

Paradise Lost (1974) (TV)

Houston, We've Got a Problem (1974) (TV)—Narrator, off-screen

Crazy Joe (1974)—Don Vittorio

Indict and Convict (1974) (TV)—DeWitt Foster

Cinderella Liberty (1973)—Lynn Forshay

The Chill Factor (1973) (TV)—Dr. Frank Enari

The Typists (1971) (TV)—Paul Cunningham

Long Live Your Death (1971)—Max Lozoya

Romance of a Horsethief (1971)—Kifke

Zigzag (1970)—Mario Gambretti

The People Next Door (1970)—Arthur Mason

The Angel Levine (1970)—Store clerk

The Adventures of Gerard (1970)—Napoleon

Mackenna's Gold (1969)—Ben Baker

The Brain (1969)—Frankie Scannapieco

Ace High (1968)—Cacopoulos

A Lovely Way to Die (1968)—Tennessee Fredericks

How to Save a Marriage (and Ruin Your Life) (1968)—Harry Hunter

The Tiger Makes Out (1967)—Ben Harris

The Good, the Bad and the Ugly (1967)—Tuco

How to Steal a Million (1966)—Davis Leland

The Poppy Is Also A Flower (1966) (TV)—"Happy" Loccarno

Genghis Khan (1965)—Shah of Khwarezm

Lord Jim (1965)—The General

Kisses for My President (1964)—Valdez

The Moon-Spinners (1964)—Stratos

Act One (1963)—Warren Stone

The Victors (1963)—Sergeant Craig

How the West Was Won (1962)—Charlie Gant

Hemingway's Adventures of a Young Man (1962)—John

The Misfits (1961)—Guido

The Magnificent Seven (1960)—Calvera

Seven Thieves (1960)—Poncho

Lullaby (1960) (TV)

The Lineup (1958)—Dancer

Where Is Thy Brother? (1958) (TV)—Dan

Baby Doll (1956)—Silva Vacarro

Play Credits

Down the Garden Paths (2000)—Mr. Garden

Visiting Mr. Green (1997)—Mr. Green

The Flowering Peach (1994)—Noah

The Price (1992)—Gregory Solomon

Café Crown (1989)—David Cole

Twice Around the Park (1982–83)—Gus Frazier

Diary of Anne Frank (1978–79)

Saturday Sunday Monday (1974)

The Waltz of the Toreadors (1973)—General St. Pé

Promenade, All! (1972)—Ollie H; Wesley

Staircase (1968)—Charles Dyer

Luv (1964–67)—Milt Manville

Rhinoceros (1961)—Berrenger

The Cold Wind and the Warm (1958–59)—Willie

Major Barbara (1956–57)—Bill Walker

The Teahouse of the August Moon (1954–56)—Sakini

Camino Real (1953)—Kilroy

Mademoiselle Colombe (1953)—Julien

The Rose Tattoo (1951)—Alvaro Mangiacavallo

Mister Roberts (1948–51)

Antony and Cleopatra (1947–48)—Diomedes, the soothsayer; Messenger

Alice in Wonderland (1947)—Duck; Two of Spades; Other Voices

Yellow Jack (1947)

Androcles and the Lion (1946–47)—Spintho

What Every Woman Knows (1946–47)—ensemble

King Henry VIII (1946–47)—Cromwell

Skydrift (1945)

Acknowledgments

GREGORY CATSOS—for his interviewing skill and research work.

WILLIAM PHILLIPS—for guidance and care in teaching me the essentials of writing.

ADAM LANGER—an editor who helped me enormously in fashioning this book.

MORLEY RUSOFF—with my thanks for believing in me.

THE PEOPLE AT HARCOURT—for not being afraid to gamble.

Index

Index

Index